D1596819

An Annotated Bibliography of European Anglicisms

AN ANNOTATED BIBLIOGRAPHY OF EUROPEAN ANGLICISMS

Edited by

MANFRED GÖRLACH

OXFORD
UNIVERSITY PRESS

Great Clarendon Street, Oxford OX2 6DP

Oxford University Press is a department of the University of Oxford.
It furthers the University's objective of excellence in research, scholarship,
and education by publishing worldwide in

Oxford New York

Auckland Bangkok Buenos Aires Cape Town Chennai
Dar es Salaam Delhi Hong Kong Istanbul Karachi Kolkata
Kuala Lumpur Madrid Melbourne Mexico City Mumbai Nairobi
São Paulo Singapore Taipei Tokyo Toronto

with an associated company in Berlin

Oxford is a registered trade mark of Oxford University Press
in the UK and in certain other countries

Published in the United States
by Oxford University Press Inc., New York

First published 2002

British Library Cataloguing in Publication Data
Data available

Library of Congress Cataloging in Publication Data
Data applied for

ISBN 0-19-924882-6

1 3 5 7 9 10 8 6 4 2

Typeset in Times NR MT by
Jayvee, Trivandrum, India
Printed in Great Britain
on acid-free paper by
Biddles Ltd., Guildford & King's Lynn

Contents

List of Contributors

Dr Nevena Alexieva
English Department
Sofia University
Tsar Osvoboditel Blvd 15
1000 Sofia
BULGARIA

Keith Battarbee
Department of English
University of Turku
SF-20014 Turku
FINLAND

Prof. Dr Amand Berteloot
Institut für Niederländische Philologie
Universität Münster
Alter Steinweg 6–7
D-48143 Münster
GERMANY

Prof. Dr Ulrich Busse
Institut für Anglistik und Am.
Martin-Luther-Universität
Dachritzstr. 12
D-06108 Halle
GERMANY

Ilinca Constantinescu
Institutul de Lingvistică
Calea 13 Septembrie Nr. 13
RO-76117 București
ROMANIA

Dr Judit Farkas
Department of English Linguistics
Eötvös Lorand University
Ajtosi Dürer sor 19
H 1146 Budapest
HUNGARY

Prof. Dr Rudolf Filipović†

Prof. Dr Manfred Görlach
Englisches Seminar
Universität zu Köln
Albertus-Magnus-Platz 1
D-50923 Köln
GERMANY

Dr art. Anne-Line Graedler
Dept. of British and American Studies,
University of Oslo
PO Box 1003, Blindern
N-0315 Oslo
NORWAY

Prof. John Humbley
UFR EILA
Université Paris 7 Denis Diderot
F 75005 Paris
FRANCE

Prof. Veronika Kniezsa
Department of English
Linguistics
Eötvös Lorand University
Ajtosi Dürer sor 19
H 1146 Budapest
HUNGARY

Prof. Dr Guðrún Kvaran
Institute of Lexicography
Neshagi 16
IS 107 Reykjavik
ICELAND

Prof. Dr Elżbieta Mańczak-Wohlfeld
Uniwersytet Jagielloński
Inst. Filologii Angielskiej
Ul. Mickiewicza 9/11
PL-31-120 Kraków
POLAND

Prof. Tamara V. Maximova and
Dr Helen Pelikh
English Department
Volgograd University
2 Prodolnaya 30
400062 Volgograd
RUSSIA

Prof. Virginia Pulcini
Università degli Studi di Torino
Facoltà di Lingue e Letterature
Straniere
Dipartimento di Scienze del
Linguaggio
Via S. Ottavio 20
10124 Torino
ITALY

Prof. Félix Rodríguez González
Dep. de Fil. Anglesa
Universitat d'Alacant
Ap. Correus 99
E-03080 Alacant
SPAIN

Prof. Knud Sørensen
Råhoj Alle 12
DK-8270
Hójbjerg
DENMARK

Ekaterini Stathi
Messogion 73 B
GR 15126 Athens
GREECE

Dr Ariadna Ştefănescu
Institutul de Lingvistică
Calea 13 Septembrie Nr. 13
RO-76117 Bucureşti
ROMANIA

Ásta Svavarsdóttir
Institute of Lexicography
Neshagi 16
Reykjavik 101
ICELAND

Nicoline van der Sijs
Hooghiemstraplein 103
NL-3514 AX Utrecht
THE NETHERLANDS

INTRODUCTION

English has had a profound lexical impact on various languages of the world, and this development has generated both intensive public interest and a great number of more or less scholarly investigations. Somewhat surprisingly, however, there has never been a comprehensive bibliography devoted to anglicisms. The best approximation we have are references included in books and articles (such as the impressive list for German in Carstensen and Busse (1993–5)), or lists made on the basis of somewhat restricted available information (as in various publications by the late Rudolf Filipović). The data included in this bibliography are, however, selected and not intended to be comprehensive.

We have tried to restrict our references to the following types of works (books and articles):

a) dictionaries of anglicisms;
b) a selection of foreign-word dictionaries, etymological dictionaries, and general dictionaries, concentrating on those we found most helpful in the compilation of *A Dictionary of European Anglicisms*;
c) books and articles devoted to the influence of English on the language in question, whether English is exclusively treated or included in an informative, comparative way;
d) works restricted to individual levels of the English influence (graphemics, phonology, morphology, etc.);
e) works dealing with the English influence in specific fields, in individual styles, regions, or social classes;
f) corpus-oriented studies, such as major investigations of anglicisms in newspaper or advertising language;
g) major works documenting earlier influences of English and the cultural background.

The selection of the one hundred or so most important works on anglicisms was particularly difficult in a language such as German which has some one thousand titles to choose from. We hope to have found a compromise selecting works which are comprehensive, clear, innovative, reliable, and accessible. For languages lacking an extensive scholarly tradition, contributors were able to be more liberal in their admission of titles, but even here we have aimed at restricting the number of works written by an individual scholar assuming that there will be a certain amount of repetition in data and arguments. All chapters were written by *A Dictionary of European Anglicisms* contributors or scholars closely associated with the project. Since Albanian had no relevant literature worth mentioning we have gratefully taken up K. Sørensen's offer to contribute a section on Danish. But there was not enough evidence available on other languages (such as Swedish, Czech, or Portuguese) to justify a separate section on these languages. Titles are included under the headings of the language treated in the work. More general discussions are listed in an introductory chapter which also includes monographs comparing the influence in more than one language (with cross-references from the chapters devoted to the individual language—such titles are asterisked, e.g. *Yang 1990). Asterisks are also used for collections of papers comprising several articles on different languages; the individual papers are listed under their authors in the specific chapters, but the collection, and the cross-reference to it, are asterisked.

All the entries are numbered consecutively for easy reference giving language sigil plus number. The literature mentioned is as up-to-date as possible. However, the active collection of titles ended in 1995 (as in the dictionary data in the *Dictionary of European Anglicisms*). Although we have admitted some important publications after 1995, only a few have been suggested by the compilers, as can be seen from the small number of more recent entries.

The bibliographical details given are as complete as possible; we have tried to inspect as many publications quoted as possible so as not to rely on second-hand information. The author is followed by the year and the title of the work; these are translated into English unless they are in French, Spanish, Italian, and German (which we take are widely understood). The short descriptions concentrate on contents, but some include evaluative remarks in order to indicate whether a publication is worth inspecting. Only where the research is too meagre, have we compromised in listing unpublished (and therefore largely inaccessible) works, as is the case with Norwegian *hovedfag* theses, or with Russian *avtoreferats*. We have also advised contributors not to list studies of individual anglicisms, but have accepted such entries where the total number of items was small (mainly in Eastern European languages).

By contrast we see no point in mentioning a full list of items including works dealing with languages covered by the *Dictionary of European Anglicisms* where they are in close-contact situations; the dictionary therefore excludes evidence from Quebec French, Puerto Rican Spanish, and the like, and so does this volume, except for a few titles with more general reference. We have also omitted:

a) ephemeral journalistic articlettes in newspapers and magazines or discussions of individual words;
b) entries in general encyclopedias;
c) papers written in foreign languages neither easily understood nor accessible to the general user;
d) papers devoted to related topics whose focus is outside the proper field (etymology, language contact, pidginization, historical linguistics, non-European languages, general aspects of cultural history, the development of individual disciplines ranging from horse-breeding to aeronautics, and general dictionaries, to name a few categories). All these may provide valuable information, factual or linguistic, on individual items, but they do not belong in a specialized bibliography.

Part I

General Problems in Language Contact and Studies of More than One Language

Note: Cross-references to relevant titles in this section are listed under the individual language headings in Part II.

1. Alexiev, Bojan (1992), 'The Conceptual Structure of Terms as the Tertium Comparationis in Contrastive Terminology', *International Classification*, 19 (2): 91–2.

   The paper discusses the issue of determining the proper tertium comparationis for contrasting equivalent terminological units from two languages. Taking into account the monosemic and mononymic character of the 'ideal' term, a common conceptual structure of the two contrasted terms is assumed, often expressed linguistically by a common definition.

2. Algardy, Françoise, Pierre Lerat, and Jean-Pierre van Deth (1987), 'La fertilisation terminologique des langues romanes: Actes du colloque de Paris, Octobre 1986', *Meta*, 32 (3): 217–370.

   This conference took up the question of how Romance-language terminology (mainly French) reacts to English influence, and concluded that it has been an enrichment (terminologies have been 'cross-fertilized'), though the influence is not without danger.

3. Ammon, Ulrich, K. J. Mattheier, and P. H. Nelde (eds.) (1994), *English only? in Europa / in Europe / en Europe* (Sociolinguistica, 8), 212 pp.

   The book contains nine articles dealing with the general situation (Ammon: 1–14), the state of play in France (Truchaut: 15–25), in Eastern Europe (Domaschnew: 26–43), and in Switzerland (Dürmüller: 65–72), followed by 'the American perspective' (Fishman: 65–72), a general treatment of language policy (Phillipson and Skutnabb-Kangas: 73–87), and English in the (institutions of the) European Community (Volz: 88–100; Schlossmacher: 101–22; Gellert-Novak: 123–35). Bibliographies are attached to individual chapters. Languages used: English, French, and German.

4. Bergman, Karl (1912), *Die gegenseitigen Beziehungen der deutschen, englischen und französischen Sprache auf lexikologischem Gebiete* (Dresden and Leipzig).

   Of limited historical interest.

5. Braun, P. (ed.) (1979), *Fremdwort-Diskussion* (UTB 797; Munich: Fink), 363 pp.

The collection contains twenty-one articles, of which eight are devoted to anglicisms in a straightforward way (5, 14, 15, 17, 18, 19, 20, 21). The editor aims at a wider audience; English influences are explicitly or implicitly placed into a European context of language and culture contact.

6. —— Burkhard Schaeder, and Johannes Volmert (eds.) (1990), *Internationalismen. Studien zur interlingualen Lexikologie und Lexikographie* (RGL 102; Tübingen: Niemeyer), 193 pp. (Review: Görlach, *IJL* 5 (1992), 77–8).

The eight papers in the volume represent a preliminary report on a research project, 1986–88, which was expected to lead to a dictionary; publication was announced for 1993, but the project has obviously been cancelled. The authors draw attention to lexical equivalents of various etymologies across language boundaries in West European languages; some shared 3,500 items are claimed to be found in school dictionaries. The author's tenets are illustrated by entries under the letter *F* (95–122) and an analysis of theatre terms (123–62).

7. Browne, Wayles (1991), 'Language Contact: Some Reactions of a Contactee', in *Ivir and Kalogjera (eds.), 69–71.

The article shows some reactions on how a native speaker of English feels about various changes which anglicisms go through in the borrowing language.

8. Bruguière, Michel (1978), *Pitié pour Babel: un essai sur les langues* (Paris).

After some remarks on French language policy, Bruguière claims that a single international language does not exist and never will. The solution of linguistic problems will contribute to the solution of other international problems.

9. Burger, Antje (1979), 'Die Konkurrenz englischer und französischer Fremdwörter in der modernen deutschen Pressesprache', in *Braun, 246–72 (first in: *Muttersprache*, 76 (1966), 33–48).

Burger investigates how older French loanwords in German are affected by more recent anglicisms. There may be a wavering between the two competing words, the French word may be pushed out, or the two may survive in different meanings—categories which are illustrated with seven, four and eight word-pairs, and with another eight in which the equivalence of the English and French item is less clear.

10. Caputo, Ambra, Enrico, and Masucci (1987), 'Néologismes et contact des langues', *Meta*, 32 (2): 267–72.

A comparison of anglicisms in the French and Italian press suggests that an entire discourse model is being borrowed rather than simply elements; a dominant dynamic process is manifest in which borrowings are incorporated into both languages and largely transformed.

11. Carstensen, Broder (1986), 'Euro-English', in Dieter Kastovsky and Aleksander Szwedek (eds.), *Linguistics across Historical and Geographical Boundaries: In Honor of Jacek Fisiak*, Vol. 2: *Descriptive, Contrastive and Applied Linguistics* (Trends in Linguistics. Studies and Monographs 32; Berlin: Mouton de Gruyter), 827–35.

Adding to his former articles on morphological, lexical and semantic pseudo-loans (cf. German nos. 20, 22, 26) Carstensen supplies further German, and non-German examples of pseudo-loans which he calls 'Euro-English'. He concludes that the English language can be used as an open lexical reservoir from which words or their meanings may be borrowed at random.

12. Clyne, Michael G. (1975), *Forschungsbericht Sprachkontakt. Untersuchungsergebnisse und praktische Probleme* (Monographien Linguistik und Kommunikationswissenschaft 18; Kronberg: Scriptor).

13. *Circuit*, 41 (1993) (Montréal).

This special issue on English in Europe has articles on France, the Netherlands, Germany; Euro-English; English in science; English at the Paris Language Fair.

14. Denison, Norman (1980), 'English in Europe, with Particular Reference to the German-speaking Area', in W. Pöckl (ed.) *Europäische Mehrsprachigkeit. Festschrift Wandruszka* (Tübingen: Niemeyer).

15. Filipović, Rudolf (1959), 'Consonantal Innovations in the

Phonological System as a Consequence of Linguistic Borrowing', *Studia Romanica et Anglica Zagrabiensia* (EEEL 4) 7: 39–62.

The author discusses the effects of phonemic redistribution caused by English loanwords in Croatian. He analyses consonant clusters in initial, medial, and final positions.

16. Filipović, Rudolf (1971), *Kontakti jezika u teoriji i praksi* (Language Contacts in Theory and Practice) (Zagreb: Školska knjiga) (Zagreb: The School Book), xvi + 142 pp.

'Teaching methods' is followed by 'Contrastive Analysis'. In Part Three, 'Languages in Contact and Linguistic Borrowing', the author traces the origins of the discipline from the nineteenth century to Leopold, Haugen, and Weinreich. Then bilingualism is discussed as the basis of language contacts and the adaptation of English words at three levels (phonological, morphological and semantic) analysed.

17. —— (1974), 'A Contribution to the Method of Studying Anglicisms in European Languages', *Studia Romanica et Anglica Zagrabiensia*, 37: 135–48. (EEEL 4)

Four methodological principles are formulated: 1) the corpus should be multilingual if we want to formulate and explain some general principles of linguistic borrowing; 2) texts should be typical representatives of their groups; 3) the type of contact has to be examined carefully (oral or written, BrE or AmE etc.); 4) the intermediary language often helps in solving some etymological questions.

18. —— (1977*a*), 'Some Basic Principles of Languages in Contact Reinterpreted', *Studia Romanica et Anglica Zagrabiensia*, 43–44: 157–66. (EEEL 4).

Some basic principles of language borrowing are made more precise and finally reinterpreted taking into account genetically different languages and conditions typical of cultural or intimate borrowing. Closely related to these factors are the levels on which the analysis of linguistic borrowing can be carried out.

19. —— (1977*b*), 'Primary and Secondary Adaption of Loanwords', *Wiener Slavistisches Jahrbuch*, 22: 116–25.

20. —— (1977*c*), 'English Words in European Mouths and Minds', *Folia Linguistica*, 10: 195–206.

The project *The English Element in European Languages* (EEEL 4) is sketched; it envisaged a monograph under the same title and an *Etymological Dictionary of English Loan Words in European Languages*.

21. —— (1980), 'Transmorphemization: Substitution on the Morphological Level Reinterpreted', *Studia Romanica et Anglica Zagrabiensia*, 25: 1–8. (EEEL 4).

Transmorphemization is defined as a form of substitution which regulates all the changes which appear in the adaptation of bound morphemes as they pass from the donor language to the borrowing language. There are three types or stages of transmorphemization: a) zero transmorphemization according to the formula free morpheme + zero morpheme; b) compromise transmorphemization, in which the compromise replica keeps the bound morpheme of the donor language, and c) complete transmorphemization, which means complete integration into the borrowing language with the replacement of the donor language's bound morpheme by a synonymous bound morpheme of the borrowing language.

22. —— (1981*a*), 'Morphological Categories in Linguistic Borrowing', *Studia Romanica et Anglica Zagrabiensia*, 26 (1–2): 197–207.

The author distinguishes between primary adaptation (loanwords remain in the same word class) and secondary adaptation (the word class of a loanword is changed). Three parts of speech are analyzed in order to show the changes in anglicisms and their consequences.

23. —— (1981*b*), 'Transphonemization: Substitution on the Phonological Level Reinterpreted', in W. Pöckl (ed.), *Europäische Mehrsprachigkeit. Festschrift Wandruszka* (Tübingen: Niemeyer), 125–33.

Three types of transphonemization result from phonological differences between donor and receiving language distinguished: complete, partial, and free transphonemization.

24. —— (1982*a*), 'Phonologization and Activation of Latent Phonemes in Linguistic Borrowing (Reinterpretation of "Phoneme Importation")', *Journal of the International Phonetic Association*, 12: 36–47.

Filling an empty space in the phonological system of the borrowing language as a consequence of language contact is possible either through phonologization (if a corresponding allophone exists) or through the activation of a latent phoneme.

25. Filipović, Rudolf (ed.) (1982*b*), *The English Element in European Languages*, vol. 2: *Reports and Studies* (EEEL 4; Institute of Linguistics, Faculty of Philosophy, University of Zagreb), xvi + 501 pp.

The collection contains seventeen articles (listed separately in the 'national sections') dealing with the impact of English on the following languages: Albanian (Nuhiu, Mehmeti), Czech (Poldauf), Danish (Sørensen), Dutch (Gerritsen), Finnish (Orešnik), German (Muhvić-Dimanovski), Hungarian (Jakobs-Németh), Icelandic (Eiriksson), Latvian (Bulduněiks), Lithuanian (Pažūsis), Norwegian (Schmidt), Romanian (Băncilă and Chiţoran), 'Serbo-Croatian' (Velčić, Vilke), Slovak (Lenhardt), Turkish (Başkan). Problems of phonological and morphological adaptation predominate, but there are also general treatments devoted to individual subject areas. The special value of this volume is that it includes languages for which relevant research is extremely rare.

26. —— (1983), 'An Etymological Dictionary of Anglicisms in European Languages', in P. H. Nelde (ed.), *Theory, Methods and Models of Contact Linguistics* (Bonn: Dümmler), 59–68.

The Dictionary is to be compiled according to eight basic principles: the choice of receiving languages; the parts of speech included; the levels of analysis; the fourth primary and secondary adaptation of anglicisms; the analysis of the phonological form; the substitution on the phonological level; the adaptation of the citation form, and the adaptation of meaning.

27. —— (1984), 'Can a Dictionary of *-isms* be an Etymological Dictionary?', in R. R. K. Hartmann (ed.), *LEXeter '83. Proceedings* (Tübingen: Niemeyer), 73–9.

A dictionary of *-isms* may be labelled 'etymological' even if it does not give historical etymologies of English words which are sources of anglicisms. Since it provides for each recorded anglicism the synchronic source in English and a detailed analysis on three levels, the etymological dictionary meets some of the criteria given in Malkiel's *Tentative Typology of Etymological Dictionaries*.

28. —— (1984–5), 'Odnos posrednog i neposrednog posuđivanja u teoriji kontaktne lingvistike' (The Relation between Direct and Indirect Borrowing in Contact Linguistic Theory), *Zbornik za Filologiju i Lingvistiku*, 27–28: 861–7.

The relationship between indirect and direct borrowing is one of the crucial problems in contact linguistics. The article is based on the results of research on the contacts between English and European languages in Europe and the USA. The contact of English with other European languages depends on the milieu in which it is realized, its function in this milieu and the relationship between the languages in contact. If one of these elements is changed, the type of contact also changes.

29. —— (1985), 'Pseudoanglicisms in European Languages—a Sociolinguistic Analysis', in Pieper and Stickel (eds.), *Festschrift für Werner Winter. Studia Linguistica Diachronica et Synchronica* (Berlin: Mouton de Gruyter), 249–55.

The author presents a few sociological factors that create conditions and needs for coining new expressions. Such an analysis requires carefully collected corpora in situations where new sociological factors are likely to appear.

30. —— (1986), *Teorija jezika u kontaktu. Uvod u lingvistiku jezičnih dodira.* (Theory of Languages in Contact. An Introduction to Contact Linguistics) (Jugoslavenska akademija znanosti i umjetnosti, Školska knjiga), 322 pp. (Review: Ivir, *SRAZ* 35 (1990), 183–6).

The author introduces his new terminology: adaptation on the phonological level is called transphonemization (phoneme substitution) and is further analyzed as zero, partial and free. Adaptation on the morphological level or transmorphemization (morpheme substitution) can be zero, partial or complete. Adaptation on the semantic level involves zero semantic change, semantic extension and semantic restriction in terms of the number of meanings and in terms of the number of semantic fields. Another conceptual and methological contribution concerns the distinction between primary and secondary changes affecting borrowed items and, consequently, between primary and secondary adaptation.

31. Filipović, Rudolf (1988), 'Contact Linguistics: Retrospect—Prospect', in Josef Klegraf (ed.), *Essays on the English Language and Applied Linguistics on the Occasion of Gerhard Nickel's Sixtieth Birthday* (Heidelberg: Groos), 342–56.

Further investigation of bilingualism and multilingualism, language acquisition, language conflict, language loss, language planning, etc. will bring about new results and show its prospects, i.e. directions of its further development and the relations it will bear on general linguistics.

32. —— (1989), 'Some Contributions to the Theory of Contact Linguistics', in M. Radovanović (ed.), *Yugoslav General Linguistics* (Amsterdam and Philadelphia: John Benjamins), 47–71.

The concepts of *primary* and *secondary* changes are explained and new terms introduced: *transphonemization* for substitution on the phonological level and *transmorphemization* for substitution on the morphological level. The fourth innovation introduced is the so-called *phonologization* and *activation of latent phonemes* which explains and redefines the phenomenon previously called phonemic importation.

33. —— and M. Bratanić (eds.) (1990), *Proceedings of the Symposium 16.1. 'Languages in Contact' of the Twelfth International Congress of Anthropological and Ethnological Sciences, Zagreb University, July 25–27, 1988* (Institute of Linguistics, University of Zagreb), xiii + 378 pp.

A collection of papers dealing with some theoretical questions and study of anglicisms in various languages read at the symposium.

34. —— (1991), *The English Element in European Languages*, vol. 3: *Reports and Studies* (Institute of Linguistics, University of Zagreb), viii + 164 pp.

A collection of articles dealing with anglicisms in various European languages.

35. —— (1992), 'Metonimija u funkciji formiranja anglicizama u evropskim jezicima' (Metonymy in the Function of Forming Anglicisms in European Languages), *Suvremena lingvistika*, 34: 63–72. (EEEL 4).

The author analyses anglicisms in European languages which are formed following the types of metonymy: inventions and discoveries are named after the person responsible while various things and products are named after their place of origin. The author presents five groups of English appellatives which are transferred into anglicisms in six European languages.

36. —— (1992–93), 'Porijeklo anglicizama: etimologija i razvoj' (The Origin of Anglicisms: Etymology and Development), *Filologija*, 20–21: 75–85.

The author introduces two degrees of etymology: primary (historical) and secondary, e.g. the immediate source of an anglicism.

37. —— (1995*a*), 'Linguistic Purism versus Linguistic Borrowing in a Changing Europe', in K. Sornig *et al.* (eds.), *Linguistics with a Human Face. Festschrift für Norman Denison zum 70. Geburtstag* (Grazer Linguistische Monographien 10), 53–61.

The article compares recent trends of purism in French and Croatian, with an outlook on German; specimens are provided of anglicisms and their suggested Croatian replacements.

38. —— (1995*b*), 'Some Problems in Compiling an Etymological Dictionary of Anglicisms', *On Languages and Language—The Presidential Addresses of the 1991 Meeting of the Societas Linguistica Europaea* (Berlin and New York: Mouton de Gruyter), 127–43.

The analysis of anglicisms in the dictionary is carried out on four levels: orthographic, phonological, morphological and semantic. Consequently, the dictionary entry is an English word, the model and the source from which an anglicism is developed, and not an anglicism as is the case in the majority of traditional dictionaries of anglicisms. The original adaptation was refined by introducing a) a distinction between primary adaptation and secondary adaptation; b) three types of transphonemization; c) three degrees of transmorphemization; and d) five categories of semantic extension.

39. Galinsky, Hans (1977), 'Amerikanisch-englische und gesamtenglische Interferenzen mit dem Deutschen und anderen Sprachen der Gegenwart', in Herbert Kolb and Hartmut Lauffer (eds.), *Sprachliche Interferenz. Festschrift für Werner Betz zum 65. Geburtstag* (Tübingen: Niemeyer), 463–517.

This detailed and thorough report on writings on AmE and general English influences on German and other European languages covers three decades from 1945 onwards. Galinsky has organized his report in three parts starting with works dealing with AmE interferences (comprehensive, lexical, and morphological studies). This is followed by works treating general English influences on German and concluded by a brief summary on AmE and general English influences on other contemporary European languages.

40. GÖRLACH, MANFRED (1994), 'A Usage Dictionary of Anglicisms in Selected European Languages', *IJL* 7: 223–46.

The first and most comprehensive description of the *UDASEL* (= *DEA*) project, discussing problems and methods of compilation and including pilot studies to test the currency of selected items and specimen entries.

41. —— (1997*a*), 'Is Airbagging Hip or Megaout? A New Dictionary of Anglicisms', in Martin Pütz (ed.), *Language Choices: Conditions, Constraints, and Consequences* (Amsterdam and Philadelphia: John Benjamins), 91–111.

A progress report of the *UDASEL* (= *DEA*) project concentrating on a problem of recent imports into German.

42. —— (1997*b*), 'The *UDASEL*: Progress, Problem and Prospects', in Zygmunt Mazur and Teresa Bela (eds.), *New Developments in English and American Studies: Continuity and Change* (Krakow: University), 561–79.

The most recent report on the *UDASEL* nearing completion.

43. —— (1997*c*), 'Usage in the *UDASEL*', in Jacek Fisiak (ed.), *Festschrift for Roger Lass: Studia Anglica Posnaniensia*, 31: 67–77.

The categories used to define currency and acceptability of anglicisms in sixteen European languages are discussed on the basis of the evidence available by 1996.

44. —— (1998), 'Purism and the *UDASEL*', in *Festschrift for Rudolf Filipović. Suvremena lingvistika*, 41–42 (Zagreb: Institute of Linguistics), 163–83.

45. —— (1999), 'Recent dictionaries of anglicisms' (Review article), *IJL* 12:147–54.

The survey analyses the dictionaries compiled by Carstensen/

Busse (German, 1993–6), Sørensen (Danish, 1997), Graedler and Johansson (Norwegian, 1997), Rodriguez (Spanish, 1997), Mańczak-Wohlfeld (Polish, 1994), Filipović (Croatian, 1990), and Maximova (Russian, 1998), comparing methods and contents; a revised and expanded version of the review will be included in Görlach (fc.). The dictionaries here mentioned are also described in their respective sections below.

46. —— (fc.), *English Words Abroad: Lexical Loans in European Languages.*

The volume is to include chapters on phonological, morphological and semantic integration, purism, mediation and historical differences in language contact of English with the sixteen *UDASEL / DEA* languages.

47. Goetschalckx, Joris A. M. (1991), 'Normalisatie van terminologie: wel of geen engels?' (The normalization of terminology: plenty or no English), *Terminologie et Traduction*, 1: 195–206.

48. Gusmani, Roberto (1981/1983), *Saggi sull'interferenza linguistica* (2 vols.; Florence: Le Lettere).

49. Gutia, I., G. M. Semes, M. Zappieri, and F. Cabasino (eds.) (1981), *Contatti interlinguistici e mass media* (Collana di lingue moderne; Rome: La Gollardica Editrice).

Mostly devoted to Italian, though including some comparisons with French, this collection of studies is unique in highlighting the importance of the media as the main vector of English influence on European languages. This influence is seen as concomitant with the change to the consumer society on the American model, the language change being part of a change in civilization.

50. Hartmann, Reinhard (ed.) (1996), *The English Language in Europe* (Europa 2.3; Oxford: Intellect), 60 pp. (Review: Görlach *EWW* 18 (1997), 157–8.)

The collection includes the articles 'English in the world and Europe' (MacArthur, 3–15), 'English as a lingua franca in German-speaking countries' (Viereck, 16–23), 'English in the European Union' (Dollerup, 24–36), 'English as a donor language' (Filipović, 37–46), and 'Societal and individual bilingualism with English' (Hoffmann, 47–60). Informative, aimed at a general readership.

51. HAUGEN, EINAR (1950), 'The Analysis of Linguistic Borrowing', *Language*, 26: 210–31.

One of the classic studies of borrowing and language contact.

52. HÖFLER, MANFRED (1980), 'Für eine Ausgliederung der Kategorie "Lehnschöpfung" aus dem Bereich sprachlicher Entlehnung', in W. Pöckl (ed.), *Europäische Mehrsprachigkeit. Festschrift zum 70. Geburtstag von Mario Wandruszka* (Tübingen: Niemeyer), 149–53.

53. HUMBLEY, JOHN (1987), 'La pénétration de l'anglais dans le français et l'allemand de l'informatique: étude contrastive', *Contrastes*, 14–15: 263–77.

This study of popular science computer magazines in France and Germany revealed a higher proportion of direct loans in German especially in advertising. Most terms recommended by the Ministerial Commission were used in the French sources, whereas in German, the equivalent tended to be the direct loan.

54. —— (1988), 'Comment le français et l'allemand aménagent la terminologie de l'informatique', *Banque des Mots*, 85–148.

Taking the hypothesis that the overwhelming majority of terms in the computer and data-processing sectors are borrowed or adapted from English, a representative selection of this vocabulary is examined in French and German to ascertain what strategies are used. German appears to prefer direct loans (which French generally eschews, possibly as a consequence of official discouragement) but when no commercial pressure is evident, the resources of German compounding are employed to give many successful loan translations. Both languages exploit common Greek and Latin roots.

55. —— (1990*a*), 'L'intégration de l'anglicisme contemporain: étude comparative des emprunts lexicaux faits à l'anglais depuis 1945 en français, en allemand et en danois, refletés dans les dictionnaires', doctorat d'état (disponible à l'atelier de reproduction des thèses, Lille).

The thesis examines how English loans are integrated into three European languages, especially from the evidence of their presentation in dictionaries, compared with a monitor corpus of direct observations. A preliminary section deals with dictionary treatment of anglicisms in general language dictionaries and dictionaries devoted to anglicisms or foreign words. Integration is then examined for the three languages under the headings of pronunciation, spelling, morphology (gender and number in particular), and lexical integration. The glossary (A–L only) gives entries from representative dictionaries, together with complementary direct observations.

56. —— (1990*b*), 'Semantic Convergence of English Borrowings in Western European Languages', in *Filipović and Bratanić (eds.), 82–7.

Loanwords usually have a reduced semantic range compared to that in their original language and tend to take on different meanings. Anglicisms are no exception, but increasing familiarity with English in Western Europe tends to bring anglicisms in line with the semantic range of the English etymon.

57. —— (1990*c*), 'Conscience linguistique et anglicisation des langues nationales européennes (Résumé)', *Actes du XXXe colloque de la SAES* (Le Mans), 129.

58. Ivir, Vladimir (1991), 'Contrastive Methods in Contact Linguistics', in *Ivir and Kalogjera (eds.), 237–45.

The article is an attempt to define the status of contact linguistics from the point of view of its methodology. As all the analyses in contact linguistics are based on contrasting the elements of the donor language to the corresponding elements in the receiving language, the author considers the contrastive method the most productive analytical tool on all levels of investigation. It is always the comparison of two language systems regardless of the fact that it can either be the phonological, morphological, semantic, syntactic, or stylistic level. The author illustrates the results of language contact for each of these with anglicisms in Croatian.

59. —— and Damir Kalogjera (eds.) (1991), *Languages in Contact and Contrast. Essays in Contact Linguistics* (Trends in Linguistics, Studies and Monographs 54; Berlin: Mouton de Gruyter).

60. Jabłonski, Mirosław (1990), *Regularität und Variabilität in der Rezeption englischer Internationalismen im modernen Deutsch, Französisch und Polnisch. Aufgezeigt an den Bereichen Sport, Musik und Mode* (LA 240; Tübingen: Niemeyer), 233 pp. (Review Görlach, *IJL* 5 (1992), 77).

The 1988 Cologne thesis investigates the lexical impact in the fields of sports, (light) music and fashion using evidence mainly from journals and newspapers, but not in any statistically controlled way. There are chapters on spelling and pronunciation, morphology, semantics and stylistics, a summary and various appendixes, which provide a careful documentation of graphic and phonic variants: for the domains investigated, these lists provide comprehensive and reliable data.

61. Kesić-Śafar (1982), 'Semantička adaptacija engleskih, njemačkih i francuskih posudenica u Tolstojevo doba' (The Semantic Adaptation of English, German and French Loanwords in the Times of Tolstoy), *Filologija*, 10: 223–42.

62. Kirkness, Alan and W. Müller (1975), 'Fremdwortbegriff und Fremdwörterbuch', *Deutsche Sprache*, 3: 299–313.

63. Liutakova, Rumiana (1993), 'Trăsături specifice ale împrumuturilor englezeşti din linbile română şi bulgară' (Characteristic Features of the English Borrowings in Romanian and Bulgarian), *Studii şi cercetari lingvistice (SCL)*, 44 (2): 151–62.

The paper contrasts English borrowings in the two languages within a similar sociocultural context, especially in recent years. Starting from what they have in common, the paper deals mostly with the differences which are classified into loans found only in one of the languages and loans found in both, but differing in form and/or meaning.

64. —— (1997), 'Morfologichnata adaptatsiya na angliĭskite zaemki v bŭlgarski i rumŭnski' (The Morphological Adaption of English Loanwords in Bulgarian and Romanian), *Sŭpostavitelno ezikoznanie*, 2: 5–18.

The paper is based on a Ph.D. thesis, dealing with anglicisms in Romanian and Bulgarian. The author compares the morphological adaptation of loanwords in two East European languages of different families. The morphological adaptation of nouns, verbs, and adjectives in each language is considered in relation to the different phonological adaptation. In addition, transliteration into the Cyrillic alphabet is shown to be an important factor in the integration of anglicisms in Bulgarian.

65. LÜLLWITZ, B. (1972), 'Interferenz und Transferenz. Aspekte zu einer Theorie lingualen Kontaktes', *Germanistische Linguistik*, 72 (2): 155–291.

66. MAČEK, DORA (1976), 'Some Marginalia of Language Contact', *Studia Romanica et Anglica Zagrabiensia*, 41: 79–85.

Studies in linguistic contact seldom deal with interjections or onomatopoeia, which belong to the sphere of intimate borrowing, i.e. to close oral contact between two speech communities. A new mode of cultural borrowing is the influence of typically spoken elements transmitted through written texts, in the first place comics. The exclamatory and imitative words are either translated into the borrowing language, merely transcribed or even used in their original form. The author has analysed several English comics issued in Croatian in order to show this type of influence.

67. —— (1990), 'The gender of loanwords denoting occupation in Serbo-Croatian', in *Filipović and Bratanić (eds.), 93–100.

The spread of different foreign terminologies correlates with the spheres of influence of the former (world) powers Turkey, Venice, and Austria-Hungary, while French and English influence is of a later date. The author provides the reader with a concise overview of some typical occupational loan terms by language of origin and type of occupation and some purely female occupations imported together with their terms from other societies and the way in which they are adapted to the system of Croatian word-formation.

68. —— (1991), 'Between Language Contact and Language Development', in *Ivir and Kalogjera (eds.), 281–8.

So far it has been assumed that in indirect borrowing linguistic influence is limited to lexis while in direct contact of two languages the influence is present in the whole system. Recently, though, due to rapid sociological changes these relationships have undergone significant changes as well. Some innovations in Croatian usage are partly the consequence of language contact and partly of 'latent' tendencies of the borrowing language.

69. MUHVIĆ-DIMANOVSKI, VESNA (1992), 'Prevedenice—jedan oblik neologizama' (Loan Translations—A Form of Neologisms), in

Rudolf Filipović (ed.), *Rad Hrvatske akademije znanosti i umjetnosi.* (The Croatian Academy of Arts and Sciences), 93–205.

The morphological characteristics of loan translations are primarily investigated as to whether they fit into the native structure or are innovations to the system. They are within the wider frame of linguistic borrowing, and data from Croatian are compared with those in other European languages in order to explore universal tendencies in their genesis, forms and usage.

70. NELDE, P. H. (ed.) (1980), *Sprachkontakt und Sprachkonflikt* (Wiesbaden).

71. OSTERHELD, WOLFGANG (ed.) (1991), *Terminologie et Traduction*, 1: *L'Influence de l'anglais sur les autres langues communautaires* (Brussels and Luxemburg: *CECA-CEE-CEEA*).

This special issue contains articles on English influence on various European Union languages in general, and on some special languages (computer technology, medical, commercial): on Danish, German, Greek, Spanish, Italian, Dutch (technical, scientific and sports fields), and French. Most articles are in the language of the community concerned. Four articles cut across language barriers: criteria which determine acceptance or rejection of direct loans (Posthumus), standardization of terminology (Goetschalckx), anglicisms made current through the media (Wallis) and the extra-linguistic causes of English influence in Europe and the forms this influence takes (Truchot).

72. PAPP, E. (ed.) (1977), *Lehnwortforschung* (Wege der Forschung 515; Darmstadt: Wissenschaftliche Buchgesellschaft).

73. PAVLOVA, ANNA (1979), 'Za nyakoi problemi pri izuchavaneto na zaemkite' (On Some Problems in the Study of Loanwords), *Filologia* (Sofia), 5: 78–84.

The article is devoted to a basic terminological problem in the study of international vocabulary—the definition of 'internationalism'. Starting from a number of structural and semantic problems, the author arrives at the basic features necessary for a definition. Due attention is paid to the so-called 'pseudo'-international words.

74. —— (1983), 'On the Morphological and Semantic Character of

Some Lexical Equivalents in Bulgarian, French and English', *University of Sofia English Papers*, 2: 202–17.

Structural and semantic analysis is used to define the features that some words have in common. Attention is also paid to the processes of divergence.

75. —— (1991), 'Leksikalni ekvivalenti v bŭlgarski, angliĭski i frenski ezik s nachalen element *avto-/auto-*' (Lexical Equivalence in Bulgarian, English and French with *avto-/auto-* as Initial Element), *Annuaire de l'Université de Sofia*, 80: 62–115.

The publication incorporates chapters 1–4 of the author's unpublished Ph.D. thesis of the same title (University of Sofia, 1984, 164 pp.). It presents an analysis of a group of lexical equivalents in Bulgarian, English, and French with *auto-* as their initial constituent. The mechanism of the process of internationalization on a synchronic-diachronic plane is revealed and the depth of that process determined by means of etymological word-formation and contrastive semantic analysis as well as through modelling derivational word-formation. A clear idea of word-formation hierarchy is formed and inter-language parallels are brought out by applying the theory of word generation.

76. —— (1992), 'Mezhduezikova leksikalna ekvivalentnost i nyakoi ot neĭnite proyavi v rechnika na turizma' (Lexical Equivalence across Languages and Some of its Manifestations in the Vocabulary of Tourism), *Filologia* (Sofia), 25–26: 127–37.

Three languages have been included in the study of the internationalization of the vocabulary of tourism. For an anglicism to be successful, it is claimed, the presence of a lexeme with at least one shared meaning in no less than three languages belonging to different language groups is the minimal condition, provided there is sufficient phonetic similarity as well. Detailed structural and semantic analyses of three international terms of relatively high frequency of occurrence illustrates the method used.

77. Phillips, Diana (1995), 'Recent English Financial Terms in French-language, Dutch-language and German-language Financial Publications: Borrowing versus Translation', *ASp, la Revue du GERAS*, 81–9.

When using financial terminology Dutch tends to borrow rather than to translate (as does German, though to a lesser extent than French in which every effort is made to avoid the anglicism).

78. Plümer, Nicole (2000), *Anglizismus—Purismus—Sprachliche Identität. Eine Untersuchung zu den Anglizismen in der deutschen und französischen Mediensprache* (Frankfurt/M.: Peter Lang), xiii + 320 pp.

Recent attitudes towards loanwords in Germany and France and French linguistic legislation are surveyed before the choice of the base for analysis (four weeks' output of two German and two French dailies plus the major news programme of one TV channel each) is justified in detail—the resulting corpus is almost 500,000 printed words for German and French, and some 23,000/37,000 words on TV. Loanwords (including internationalisms) and calques are included—but older loanwords and acronyms omitted. The results are not surprising: 1,383 items for German contrast with 750 for French, at least a partial consequence of French official attitudes. Paths of integration are described in great detail. The corpus used appears to be somewhat limited for reliable comparisons, and computer-assistance not really justified for a study of this size.

79. Poplack, Shana and Alicia Pousada (1982), 'Competing Influences on Gender Assignment: Variable Process, Stable Outcome', *Lingua*, 57: 1–28.

80. Rinner-Kawai, Yumiko (1991), *Anglo-amerikanische Einflüsse auf die deutsche und japanische Sprache der Werbung. Eine Untersuchung von Publikumszeitschriften* (Freiburg: Hochschulverlag).

This contrastive study of the Anglo-American influence on the German and the Japanese languages of advertising is based on a corpus of seven German and ten Japanese magazines yielding a total of 4642 advertisements per language. Substitutions are excluded from the analysis. The author investigated the morphology, frequency according to domains, and the (stylistic) functions of anglicisms; he found that English has affected Japanese more than German, which, however, has not led to puristic efforts.

81. Sandfeld, Jensen Kristian (1912), 'Notes sur les calques linguistiques', in *Festschrift Vilhelm Thomsen* (Leipzig), 166–73.

82. SCHELER, MANFRED (1973), 'Zur Struktur und Terminologie des sprachlichen Lehnguts', *Die Neueren Sprachen*, NF 22: 19–26.

83. SCHMITT, PETER A. (1985), *Anglizismen in den Fachsprachen. Eine pragmatische Studie am Beispiel der Kerntechnik* (Anglistische Forschungen 179; Heidelberg: Winter).

84. SPITZER, LEO (1918), *Fremdwörterhatz und Fremdvölkerhaß: Eine Streitschrift gegen die Sprachreinigung* (Vienna: Manz), 66 pp.

85. TARDEL, HERMANN (1899), 'Das englische Fremdwort in der modernen Sprache', in *Festschrift der 45. Versammlung deutscher Schulmänner und Philologen* (Bremen), 359–420.

86. TASEVA, YOANA (1994), 'Phonological Adaptation of English Loanwords in Modern Japanese and Bulgarian', unpublished diploma paper (University of Sofia).

The paper represents a cross-language investigation of the phonological adaptation of anglicisms in two typologically different languages. It offers a consistent and fairly exhaustive analysis of the rendition of all basic phonological units of the anglicisms and of their accentual characteristics in a European and an Asian language. The analysis confirms in a convincing way the auditory impression that anglicisms in Japanese deviate considerably from their English phonological prototypes as a result of a specific adaption by means of the *mora*, the basic Japanese phonological unit.

87. TESCH, GERD (1978), *Linguale Interferenz. Theoretische, terminologische und methodische Grundfragen zu ihrer Erforschung* (TBL 105; Tübingen: Narr), 302 pp.

Tesch gives the most thorough discussion of methods used in describing language contact and its consequences, and possible classifications of the phenomena involved. On the basis of some five hundred studies (listed pp. 262–93) he surveys and critically comments on suggested approaches and solutions. Although the discussion of German conditions predominates, all major European languages are included.

88. THOMAS, GEORGE (1991), *Linguistic Purism* (London: Longman), 250 pp.

Thomas provides a general description of the phenomenon on

the basis of the history of language development and planning of some twenty European languages (with particular attention to Slavic languages), with some account of Africa and Asia. His discussion concentrates on definitions, typologies, processes, and an analysis of the language situation, extralinguistic factors, the diachronic aspect, and the effects of purism. Many data are adduced to support Thomas' very abstract arguments; his objective is a synchronic contrastive analysis, so that the complex histories of the languages treated must remain shadowy in a book of this size.

89. Truchot, Claude (1990), *L'Anglais dans le monde contemporain* (Paris: Robert). (Review Görlach, *EWW* 12 (1991), 315–16).

After a review of the place of English especially in non-native English-speaking countries of the world, Truchot examines how English has influenced other languages and how it is itself influenced, and finishes with considerations on how to set up language-planning in Europe in order to strike the right balance between vehicular English and other national and regional languages.

90. —— (1991), 'L'Anglais et les langues européennes', *Terminologie et traduction*, 1: 93–115.

91. Viereck, Wolfgang and Wolf-Dietrich Bald (eds.) (1986), *English in Contact with Other Languages* (Budapest: Ak. Kiadó), 589 pp. (Review Görlach, *ZDL* 55 (1988), 76–8).

The volume, a festschrift on the occasion of Carstensen's sixtieth birthday, combines twenty case studies of the impact of English on European languages (see the detailed descriptions in the individual chapters) with nine on languages from other continents. The collection is the most comprehensive of its kind to date. The quality of the contributions is high; many summarize the state of play of the mid-eighties. However, comparability of the data is impaired by the fact that not all authors stuck to the pattern prescribed by the editors.

92. Wallis, Brian (1991), 'Linguistic and Cultural Borrowings from English in Commercials on French and German Television', *Terminologie et traduction*, 1: 61–73.

93. Weinreich, Uriel (1953), *Languages in Contact* (New York).

Possibly the most influential book on the topic to date which had an enormous impact on studies in the field of contact.

94. —— (1970), *Languages in Contact. Findings and Problems* (The Hague/ Paris: Mouton), 245 pp.

95. ZANDVOORT, R. W. (1970), 'English Linguistic Infiltration in Europe', in R. W. Zandvoort, *Collected Papers*, vol. II (Groningen: Wolters-Noordhoff), 165–71.

The paper, first read at the tenth Congress of the International Federation for Modern Languages and Literatures at Strasbourg, 30 August 1966, takes up Sapir's views (in *Language* 1921) of the world-wide impact of English, discussing the various forms of lexical infiltration of West European languages, in particular Dutch, which 'is essentially changed by the importation of a few hundreds of English words'. Zandvoort's urgent call for a contrastive study of how European languages are affected went unheeded: his hope that such a project 'might be sponsored by the Council of Europe' has the frustrated footnote attached: 'Unfortunately, it turned out that the Council was not interested'.

Part II

Studies Devoted to Anglicisms in Individual Languages

Albanian (Manfred Görlach)

(see also *25)

1. MEHMETI, ISMAIL (1982), 'A Morphological and Semantic Analysis of the Adaptation of Anglicisms in Albanian', in *Filipović (ed.), 28–56.

2. NUHIU, VEJSEL (1982), 'The English Element in Albanian—a Phonological Analysis', in *Filipović (ed.), 1–27.

Bulgarian (Nevena Alexieva)

(see also *63, *64, *75, *86)

1. Alexiev, Boyan (1988), 'Termini ot angliĭski proizkhod za nazovavane na khronostratigrafski edinitsi v bŭlgarskata geolozhka terminologiya' (Terms of English Origin for Designating Chronostratigraphic Units in Bulgarian Geological Terminology), *Bŭlgarski ezik*, 1: 61–6.

A phonological contrastive analysis is applied to identify deviations from the rules of transcribing some Bulgarian terms of English origin, which are presented in a table with their existing forms, etymologies, phonetic transcriptions, and recommended forms. The deviations result either from the old practice of transliterating rather than transcribing English borrowed names, or from the influence of a mediating language (French or Russian). Recommendations on correct transcriptions are proposed to remove undesired doublets and enhance terminological standardization.

2. Alexieva, Nevena (1977), 'Gramatichni i semantichni faktori pri opredelyane roda na angliĭskite zaemki v bŭlgarski ezik' (Grammatical and Semantic Factors in Determining the Gender of English Loanwords in Bulgarian), *Sŭpostavitelno ezikoznanie*, 2 (4–5): 44–54.

The paper deals with the various grammatical and semantic factors which influence the gender assignment of English loanwords in Bulgarian. The corpus consists of 180 nouns, the gender of 77 per cent of which is morphosemantically determined. This figure indicates that meaning has an active role to play even in a language like Bulgarian, which has a well-developed system of formal gender marking in nouns.

3. —— (1983), 'Derivational Characteristics of English Loanwords in Bulgarian', *University of Sofia English Papers*, 2: 29–58.

The paper examines the derivational activity of sixty-four English loanwords which have produced about three hundred derivatives in Bulgarian, in comparison with that of their English correlatives, with about nine hundred derivatives. A generative approach to derivational relations is applied. The general tendency towards structural simplification and loss of semantic motivation in the process of borrowing reorganizes the derivational structure of the loanwords in comparison with their native correlatives, but it does not impair their ability to take part in word-formation as members of a new language system.

4. —— (1986), 'Some Observations on the Lexico-Semantic Assimilation of English Loanwords in Bulgarian', *Godishnik na Sofiĭskiya universitet/Annuaire de l'Université de Sofia*, 75 (4): 96–128.

The synchronic study of some three hundred English loanwords and their derivatives in Bulgarian offers a semantically-based classification comprising three groups: a) English loanwords (85 per cent); b) loanwords of non-English origin (15 per cent); c) derivatives from loanwords (produced by 29 per cent of the loanwords). Subgroups a) and b) reflect the deepening structural and lexico-semantic assimilation of the loanwords, caused either by an intermediary language, or by the interaction of the loanwords with the Bulgarian lexical subsystem.

5. —— (1987), 'English Synchronic and Diachronic Loanwords in Bulgarian', *University of Sofia English Papers*, 3: 29–41.

The paper analyses the relation between synchrony and diachrony in borrowing. Synchrony manifests itself in a partial, formal, and semantic correspondence between loanwords and their etymons. Diachrony reflects the development of new meanings by loanwords, the simplification of compound etymons and the creation of pseudo-anglicisms. The different stages of lexico-semantic assimilation are represented graphically on a scale which comprises six groups.

6. —— (1991), '*Desen i dizaĭn*—sinkhronno-diakhronna sŭpostavka v semantichen plan', (*Dessin* and *Design*—a Semantically-Based Synchronic and Diachronic Contrastive Study), *Sŭpostavitelno ezikoznanie*, 16: 15–23.

The analysis of *desen* and *dizaĭn*, borrowed from *dessin* and *design*, traces the semantic development of their common etymon in Italian, French, and English. The specific nature of the semantic changes of each loanword is considered in connection with the semantic conditions offered by each receiving language.

7. Alexieva, Nevena (1994), 'New, Metaphorically Extended, Meanings of Anglicisms in Bulgarian', *Chuzhdoezikovo obuchenie*, 1: 61–4.

The comparison between the extended meanings and those of the English etymons reveals discrepancies which are rooted in the nature of lexical borrowing. Different types of social, psychological and semantic motivation underlie the varying divergence between the anglicisms and their English etymons in the creation of new meanings.

8. Andreĭchin, Lyubomir and Valentin Stankov (eds.) (1951–), *Bŭlgarski ezik* (Sofia: The Bulgarian Academy of Sciences Publishers).

This bimonthly journal has a regular section 'Language Culture', dedicated to the problems of the 'correct usage' of Bulgarian. The articles on the usage of loanwords, now mostly anglicisms, are often puristically biased.

9. Bosilkov, Lyubomir (1974), 'English Sports Vocabulary in Bulgarian', unpublished M.A. paper (University of Sofia), 64 pp.

The paper examines the phonological, grammatical and lexical aspects of the adaptation of English sports loanwords to Bulgarian, the only terminological group which enjoys considerable popularity even outside its specific domain.

10. Dachkova, Lydia (1994), '*Trilŭr, ekshŭn, khit, khevimetŭl.* Tova na Bŭlgarski li e?' (*Thriller, action, hit, heavy metal.* Do I Read Bulgarian?), *Sotsiolingvistika*, 1: 132–6.

The paper analyses the spread of new anglicisms in Bulgarian among teenagers and the sociolinguistic factors which affect their integration, underlining the mutual influence of learning English and the adoption of English borrowings.

11. —— (1997*a*), 'Let's Make Things Better! Let It Be!', *Sotsiolingvistika*, 3: 158–69.

The paper analyses the usage of borrowings, mainly anglicisms, in a specific social context—the slogans used in protest rallies in early 1997. The main sources of borrowing are pop-songs, commercials and computer language. The usage of anglicisms in this context is due to an attempt to find an attractive form of expression and an adequate means of communication with the participants and foreign journalists, as well as to a desire to stress the analogy between this and similar events abroad.

12. —— (1997*b*), 'Nyakoi tendentsii v protsesa na zaemane na chuzhdi dumi v sŭvremenniya bŭlgarski ezik' (Some Tendencies in the Borrowing of Foreign Words in Present-Day Bulgarian), *Chuzhdoezikovo obuchenie*, 1 (2): 34–40.

The paper analyses loanwords found in texts and advertisements in periodicals in 1995/96. The study empirically confirms that the main source of modern borrowings is English. There is also a tendency to borrow nonce-words from Russian. While English loans fulfil two functions—to designate new concepts and to provide stylistic variation, those from Russian, as well as some reactivated Turkish loans, are typically used for variation.

13. Danchev, Andrei (1978, ^{2}1982, ^{3}1994), *Bŭlgarska transkriptsiya na angliĭski imena* (Bulgarian Transcription of English Names), (Sofia: Narodna Prosveta; third ed.: Sofia: Open Society Fund Publishers), 222 pp.

The first part of the book discusses the linguistic and extralinguistic factors that determine the most suitable Bulgarian forms. The second part consists of an indexed Bulgarian spelling and pronunciation dictionary of English names of persons, places, businesses, news media, sports clubs, etc. Numerous loanwords have also been included.

14. —— (1981), 'Anglitsizmite v bŭlgarskiya ezik' (Anglicisms in Bulgarian), *Sŭpostavitelno ezikoznanie*, 6 (3–5): 190–204.

This is a brief review of the study of anglicisms in Bulgarian and of some methodological problems such as the dating and origin of various anglicisms. It also considers the typology of their adaptation, as well as their Bulgarian transcription and pronunciation.

15. —— (1983), 'Review of: *Leksikata ot angliĭski proizkhod v noviya Rechnik na chuzhdite dumi v bŭlgarskiya ezik* (M. Filipova-Baĭrova, S. Boyadzhiev, El. Mashalova, G. Kostov)', (*The Lexis of English Origin in the New Dictionary of Foreign Words* = Ilchev *et al.* (eds.) (1982)), *Bŭlgarski ezik*, 33 (4): 363–8.

The review considers the corpus of English loanwords in Bulgarian included in the Dictionary and offers a number of corrections as well as some new loanwords that have been omitted.

16. DANCHEV, ANDREI(1986), 'The English Element in Bulgarian', in *Viereck and Bald (eds.), 7–23.

This survey considers the quantitative and qualitative aspects of the influence of English on Bulgarian, the channels of penetration and the dating of anglicisms, as well as their phonological, morphological, and semantic adaptation. Finally, there is a brief note on public attitudes. The comprehensive article is the most easily accessible account on the topic to date.

17. —— (1988), 'Segmental Phonology of the Bulgarian English Interlanguage(s)', in Andrei Danchev (ed.), *Error Analysis: Bulgarian Learners of English* (Sofia: Narodna Prosveta), 156–75.

The study is based on a large corpus of both learner errors and English loanwords in Bulgarian. The phonological adaptation patterns of various English segmental phonemes are examined and recommendations for their Bulgarian spelling and pronunciation are offered.

18. —— (1989), 'On the Contrastive Phonology of the Stressed Vowels in English and Bulgarian', in Jacek Fisiak (ed.), *Papers and Studies in Contrastive Linguistics*, 25: 156–75.

Unlike most studies in the area of contrastive phonology, this one is based on an extensive corpus of empirical data including numerous loanwords.

19. —— (1993*a*), 'The Perception and Production of English /æ/ by Bulgarians', in Leslie Collins (ed.), *The Second Anglo-Bulgarian Symposium, Blagoevgrad, September 1985* (University of London, School of Slavonic and East European Studies), 314–45.

The paper deals with one of the most difficult problems in English-Bulgarian language contact. A large number of loanwords are included and the various adaptation patterns are examined from different linguistic, socio-linguistic and cross-linguistic angles.

20. —— (1993*b*), 'A Note on Phrasemic Calquing', in Palma Zlateva (ed.), *Translation as Social Action: Russian and Bulgarian Perspectives* (London and New York: Routledge), 57–62.

The paper examines the calquing and adoption in Modern Bulgarian of English idiomatic phrases of the 'to rock the boat' type. There has been constant infiltration of such phrases into current

Bulgarian usage, especially after 1989. Public attitudes have been divided between accepting and rejecting such literal translations.

21. —— MICHAEL HOLMAN, EKATERINA DIMOVA, and SAVOVA MILENA (1989), *Angliĭski pravopis i izgovor na imenata v bŭlgarskiya ezik* (An English Dictionary of Bulgarian Names: Spelling and Pronunciation) (Sofia: Nauka i Izkustvo Publishers), 288 pp.

This dictionary contains the English transliteration and phonetic transcription of approximately 15,000 Bulgarian names of persons, places, institutions, etc. It is meant to facilitate written and oral communication in situations of Bulgarian-English language contact. The principles governing the selection of English forms to render Bulgarian names are reviewed in detail in the introductory section. They are quite close to those adopted for the transliteration of the Bulgarian entries in *UDASEL/DEA*.

22. DAVCHEVA, LEAH (1975), 'Morphological Assimilation of English Loanwords in Bulgarian', unpublished M.A. paper (University of Sofia), 55 pp.

A corpus of 850 loanwords serves to illustrate the stages of their morphological assimilation, as well as the nature and trends of this adaptation. It is governed by two tendencies which are not diametrically opposed, *viz.* preservation of the original formal structure and activity of the Bulgarian grammatical system. The majority of borrowings are nouns, which acquire the Bulgarian categories of gender and number; verbs and adjectives enter their respective paradigms and are inflected accordingly. The paper also examines the derivational potential of anglicisms.

23. DESPOTOVA, VERA (1980), 'Vokalna interferentsiya v angliĭskoto proiznoshenie na bŭlgarite (Akustichen analiz)' (Vowel Interference in the English Pronunciation of Bulgarians (Acoustic Analysis)), unpublished Ph.D. thesis (University of Sofia), 192 pp.

This is a study of the perception of vowel interference and of a foreign accent in Bulgarians' pronunciation of English. The author's conclusions are based on the laboratory analysis of experimental data. Vowel interference can lead to loss of phonemic distinctions between pairs of English words, or only to phonetic deviations, which are perceived as a 'foreign accent'. The difficulties in acquiring the pronunciation of the English vowels are experimentally proved to be rooted in the considerable differences between the English and Bulgarian vocalism. The findings of this study also help to explain the spontaneous changes English vowels undergo in borrowed words.

24. DIMITROVA, VANYA (1975), 'Phonological Assimilation of English Lexical Borrowings in Bulgarian', unpublished M.A. paper (University of Sofia), 70 pp.

This is a corpus-based study of the phonological assimilation of English borrowings with regard to phonemic substitution and changes in the accentual and syllabic structures as the result of adaptation to the Bulgarian phonological system. The most prominent changes consist in the monophthongization of diphthongs and the neutralization of the phonological opposition between voiced and voiceless consonants in word-final position. The author also takes into account the influence of mediating languages.

25. DOBREVA, DENKA (1987), 'Angliĭskite zaemki v bŭlgarskata veterinarnozootekhnicheska leksika' (English Loanwords in Bulgarian Veterinary-Zootechnical Terminology), unpublished Ph.D. thesis (University of Plovdiv), 355 pp.

This comprehensive study of anglicisms in veterinary terminology traces their origin and offers a thorough phonological, morpho-syntactic and semantic analysis of the adaptation of 995 loanwords, calques, and semicalques. It also provides sociological information about specialists' attitudes to these loan terms and recommendations for the appropriate use of the three different types.

26. GABEROFF, IVAN ([3]1999), *Rechnik na chuzhdite dume v bŭlgarski* (Dictionary of Foreign Words in Bulgarian) [= *DFW 1999*] (Sofia: BAN/The Bulgarian Academy of Sciences), 944 pp.

This is the latest of a long series of such dictionaries, initiated more than a century ago. It contains some 40,000 entries, also including set phrases. The author covers traditional, as well as most recent established borrowings, which are mostly anglicisms. The lemmas are provided with grammatical and stylistic labels and with recommendations for their correct usage. The history of the loans is traced from the etymon into Bulgarian. A bibliography on the topic lists the most important national dictionaries of this type and selected works on borrowing.

27. Georgiev, Vladimir *et al.* (1971–), *Bŭlgarski etimologichen rechnik* (Bulgarian Etymological Dictionary) (Sofia: BAN/The Bulgarian Academy of Sciences).

This multi-volume dictionary provides detailed information about the origins, meanings and derivatives of native or borrowed words. The development of indirect borrowings is traced through intermediary languages.

28. Ilchev, Stephan, Maria Filipova-Baĭrova *et al.* (eds.) (1982), *Rechnik na chuzhdite dumi v bŭlgarskiya ezik* (Dictionary of Foreign Words in Bulgarian = *DFW*) (Sofia: BAN/The Bulgarian Academy of Sciences), 1015 pp. Cf. Milev [4]1978.

This is the modern academic, and truly comprehensive Bulgarian dictionary of foreign words dating from the 1930s. It offers diachronic and synchronic information about the sources and stages of development of the loanwords through successive intermediary languages and precise basic and extended meanings of words in general use and specialized terms.

29. Kaburov, Georgi (ed.) (1983), *Terminologichen rechnik po fizicheska kultura i sport* (Dictionary of Physical Culture and Sports Terms) (Sofia), 527 pp.

The dictionary includes 4533 Bulgarian sports terms. In the introduction the author pays special attention to entries of foreign origin (mostly English) and to their interpretation in Bulgarian.

30. Karastoĭcheva, Tsvetana (1980), 'Za rolyata na chuzhdoezikoviya element pri izgrazhdane na bŭlgarskiya mladezhki sleng' (On the Role of the Foreign Language Element in the Formation of Bulgarian Youth Slang), in Petŭr Pashov and Valentin Stankov (eds.), *Problemi na ezikovata kultura* (Problems of Language Culture) (Sofia), 214–25.

The paper examines the complex influence of borrowed elements on the most active present-day Bulgarian sociolect. In search of expressiveness and fashionableness youth slang consciously and extensively adopts and calques English elements from the phonological, grammatical and lexical levels. Slang borrowings are characterized by more thorough semantic changes in comparison with anglicisms in standard Bulgarian.

31. Kondova, Vera (1971), 'English Borrowings in Bulgarian

Maritime Terminology', unpublished M.A. paper (University of Sofia), 54 pp.

The paper studies the most common loanwords of English origin in Bulgarian maritime terminology, their present form under the conditions of professional bilingualism, and the influence of intermediary languages.

32. Kondova, Vera (1984), 'Anglitsizmite v terminologichniya rechnik po fizicheska kultura i sport' (Anglicisms in the Dictionary of Physical Culture and Sports Terms), *Nauchni trudove*, 25 (4): 35–8.

The paper examines the anglicisms in the dictionary, their presentation and definitions, and their phonological, morphological, and semantic adaptation to Bulgarian.

33. —— (1986), 'Nyakoi nablyudeniya vŭrkhu upotrebata na anglitsizmi v bŭlgarskata sportna terminologiya' (Some Observations on the Use of Anglicisms in Bulgarian Sports Terminology), *Proceedings of the Second National Conference on the Theory and Practice of Scientific and Scientific-technical Texts* (University of Sofia), 168–73.

The paper examines 127 sports terms of English origin and 192 derivatives in the speech of 147 persons and in written texts. Doublet forms resulting from parallel direct transfer and calquing are noted. The speakers' lexical choices are viewed as an indicator of their professional involvement, education and age.

34. —— (1994), 'Nyakoi tendentsii v razvitieto na bŭlgarskata sportna rech kato profesionalen sotsiolekt' (Some Tendencies in the Development of Bulgarian Sports Speech as a Professional Sociolect), *Proceedings of the Scientific Conference to Mark the Fiftieth Anniversary of the National Sports Academy*, 94–8.

The paper studies the position of loanwords in Bulgarian sports terminology in spoken and written uses. Their occurrence in speech reflects the professional involvement of the speaker, and his attitude towards a changing social situation.

35. Maslov, Yuriĭ (1982), *Grammatika na bŭlgarskiya ezik* (A Grammar of the Bulgarian Language) (Sofia: Nauka i izkustvo Publishers), 402 pp.

36. Milev, Aleksandŭr *et al.* ([4]1978), *Rechnik na chuzhdite dumi v bŭlgarskiya ezik* (Dictionary of Foreign Words in Bulgarian = *DFW*) (Sofia: Nauka i izkustvo Publishers), 895 pp.

This latest edition of a series of dictionaries considers only the ultimate provenance of the foreign words and hence treats most as deriving from Greek or Latin. The authors distinguish between well-integrated 'loanwords' and 'aliens', which are still felt as foreign. Only aliens are included. Cf. Ilchev 1982.

37. MOLHOVA, JANA (1979), 'Angliĭskite zaemki v bŭlgarskiya ezik' (English Loanwords in Bulgarian), in Khristo Pŭrvev (ed.), *Pomagalo po bŭlgarska leksikologiya* (Readings in Bulgarian Lexicology) (Sofia), 227–38.

The article is a general survey of the major thematic groups of English loanwords in Bulgarian, and of their phonological, grammatical, derivational and semantic assimilation.

38. —— (1982), 'English Borrowings in Bulgarian', *Proceedings of the Bulgarian-American Conference, Boston, 11–14 Oct. 1982.*

The paper represents one of the earliest surveys of the lexical impact of English on Modern Bulgarian. It considers the different types and rates of adaptation of anglicisms to Bulgarian, paying particular attention to the various intra- and extralinguistic factors on which the rate of assimilation depends. The author proposes four degrees of integration, which roughly correspond to the cline of symbols ((0) to (3)) adopted in the *DEA*.

39. MOSKOV, MOSKO (1958), *Borbata protiv chuzhdite dumi v bŭlgarskiya knizhoven ezik* (The Struggle against Foreign Words in the Bulgarian Literary Language) (Sofia: BAN/The Bulgarian Academy of Sciences Publishers), 147 pp.

The book offers a historical survey of Bulgarian purism in the nineteenth and the first half of the twentieth century. The author, who accepts the inevitability of lexical borrowing, is critical of extremely purist attitudes, favouring a distinction between established loans and 'aliens'.

40. MOSKOVSKA, MARTA (1981), 'Formalno skhodni dvoĭki dumi v angliĭski i bŭlgarski ezik (semantichni i funktsionalni kharakteristiki)' (Formally Similar Pairs of Words in English and Bulgarian (Semantic and Functional Features)), *Sŭpostavitelno ezikoznanie i chuzhdoezikovo obuchenie*, 3: 222–37.

The analysis of formally similar pairs of words in English and

Bulgarian shows that the degree of semantic correspondence holding between them is not the only factor of organization of the semantic structure of the words; the author points out the type and number of components missing from each structure.

41. Moskovska, Marta (1982), 'Otnovo za lŭzhlivite priyateli na prevodacha i edna tyakhna funktsiya' (Again on the Translator's *faux amis* and one of their Functions), *Sŭpostavitelno ezikoznanie i chuzhdoezikovo obuchenie*, 4: 193–204.

The paper considers the relationships between members of grapho-phonemically related pairs of words (false friends) in English and Bulgarian and discusses instances of semantic modification of formally similar Bulgarian equivalents as a result of English interference.

42. —— (1995), 'The International Component in the Bulgarian Language: Some Recent Developments' (*Papers of the Fourth International Sociolinguistic Conference (INSOLICO'93), Sofia 9–12 Sept, 1993*), *Problemi na sotsiolingvistikata*, 4: 108–11.

Numerous recent developments under the influence of English indicate the change of status of the Bulgarian international equivalent and its ever increasing functional and communicative significance after 1989.

43. Pashova, Galina, B. Naimushin, and B. Veleva (2001), *Rechnik na chuzhditedumi v bŭlgarskiya ezik* (DFW = Dictionary of Foreign Words in Bulgarian) (Sofia: Hermes Publ.), 756 pp.

This dictionary is the second one in a series of new Bulgarian dictionaries designed in a handy, one-volume format for practical, daily reference. It covers the basic borrowings used at present in the economy, politics, the humanities and the arts, as well as the less specialized loan terms in the sciences. The dictionary offers new, more precise definitions of a number of established loanwords. The authors have included current new loans and have purposefully left out what they consider to be generally familiar words (e.g. *turist*, 'tourist'). Each lemma is provided with information about the source language, and about intermediary languages, when they have left their stamp on the form or meaning of the word.

44. Pencheva, Maya (1994), 'Semantichni konstanti. Kategoriyata

odushevenost' (Semantic Constants. The Category of Animacy), unpublished D.litt. thesis (Universitiy of Sofia), 638 pp.

A general typological and diachronic treatment of the semantic universal of animacy includes the crucial role of loanwords in the change of the grammatical category of gender in a number of languages (ch. 5). The historical disappearance of this category in English, and the appearance of uninflectable adjectives as well as the expansion of common gender in Bulgarian are shown to be largely connected with lexical borrowing.

45. PETKOVA, GERGANA (1996), 'The Sociolinguistic Factor of Age and the Distribution of Some Recent Borrowed Linguistic Items of English Origin in the Context of Pop Music', unpublished M.A. paper (University of Sofia), 70 pp.

Applying consistent sociolinguistic methodology, this pioneering work investigates thirty recent pop music terms in relation to six age groups, each represented by ten informants. Factors like (non-)professional involvement with pop music, sex, knowledge of English and education are also taken into account. The findings of the study are based on interviews and observations of spontaneous conversations. The questionnaire used in the interviews aims at eliciting the usage of these lexemes, the degree of their adaptation and the subjects' awareness of their meanings. The results are summarized statistically.

46. PETKOVA, VYARA (1977), 'Angliĭskite zaemki v bŭlgarskata morska terminologiya sled Vtorata svetovna voĭna i tyakhnata semantichna konfiguratsiya' (English Borrowings in the Bulgarian Maritime Terminology after World War II and their Semantic Configuration), *Sŭpostavitelno ezikoznanie*, 2 (4–5): 170–9.

Loanwords, loan-blends and calques generally narrow their meanings within the terminological field, whereas semantic loans tend to expand their meanings. Some borrowings undergo metonymic simplification.

47. —— (1981), 'Za bilingvizma i interferentsiyata v morsko-tŭrgovskata komunikatsiya' (On Bilingualism and Interference in Maritime Communication), *Sŭpostavitelno ezikoznanie*, 6: 17–24.

An attempt is made to analyse how different types of bilingualism interact and to trace the manifestations of interference. When used in Bulgarian, borrowed terms are not influenced by the bilingualism of mariners, because they are accepted as 'inherited terms'. However, some recent borrowings are transferred in forms close to those in the source language.

48. PETKOVA, VYARA (1988*a*), 'Bulgarian-English Language Contacts in Maritime Communication', unpublished Ph.D. thesis (University of Sofia), 245 pp.

This thorough study of Bulgarian-English contacts within a general linguistic and sociolinguistic framework treats: a) the bilingualism and interlanguage of Bulgarian mariners and b) the English element in maritime terminology. It is shown that professional bilingualism is due to some sociolinguistic pressure; this does not trigger any counter-pressure for the preservation of the linguistic identity of the socio-professional group because the two languages have the same social status.

49. —— (1988*b*), 'Kalkirane na angliĭski morski termini v bŭlgarskata morska terminologiya' (Loan-Translation of English Maritime Terms in Bulgarian Maritime Terminology), *Trudove na VNVMU*, 22: 1–42.

The author discusses 314 calques to show the advantages of loan-translation for the formation of motivated terms and as a means of internationalization of terms. She also describes the ways English structural patterns are translated into Bulgarian and what newly established word-formation patterns have appeared under English influence.

50. —— (1989*a*), 'Za kalkiraneto na morski termini-slovosŭchetaniya s formalna struktura /Adj + N/ v angliĭskiya ezik' (On the Loan-Translation of English Maritime Terminological Groups of the Pattern /Adj + N/), *Pŭrva Natsionalna Konferentsiya s mezhdunarodno uchastie Sofia IChS 'G. A. Nasur'* (First National Conference with International Participation—Institute for Foreign Students 'G. A. Nasur').

The analysis of maritime terminological phrases leads to the conclusion that calquing is greatly facilitated by the existence of parallel word-formation models in the two languages. It is proved that motivated terminological calques are created when the attributive adjectives are in a one-to-one lexical relationship with each other.

51. —— (1989*b*), 'Za otnoshenieto na spetsialistite kŭm zaemaneto i prevoda na angliĭski termini v bŭlgarskata morska terminologiya' (On the Mariners' Attitude towards Borrowing and Translation of English Terms in the Bulgarian Maritime Terminology), *Vtora Natsionalna Shkola po Sotsiolingvistika s mezhdunarodno uchastie: 'Metodi na sotsiolingvistichnoto izsledvane—Slŭnchev bryag* (Second National School of Sociolinguists with International Participation: Methods of Sociolinguistic Investigation).

The author points out that in face-to-face communication bilingual mariners employ more English terms, i.e. they prefer 'on-the-spot borrowings', while in written communication the established standardized terms are preferred.

52. STAMENOV, HRISTO (1979), 'Two English Loan Words in Bulgarian', *Philologia*, 6: 89–90.

The paper deals with the Bulgarian forms 'dŭnki' and 'dzhinsi' which refer to specific types of casual trousers. The origin of 'dunki' is not clear; Engl. *donkey jacket* and *dungarees* are discussed as possible sources.

53. STANKOV, VALENTIN and V. MURDAROV (eds.) (1983), *Glavoboliya s chuzhdite dumi* (Troublesome Foreign Words) (Sofia), 167 pp.

The book is a collection of articles treating various formal and semantic problems of borrowings in Bulgarian, a considerable number of which are anglicisms. The authors' viewpoints reflect the two conflicting attitudes to borrowing in contemporary Bulgarian studies—acceptance and purist objection. The latter manifests itself in dividing borrowings into acceptable *loanwords* and unnecessary *aliens*.

54. STOYANOV, STOYAN (ed.) (1983), *Gramatika na sŭvremenniya bŭlgarski knizhoven ezik (Morfologiya 2)* (Grammar of the Contemporary Bulgarian Literary Language (Morphology 2)) (Sofia: BAN/The Bulgarian Academy of Sciences Publishers), 511 pp.

The book considers the grammatical adaptation of borrowings, including anglicisms, within a general academic survey of the Bulgarian morphological system. It notes structural features influenced by lexical borrowing.

55. TILKOV, DIMITŬR (ed.) (1982), *Gramatika na sŭvremenniya bŭlgarski knizhoven ezik (Fonetika 1)* (A Grammar of the Contemporary

Bulgarian Literary Language (Phonetics 1)) (Sofia: BAN/The Bulgarian Academy of Sciences Publishers), 300 pp.

This comprehensive treatment of the Bulgarian phonological system and spelling also considers problems of the pronunciation and transliteration of loanwords, mostly anglicisms.

56. TSVETANOVA, YANKA (1978), 'English Borrowing in the Tourist Industry', unpublished M.A. paper (University of Sofia), 43 pp.

The paper examines the assimilation of English borrowings on the phonological, morphological and lexical planes. Some terms are found to remain morphologically non-assimilated, a fact which the author attributes to the need for effective communication in the domain of tourism.

57. VANKOV, LYUBOMIR (1971), 'Rannite zaemki ot angliĭski ezik v bŭlgarski' (The Early Borrowings from English into Bulgarian), *Godishnik na Sofiĭskiya universitet/Annuaire de l'Université de Sofia*, 65: 297–324.

The paper is a diachronic study of sixty-four early anglicisms in Bulgarian which entered the language in the nineteenth century. Their forms and meanings testify to their indirect borrowing through French, Russian, and Turkish, with which Bulgarian was in close contact at the time.

58. VIDENOV, MIKHAIL (1982), *Sotsiolingvistika. Bŭlgarski sotsiolingvisticheski problemi* (Sociolinguistics. Bulgarian Sociolinguistic Problems) (Sofia: Nauka i izkustvo publishers), 213 pp.

Lexical borrowing in Modern Bulgarian within the sociolinguistic situation of the last two hundred years is treated with particular attention to the present problems of borrowings, among which anglicisms predominate. The author's realistic treatment of this subject sets him apart from the majority of Bulgarian linguists, whose views on 'foreign words' are still in varying degrees puristically biased.

59. YORDANOVA, LYUBIMA (1980), *Novite dumi v sŭvremenniya bŭlgarski ezik* (Neologisms in Contemporary Bulgarian) (Sofia: Nauka i izkustvo publishers), 91 pp.

The book contains a chapter on borrowings (largely anglicisms), one of the major sources of neologisms in Bulgarian, and considers the reasons for their adaptation.

60. Zlateva, Maria (1985), *Sintagmatichni anglitsizmi v bŭlgarskiya ezik* (Syntagmatic Anglicisms in Bulgarian), unpublished Ph.D. thesis (University of Sofia), 169 pp.

Croatian (Rudolf Filipović)

(see also *16, *18, *25, *37, *45, *67)

SRAZ = *Studia Romanica et Anglica Zagrabiensia*, Zagreb

1. Broz, Ivan (1886), 'Hrvatski jezik', *Crtice iz hrvatske književnosti* ('The Croatian Language', Examples of the Croatian Literature), 1: 104–67.

2. Đurkovečki, Jožef (1826), *Jezičnica horvatsko-slavinska* (The Croatian-Slavic Vocabulary) (Pešta), 200–6 (repr. 1933) in *Građa XII* (Zagreb).

3. Filipović, Rudolf (1958), 'The Phonetic Compromise', *SRAZ* 5: 77–88.

The author discusses phonetic compromise as a transition from the foreign status of a word, or the first stage, to completely assimilated native status, or the third stage. This compromise is a general linguistic phenomenon which disappears as soon as the borrowed word is widely used. Accommodation can take three forms, as seen in a) foreign phonemes; b) foreign phonemic combinations; c) and adoption of a foreign accentual system.

4. —— (1960*a*), 'Phonemic Importation', *SRAZ* 9–10: 177–89.

Phonemic importation is phonetically conditioned. A phoneme can be imported; 1) if there is an allophone of the same kind in the borrowing language; 2) if it exists in the borrowing language as a latent phoneme; 3) if it fills a gap in the pattern; 4) if it exists in a dialect; 5) if it is a result of a phonetic law in the borrowing language; 6) if there is a tendency in the language to form certain phonemes of a category; and 7) if its true equivalent exists in the primary system, but is restricted to one position only.

5. —— (1960*b*), *The Phonemic Analysis of English Loanwords in Croatian* (Acta Instituti Phonetici, 8; Zagreb: University of Zagreb), 137 pp.

A historical survey of how purism worked in Croatia and how foreign words were borrowed is followed by 'Principles of linguistic borrowing' (based on Haugen). Pronunciation is used to distinguish three degrees of adaption: a) foreign words; b) foreign loans; c) loanwords, the distinction related to a contrastive analysis of English and Croatian phonology and stress. (Reviews: Haugen, *Language*, 56 (1960), 548–51; *Folia Linguistica*, 22 (1–2) (1988), 3–9; Strang, *Notes and Queries*, 9 (5) (1962), 190–2.)

6. —— (1961), 'The Morphological Adaption of English Loanwords in Serbo-Croatian', *SRAZ* 11: 91–103.

English words in Croatian either retain their English forms or they are morphologically adapted. Substantives are assigned to the category of gender and subjected to the Croatian system of inflections. Most adjectives have retained their original form, while new adjectives derived from English loanwords are fitted into the inflexional system of Croatian. Verbs are adapted by adding a verbal infinitive suffix and an infinitive formant.

7. —— (1967), 'Compromise Replica and Phonemic Importation', in *To Honor Roman Jakobson: Essays on the Occasion of his Seventieth Birthday*, 662–6.

The author discusses the relation between compromise replica and innovations in the distribution of consonantal phonemes and phonemic importation in the system of vowels in Croatian.

8. —— (1968), 'Semantic Extension Changes in Adaptation of English Loanwords in Serbo-Croatian', *SRAZ* 25–6: 109–19.

The author discusses some of the most typical examples of the semantic adaptation of English loanwords in Croatian. Hope's pattern of a) zero extension; b) restriction in meaning; and c) expansion in meaning does not cover all the various changes, so further subdivisions of groups b) and c) are suggested. Changes in group b) should be divided into: (1) restriction of meaning in general, i.e. the loss of some senses; and (2) restriction of meaning within one sense. Changes in group c) should be divided into: (1) expansion of meaning in general, i.e. acquiring some new senses; and (2) expansion of meaning within one sense.

9. —— (1973), 'Some Problems in Studying the English Element in the Main European Languages', *English Studies Today*, 5: 25–52, and *Studia Anglica Posnaniensia*, 4 (1–2): 141–58.

Major problems in the analysis of English loanwords are

described on four levels: stress on the phonological level, verbal aspect on the morphological level, changes in semantic extension on the semantic level, and technical vocabulary on the lexical level.

10. FILIPOVIĆ, RUDOLF (1985), 'Accentuation of English Loanwords in Serbo-Croatian', *International Journal of Slavic Linguistics and Poetics*, 32–33: 143–9.

The author tries to determine the link between some phonetic elements of an English model and the qualitative and quantitative characteristics of the musical stress of the Croatian replica, to base the loanword stress on some geographic factors and find out the trend in native word accentuation and how it is reflected in the loanword, and to link the historical development of stress in Croatian native words with loanword stress in some replicas.

11. —— (1986), 'Research Guidelines for Analysing Anglicisms in Serbo-Croatian', in *Viereck and Bald (eds.), 333–43.

The analysis of anglicisms in Croatian must be based on the fact that the contact between English and Croatian was mediated in this early phase; it is limited to the phonological, morphological, lexical, and semantic levels, and it has to take into consideration the distinction between primary and secondary changes. The analysis should use the explanatory categories of transphonemization and its three types on the phonological level, transmorphemization and its three types on the morphological level, and the changes in semantic extension (in number and in field).

12. —— (1988), 'Fonološke varijante u rječniku anglicizama u hrvatskom ili srpskom jeziku' (Phonological Variants in *The Dictionary of Anglicisms in the Croatian or Serbian Language*), *Filologija*, 16: 73–85.

Phonological variants of anglicisms can originate because: a) they follow the orthography of the model; b) anglicisms follow pronunciation of the model; c) anglicisms are formed partly according to the orthography and partly according to the pronunciation of the model; d) anglicisms are formed under the influence of the intermediary language.

13. —— (1990*a*), 'Secondary Anglicisms in a Dictionary of Anglicisms in Serbo-Croatian', *The Bell of Freedom: Essays presented to*

Monica Partridge on the Occasion of her Seventy-fifth Birthday (Nottingham: Astra Press), 1–11.

One of the functions of borrowing from foreign languages is to fill gaps in the vocabulary. This is achieved by borrowing words or expressions or by coining new words or expressions from elements of the donor language (pseudo-anglicisms).

14. —— (1990*b*), 'Morfološke varijante u "Rječniku anglicizama u hrvatskom ili srpskom jeziku"' (Morphological Variants in *The Dictionary of Anglicisms in Croatian and Serbian*), *Croatica-Slavica-Indoeuropea, Wiener Slavistisches Jahrbuch*, Ergänzungsband 8: 35–42.

Morphological variants of anglicisms in Croatian are found in borrowed nouns and verbs. In nouns, the variant can be identical with the English model or it has the plural form of the English model, or the variant is formed on the basis of the English plural form and the ending *-a* denoting gender. According to the formation of the citation form verbal anglicisms fall into two groups based on the infinitival formants: a) anglicisms formed by means of formants of the borrowing language (*-a-*, *-ova-*); and b) by means of hybrid formants (*-ira-*, *-isa-*). Both of these groups show a whole range of morphological variants.

15. —— (1990*c*), *Anglicizmi u hrvatskom ili srpskom jeziku: porijeklo—razvoj—značenje* (Anglicisms in Croatian or Serbian: Origin—Development—Meaning) (Djela JAZU, knjiga 70; Jugoslavenska akadmija znanosti i umjetnosti, Školska knjiga) (JAZU, Book 70, Yugoslav Academy of Science and Art, School Book) (Zagreb), 336 pp. (Review: Ivir, *SRAZ* 35 (1990), 183–6).

An analysis of anglicisms in Croatian based on the theoretical principles of *Filipović (1986) is followed by a dictionary of anglicisms. The analysis in the textual part and in the dictionary starts with the English etymon and then traces its adaptation on the orthographic, phonological, and morphological levels; it also records the meaning(s) of the English word taken over in the process of borrowing and its subsequent adaptation in Croatian. The presentation of the analytical information in the dictionary follows the system developed by the author: standard symbols (or formulas) have been devised providing for every aspect of borrowing and adaptation of anglicisms both in Croatian and in other languages.

16. Filipović, Rudolf (1996*a*), 'English as a Word Donor to Other Languages of Europe', in *Hartmann, 37–46.

17. —— (1996*b*), *An Annotated Bibliography (1958–1995), The English Element in European Languages* (Vol. 4, Zagreb: Institute of Linguistics), 69 pp.

18. Muhvić-Dimanovski, Vesna (1986), 'O paralelnoj upotrebi posuđenica i njihovih prevedenica' (On the Parallel Use of Loanwords and their Loan Translations), *Filologija*, 14: 247–53.

Before a loan translation has established itself in a language, it has to go through a phase in which it exists in parallel with the loanword that had served as its model. The author discusses examples of such parallel use of English loanwords and their loan translations in Croatian.

19. —— (1990), 'Some Recent Semantic Loans of English Origin in Serbo-Croatian', in *Filipović and Bratanić (eds.), 151–6.

Semantic loans have always been a very common category in linguistic borrowing and comprise a frequently used means of expressing new concepts in a language. Through its history Croatian has acquired numbers of new meanings from several languages, mostly from German and Italian. Recently though, due to extensive Anglo-American influence, most of the semantic loans that appear in Croatian are of English origin.

20. Sočanac, Lelija (1994), 'O nekim anglicizmima i pseudoanglicizmima u rječnicima hrvatskoga književnog jezika' (On some Anglicisms and Pseudoanglicisms in the Dictionaries of the Croatian Literary Language), *Filologija*, 22–3: 225–8.

The author discusses the problem of anglicisms in Croatian dictionaries, including the problem of intermediary languages, pseudoanglicisms, derivatives, compounds, etc. The problem of purism versus linguistic borrowing is also discussed.

21. Velčić, Ivana (1982), 'The English Element in Croatian Sports Vocabulary', in *Filipović (ed.), 421–39.

The majority of English sport terms have been adapted according to Croatian phonological and morphological systems, while on the semantic level quite a number of examples show changes in semantic extension. The article also contains a list of the most frequent anglicisms from sports.

(Serbo-)Croatian (Rudolf Filipović)

(This section includes studies of Serbo-Croatian—regarded as one language until a few years ago—and modern works on Croatian. There do not seem to be any recent studies contrasting anglicisms in Croatian and Serbian, exploring how the linguistic split is reflected in the field of anglicisms.)

1. ČULIĆ, ZJENA (1992), 'Engleski jezik u dodiru s hrvatskim jezikom u prevođenju znanstvenih radova' (The Contact between English and Croatian in the Translation of Scientific Papers), in M. Andrijašević and Y. Vrhovac (eds.), *Zbornik radova Hrvatskoga društva za primijenjenu lingvistiku. Strani jezik u dodiru s materinskim jezikom* (Zagreb), 139–45.

The author analyses some English equivalents of the Croatian structures from a corpus which includes the scientific register. The analysis can be considered as an introduction to a further study of the relationship between implicit and explicit coding of the same semantic functions in the two contrasted languages.

2. MAČEK, DORA (1991), 'Between Language Contact and Language Development', in *Ivir and Kalogjera (eds.), 281–8. (EEEL 4).

The author discusses innovations which appear in a language as a consequence of language contact. One of the basic principles of such a contact is the relationship between direct and indirect contact, each of which has a different effect on the language. So far it has been considered that in direct contact of two languages the influence is present in the whole system.

3. STOFFEL, HANS-PETER (1991), 'Common Features in the Morphological Adaptation of English Loanwords in Migrant Serbo-Croatian', in *Ivir and Kalogjera (eds.), 417–29.

The aim of the article is to describe some common features of the morphological adaptation of loanwords originating in North-American and New Zealand English in Croatian and Serbian spoken by immigrants.

4. VILKE, MIRJANA (1982), 'The English Element in Serbo-Croatian Technical Vocabulary', in *Filipović (ed.), 439–67.

The investigation is limited to shipping, the oil industry, high-frequency technology and nuclear physics, all abounding in anglicisms. The article also gives some interesting general remarks on technical terminology and its history. The analysis of the corpus showed two opposite trends, one leading to the internationalization and the other to linguistic purification of terminology.

Danish (Knud Sørensen)

(see also *25, *45, *55)

1. DAHL, TORSTEN (1942), 'English Influence as Reflected in the Danish Language', *Studia Neophilologica*, 14: 386–92.

2. —— (1956), 'Engelske spor i moderne dansk' (English Traces in Modern Danish), in Svend Askjær *et al.* (eds.), *Festskrift til Peter Skautrup* (Festschrift for Peter Skautrup) (Aarhus), 251–6.

3. DAVIDSEN-NIELSEN, NIELS, ERIK HANSEN, and PIA JARVAD (eds.) (1999), '*Engelsk Eller Ikke Engelsk? That is the question*', Dansk Sprognævns skrifter 28.

This book contains seven papers given by linguists at a conference held in the spring of 1998 for the purpose of discussing various problems arising from the fact that the Danish language is being (increasingly, some would say) influenced by English. The contributors do not agree on how to assess this influence: is it good, bad, or negligible? And if it is bad, what, if anything, can be done to stem the tide? To what extent is it possible to devise Danish terms as substitutes for English loanwords? Unlike Sweden, Denmark has no official language policy, and since some Danes might wish to follow Sweden's example in this respect, the book concludes with an 'action programme for furthering the Swedish language' proposed by the Swedish Language Academy (Svenska språknämnden).

4. HANSEN, ERIK and JØRN LUND (1994), *Kulturens Gesandter. Fremmedordene i dansk* (Ambassadors of Culture. Foreign Words in Danish).

This book is a general account of foreign words in Danish and includes a section on twentieth-century anglicisms.

5. JACOBSEN, HENRIK GALBERG (1994), 'Sprogændringer og sprogvurdering. Om nogle aktuelle engelskinspirerede ændringer i dansk og om vurderingen af dem' (Language Changes and their Assessment. On some topical English-inspired Changes in Danish and their Assessment), *Danske Studier*, 5–28.

This article reviews a number of English-inspired changes that have affected the Danish language over the last twenty or thirty years. These changes manifest themselves on practically all linguistic levels and provoke varied reactions. Many lay people react strongly against direct loans. As for the insidious semantic loans, the author argues that these merely facilitate developments that are already latent in Danish.

6. JARVAD, PIA (1995), *Nye ord—hvorfor og hvordan?* (New Words—Why and How) (Copenhagen: Gyldendal).

This book is a general account of new words in contemporary Danish, but it contains over a hundred pages dealing with influence from English. About 10 per cent of the new words are anglicisms, and the author sees this as a threat to Danish. As she puts it: 'We are increasingly allowing another culture and its language to govern our reality.'

7. LARSEN, FRITZ (1994), 'More than Loan-words: English Influence on Danish', *RASK* 1: 21–46.

This article focuses on covert influences, i.e. calques and semantic loans, arguing that when English influence is covert, there will be less resistance to the adoption of loans.

8. *Nordiske Sprogproblemer 1955–1967* (1956–68) (Nordic Linguistic Problems), 7 vols. (Dansk Sprognævn).

9. PETERSEN, PIA RIBER (1984), *Ny Ord i Dansk 1955–75* (New Words in Danish 1955–75). (Dansk Sprognævns Skrifter, 11)

This dictionary records and documents the use of neologisms in Danish adopted in the period 1955–75, approximately 25 per cent of which are anglicisms.

10. PREISLER, BENT (1999), *Danskerne og det engelske sprog, med et bidrag af Kjeld Høgsbro* (The Danes and the English Language. With a contribution by Kjeld Høgsbro). (Roskilde Universitetsforlag).

This book examines the social and psychological factors underlying English influence on the Danish language. A statistical survey lays bare the—mainly positive—attitudes towards that influence. It is argued that the influence comes partly from above, i.e. the educational system and the internationally orientated business world, partly from below, where it operates in a number of subcultures: hip hop, rock music, death metal, computers, and amateur radio; to those who go in for these subcultures the use of the English language is very important, as is code-switching between English and Danish. In some cases the influence from above and that from below may work together. About 20 per cent of the population have practically no knowledge of English, and it is suggested that it is up to Danish politicians to remedy this.

11. SKAUTRUP, PETER (1944–68), *Det Danske Sprogs Historie I–IV* (Linguistic History of Danish).

A comprehensive history of the Danish language which provides a chronological account of English loanwords in Danish.

12. SØRENSEN, KNUD (1971), 'Knock-out og come-back. Om trykket i en engelsk låneordstype', *Nyt fra Sprognævnet*, 7: 1–2.

This brief article discusses the end-stress in Danish in anglicisms of the *knock-out* type.

13. —— (1973), *Engelske lån i dansk* (English Loans in Danish) (Dansk Sprognævns Skrifter, 8) (Copenhagen). (Reviews: Rona, *Translatøren*, 2 (1974), 30–2; Hansen, *Danske Studier* (1975), 103–12).

This is the first monograph in Danish on the subject of anglicisms. It surveys the orthographic, phonemic, and morphological adaptation of English loanwords and briefly discusses English syntactic influence on Danish. The bulk of the book is concerned with the various types of loanword: direct loans, translation loans, semantic loans, formal adaptations, hybrids, acronyms, and pseudo-loans, and their occurrence. In conclusion a survey is given of the principal semantic areas that favour the adoption of anglicisms.

14. —— (1975), 'Om anglicismer i moderne dansk' (On Anglicisms in Modern Danish), *Nordiske Studier. Festskrift til Chr. Westergård-Nielsen* (Copenhagen), 221–31.

This article concentrates on the adoption and adaptation of English idioms in contemporary Danish.

15. —— (1978), 'Om engelske betydningslån i moderne dansk', *Danske Studier*, 134–40.

This article lists and analyses a number of semantic loans in contemporary Danish.

16. Sørensen, Knud (1981), 'Fra *Seven Gothic Tales* til *Syv fantastiske Fortællinger*' (From *Seven Gothic Tales* to *Syv fantastiske Fortællinger*), *Danske Studier*, 45–71.

This article examines a work by the bilingual writer Karen Blixen, concluding that when she writes in English, danicisms crop up from time to time, and when she translates her English text into Danish, a number of anglicisms creep in.

17. —— (1982), 'English Influence on Contemporary Danish', in *Filipović (ed.), 71–154.

This is an updated and condensed version of Sørensen (1973).

18. —— (1986), 'On Anglicisms in Danish', in *Viereck and Bald (eds.), 31–49.

After a historical survey, the author sketches the integration of English loanwords on the individual linguistic levels and summarizes borrowing vs. calquing processes evident from Danish. The author concludes that at the time of writing there were some four thousand anglicisms in Danish, and that there was in many cases an unstable equilibrium between direct loans and translation loans. A brief but informative account.

19. —— (1987), 'Engelsk indflydelse på moderne dansk syntaks' (English Influence on Modern Danish Syntax), *Møde om Udforskningen af Dansk Sprog*, 1: 135–44.

This article emphasizes the difficulty of ascertaining English syntactic influence on Danish owing to the fact that the two languages have many similar patterns.

20. —— (1989), 'Om "indirekte" anglicismer' (On 'Indirect' Anglicisms), *Møde om Udforskningen af Dansk Sprog*, 2: 291–6.

This article focuses on a spinoff of English influence: analogical but non-English formations. For instance the loanword *hooligan* has given rise to the new Danish word *roligan* 'a well-behaved football spectator' (the stem being Danish *rolig* 'quiet').

21. —— (1990), 'Sociolinguistic Relations between English and Danish since 1945', in *Filipović and Bratanić (eds.), 30–3.

22. —— (1991), 'Talegengivelse hos Dickens og hans oversætter L. Moltke', *Møde om Udforskningen af Dansk Sprog*, 3: 233–40.

This article analyses the extent to which a nineteenth-century translator of Dickens let himself be influenced by English in the rendering of speech, and particularly the use of 'private verbs'.

23. —— (1995), *Engelsk i dansk. Er det et must?* (English in Danish. Is it a must?). (Copenhagen: Munksgaard), 248 pp.

This is a fairly comprehensive survey of English influence on Danish. After an introductory chapter, in which a critical attitude is adopted towards the many superfluous or misunderstood anglicisms that are rife in contemporary Danish. There is a brief discussion of the orthography, pronunciation, and morphology of the loans, followed by a brief discussion of anglicisms prior to the twentieth century. The following chapter gives a detailed account of the different types of loans: direct loans, translation loans, hybrids, semantic loans (including an account of the way Danish prepositions are influenced by English), formal adaptions, acronyms, pseudo-anglicisms, and indirect anglicisms. One chapter deals with idioms and proverbs, one with syntactic influence from English. The final chapter presents a fairly detailed account of a number of socio-semantic fields in which English influence on Danish is particularly prominent. The book concludes with a bibliography and an alphabetical list of the approximately two thousand words and expressions dealt with.

24. —— (1997), *A Dictionary of Anglicisms in Danish* (Historisk-filosofiske Skrifter, 18; Copenhagen: Munksgaard), 405 pp.

This is the first comprehensive dictionary of anglicisms for the language. It comprises more than six thousand entries of loanwords (anglicisms in the narrower sense, and internationalisms, coined in or transmitted by English) and calques. Each entry has full lexicographic data: pronunciation, status, provenance, and meaning are indicated, as are dates of adoption, usage labels, and examples where available or relevant. All Danish sentences illustrating the use of the term are translated into English. The collection and interpretation are thorough and reliable, for both historical evidence and present-day usage. (Reviews: Algeo, *American Speech* 74 (1999), 436–8; Görlach, *IJL* 12 (1999), 150.)

Dutch (Amand Berteloot and Nicoline van der Sijs)

(see also *25, *77)

1. *ANS* = *Algemene Nederlandse spraakkunst* (General Dutch Grammar), eds. G. Geerts *et al.* (1984) (Groningen/Leuven: Wolters-Noordhoff).

2. Bense, J. F. (1924), *The Anglo-Dutch Relations from the Earliest Times to the Death of William the Third* (The Hague: Nijhoff).

This work was intended to be an introductory chapter to Bense's work on the Low Dutch element in the English vocabulary but grew to the size of an independent volume. It comprises a general survey of the Anglo-Dutch relations beginning with the Old English period to the death of William the Third in 1702. The author includes relations in industrial, commercial, political, financial, colonial, and literary domains.

3. Bezooijen, Renée van and Marinel Gerritsen (1994), 'De uitspraak van uitheemse woorden in het Standaard-Nederlands: een verkennende studie' (The Pronunciation of Foreign Words in Standard Dutch: An Investigation), in *De Nieuwe Taalgids* 87: 145–60.

The article summarizes methods and results of an empirical investigation of pronunciation variants of frequent borrowings from various languages in the process of their integration. Factors used to explain variants of the eighteen selected words include the regional and educational status of speakers, analogy effected by words similar in form or content, and the loanwords' phonetic structure, frequency, and date of acceptance into Dutch.

4. Bot, Kees de (1997), 'Nederlands en Engels kunnen goed naast elkaar bestaan' (Dutch and English can Coexist), in *Taalschrift* 1: 28–9.

This paper summarizes the findings of an investigation of four aspects relating to attitudes towards Dutch, English, German and Turkish, *viz*: How important are these languages? Is there any interest in learning them? What is the general attitude towards them? Is any of these a threat to Dutch?

5. Bremmer, Rolf H., Jr. (1989), 'Is de Nederlandse meervouds *-s*

van Engelse komaf?' (Is the Dutch Plural Ending -*s* of English Origin?), *Amsterdamer Beiträge zur älteren Germanistik*, 28: 77–91.

6. CLAUS, P. and J. TAELDEMAN (1989), 'De infiltratie van Engelse (leen)woorden in het Nederlands en in Nederlandse woordenboeken' (The Infiltration of English Loanwords in Dutch and Dutch Dictionaries), in S. Theissen and J. Vromans (eds.), *Album Moors* (Liège: CIPL), 11–30.

The impact of English loanwords on the Dutch language and its representation in Dutch dictionaries is investigated on the analysis of a comprehensive selection of Dutch and Flemish newspapers and magazines. The anglicisms were classified according to usage levels and domains such as sports, music, literature, film, society, fashion, economy, and technology.

7. COHEN, A. (1958), 'Het Nederlands diminutiefsuffix: een morfonologische proeve' (The Dutch Diminutive Suffix: A Morphonological Study), *De Nieuwe Taalgids*, 51: 40–5.

8. COHEN, HARRY (1996), 'Coca versus Cola. Verschillen tussen Nederland en België in het gebruik van Engelse leenwoorden' (Differences Between the Netherlands and Belgium in the Use of English Loanwords), in Sijs (1996: 307–12).

Differences exist in pronunciation, plural formation, spelling, and frequencies of anglicisms; reasons for this divergence are summarized at the end.

9. COLLINS, BEVERLEY and INGER MEES (1981), *The Sounds of English and Dutch* (The Hague: Leiden UP).

10. CONINCK, R. H. B. DE (1970), *Groot uitspraakwoordenboek van de Nederlandse taal* (Comprehensive Pronunciation Dictionary of the Dutch Language) (Antwerpen, Utrecht: De Nederlandsche Boekhandel).

11. *Eindvoorstellen van de Nederlands-Belgische Commissie voor de Spelling van de Bastaardwoorden* (Final Proposals of the Dutch-Belgian Commission for the Spelling of Loanwords) (1969) (Brussels/s' Gravenhage: Staatsuitgeverij).

12. ENDT, E. (1974), *Bargoens woordenboek* (Dictionary of Cant) (Amsterdam: Rap).

The dictionary comprises cant words of the 1950s and 1960s;

entries include definitions, etymologies, and usage labels. The ratio of anglicisms in this lexical layer in modern Dutch is particularly high.

13. Geerts, G. (1970), 'De nominale klassifikatie van ontleningen' (The Nominal Classification of Borrowed Nouns), in *De Nieuwe Taalgids*, Van-Haeringen-nummer, 43–53.

The paper investigates differences in gender assignment between standard Dutch and its dialects. Most of these nouns are borrowed, and Geerts shows that differences have to do with the source language, using a great number of French, English, and German words to prove his hypothesis.

14. —— (1975), 'Het genus van Engelse leenwoorden in het Duits en in het Nederlands' (The Gender of English Loanwords in German and Dutch), in R. Jansen-Sieben, S. De Vriendt, and R. Willemyns (eds.), *Spel van zinnen. Album A. van Loey* (Brussel: Ed. de l'Univ.), 115–23.

Geerts tries to categorize gender assignment and to establish trends of the past few decades.

15. —— (1996), 'De genusbepalende eigenschappen van Engelse leenwoorden in het Nederlands' (Gender-Determining Factors of English Loanwords in Dutch) in *Verslagen en Mededelingen v.d.K. Academie voor Nederlandse Taal- en Letterkunde* 1996 (2/3), 137–46.

Gender assignment of anglicisms in Dutch is summarized on the basis of examples and ratios by other linguists. Most are assigned to the *de* class (M/F), and semantic and formal factors are named that might favour attribution to the *het* (N) class (including a comparison with German). These factors include:

- the existence of an etymologically related word
- classification in a semantic category
- presence of certain suffixes
- the existence of an equivalent not etymologically related.

16. Gerritsen, Johan (1982), 'English Influence on Dutch', in *Filipović (ed.), 154–80.

17. —— (1983), 'English Influence on Dutch', in J. Hasler (ed.), *Anglistentag 1981. Vorträge* (Trierer Studien zur Literatur, 7; Frankfurt: Lang), 9–21.

18. —— (1986), 'Dutch in Contact with English', in *Viereck and Bald (eds.), 51–64.

The author sketches the state of diachronic research and the new start, from 1964, of the synchronic analysis of anglicisms, concentrated in the Groningen School (Zandvoort, Gerritsen, Posthumus).

19. —— (1991), 'English Influence on Dutch', in *Filipović (ed.), 80–90.

20. GERRITSEN, MARINEL (1996), 'Engelstalige productadvertenties in Nederland: onbemind en onbegrepen' (English Commercial Advertisements in the Netherlands: Disliked and Misunderstood). In R. van Hout and J. Kruijsen, *Taalvariaties.* (Dordrecht: Foris), 67–83.

The article is a part of a larger investigation of advertisements in the Netherlands, Germany, France, and Italy. It concentrates on three aspects:

a) the proportion of advertisements in Dutch newspapers and journals entirely or partly in English;
b) the comprehension of these;
c) attitudes to advertisements in English.

21. GUSSENHOVEN, C. (1952), 'Concentratie door diminuering' (Concentration through Shortening), *De Nieuwe Taalgids*, 45: 194–9.

22. —— (1971), 'Het achtervoegsel -*ing*: mogelijkheden en beperkingen' (The Suffix -*ing*: Possibilities and Restrictions), *De Nieuwe Taalgids*, 64: 449–68.

23. —— (1981), 'Voiced Fricatives in Dutch: Sources and Present-day Usage', *Proceedings of the Institute of Phonetics of the Catholic University*, Nijmegen: Inst. of Phonetics, 5: 84–95.

24. HEEROMA, K. (1952), 'Oudengelse invloeden in het Nederlands' (Old English Influences in Dutch), *Tijdschrift voor Nederlandse Taal- en Letterkunde* 70: 257–75.

The analysis is based on a linguistic analysis concentrating on dialectal and lexicological aspects.

25. HOOG, W. DE (1909), *Studiën over de Nederlandsche en Engelsche taal- en letterkunde en haar wederzijdschen invloed* (Studies in Dutch

and English Linguistics and Literature and their Reciprocal Influence) (Dordrecht: Revers).

26. HOPPENBROUWERS, C. A. J. (1980), 'De meervoudsvorming in het Nederlands' (Plural Formation in Dutch), in Th. F. Jansen and N. F. Streekstra (eds.), *Grenzen en domeinen in de grammatica van het Nederlands* (Groningen: Nederlands Instituut).

Basing his statements on his earlier analysis of plural formation, the author formulates rules and regularities, appending a chapter on the inflexion of loanwords.

27. KOBAYASHI, SAYURI (1995), *The Role of Foreign Language Education in the Netherlands* (Osaka).

Kobayashi deals with general foreign language provisions in the Dutch educational system defining what role foreign language teaching in the multicultural Dutch society plays as a part of a future citizen's education.

28. KOENEN, LIESBETH and RIK SMITS ([2]1992), *Peptalk. De Engelse woordenschat van het Nederlands* (Peptalk: The English Vocabulary of Dutch) (Amsterdam: Nijgh and Van Ditmar) (The first edition has the authors' names reversed).

The 3600 words and idioms of this second edition of *Peptalk and Pumps* provide an excellent survey of the English influence.

29. KRUISINGA, E. (1938), *Het Nederlands van nu* (Present-Day Dutch) (Amsterdam: Wereldbibliotheek).

30. LENNEP, G. L. VAN (1988), *Verklarend oorlogswoordenboek* (Explanatory War Dictionary) (Amsterdam).

31. MAK, J. J. (1945), 'Oorlogswinst der Nederlandse taal' (War Acquisitions of the Dutch Language), *De Nieuwe Taalgids*, 38: 163–72.

32. *NEN 5050*. (1994), *Goed woordgebruik in bedrijf en techniek. Woordenlijst met taalkundige aanwijzingen* (Good Usage in Business and Technology; Word-List with Linguistic Advice) (Delft: Nederlands Normalisatie Instituut).

General remarks on spelling, pronunciation, pluralization, compounding, etc. are followed by a word-list suggesting Dutch alternatives to disliked foreign words and idioms; many words are also accompanied by glosses and explanations.

33. NIEROP, M. VAN (1975), *Nieuwe woorden* (New Words) (Hasselt: Herdeland-Orbis).

34. PHILIPPA, M. (1981), 'Volksetymologie' (Folk Etymology), in J. Renkema (ed.), *Taalschat. Een keur van artikelen uit het maandblad Onze Taal van 1931–1981* (Vocabulary. A Selection of Articles from the Journal *Onze Taal* from 1931–1981) (Dordrecht).

35. —— (1987), 'Noordzeegermaanse ontwikkelingen. Een keur van fonologische, morfologische en syntactische parallellen op Noord- en Noordzeegermaans gebied' (North Sea Germanic Developments. A Selection of Phonological, Morphological, and Syntactic Parallels in North and North Sea Germanic), unpublished dissertation (Amsterdam).

36. POSTHUMUS, JAN (1986), *A Description of a Corpus of Anglicisms* (Groningen: Anglistisch Instituut), 195 pp.

The author first gives a detailed discussion of how English items become adapted in Dutch—as loanwords, calques or blends, in spelling, pronunciation, morphology, and derivation. He then gives a list of 829 words (plus hundreds of compounds) with contexts, collected from the Dutch weekly *Elseviers Weekblad* and the daily *De Telegraaf*. The individual entries contain information on formal and grammatical characteristics, meaning, relation to foreign model or source-form, date of borrowing, field of usage and stylistic function. Posthumus admits the limitations of his corpus; otherwise his study is exemplary for its reliability and common sense.

37. —— (1988), 'De uitspraak van Engelse leenwoorden' (The Pronunciation of English Loanwords), *Onze Taal* 57: 112–13.

Posthumus formulates a few guidelines but decides that it is up to the individual to decide on the pronunciation of current anglicisms and speakers should not worry about a Dutch accent.

38. —— (1989*a*), 'Over floppy's, guppy's en yuppies. Schijnbare verkleinwoorden uit het Engels' (On Floppy's, Guppy's and Yuppies; Seeming Diminutives from English), *Onze Taal* 58: 123.

Posthumus depicts in what way Dutch morphological rules are applied to English loans. Words like *floppy* or *guppy* look like diminutives to Dutch users who create backformations like *flop*/*flopje* or *gup*/*gupje*.

39. Posthumus, Jan (1989*b*), 'Hybridische woorden. Engels-Nederlandse samenstellingen' (Hybrids: English-Dutch Compounds), *Onze Taal* 58: 219.

Posthumus traces the language processes that establish hybrids consisting of Dutch and English elements. He recommends considering them as normal elements in the Dutch language.

40. —— (1991*a*), 'De acceptatie van Engelse leenwoorden in het Nederlands' (The Acceptance of English Loanwords in Dutch), *Terminologie et Traduction*, 1: 163–93.

The first part deals with factors influencing the acceptance of anglicisms, in particular speaker needs and language-internal assimilation. The second part analyses, on the basis of four sports disciplines imported from anglophone countries, how far the terminology has remained English or has been translated.

41. —— (1991*b*), 'Hoe komen wij tot namaak-buitenlands?' (How to Explain Pseudo-Foreign), *Onze Taal* 60: 11–13.

The author discusses loanwords which have changed their meaning, being formally adapted to Dutch. He categorizes them according to the factors that determined their semantic integration.

42. Reinsma, R. (1975), *Signalement van nieuwe woorden* (Description of New Words) (Amsterdam/Brussels: Elsevier).

43. Renkema, J. (1979), *Schrijfwijzer. Handboek voor duidelijk taalgebruik* (A Guide to Clear Written Style) (The Hague: Staatsuitgeverij).

44. Rijpma, E. and F. G. Schuringa ([24]1972), *Nederlandse spraakkunst* (Dutch Grammar), ed. Jan v. Bakel (Groningen: Wolters-Noordhoff).

45. Royen, G. (1946), *Ongaaf Nederlands* (Impure Dutch) (Mededelingen der Koninklijke Nederlandse Akademie van Wetenschappen, afd. Letterkunde. Nieuwe Reeks, deel 4, no. 10; Amsterdam: Noord-Hollandsche Uitg. Maatschappij).

46. Salleveldt, Henk [= Leen Verhoeff] (1978), *Het woordenboek van Jan Soldaat* (Dictionary of Soldiers' Jargon) (Alphen aan den Rijn: Sijthoff).

47. ——(1980), *Het woordenboek van Jan Soldaat in Indonesië* (Dictionary of the Language of Dutch Soldiers in Indonesia) (Alphen aan den Rijn: Sijthoff).

48. Schultink, H. (1962), *De morfologische valentie van het ongelede adjectief in modern Nederlands* (The Morphological Valency of the Simple Adjective in Modern Dutch) (The Hague).

49. Schutter, G. de (1996), 'De woordenschat van het Nederlands en van het Engels. Een vergelijkende studie' (Dutch and English Lexis. A Contrastive Study), in *Verslagen en Mededelingen van de Koninklijke Academie voor Nederlandse Taal- en Letterkunde*, 41–60.

The author attempts to trace diverging developments in the two closely related languages by looking at genetically related words but also loanwords borrowed from the other language, and from other languages, contrasting core vocabulary and more marginal expressions.

50. Sijs, Nicoline van der (1996), *Leenwoordenboek. De invloed van andere talen op het Nederlands* (Dictionary of Foreign Words. The Influence on Dutch of Other Languages) (Den Haag: SDU Uitg.)

The reference book was compiled for interested laymen as well as for linguists, with an extensive index section at the end. The author attempts an objective survey of the contacts other languages had with Dutch as a reflex of cultural history. This is followed by information on the dates of loans, reasons for borrowing and the integration of loanwords.

51. Sterkenburg, P. G. J. van *et al.* (eds.) (1984), *Van Dale Groot woordenboek van hedendaags Nederlands* (Comprehensive Dictionary of Present-Day Dutch) (Utrecht, Antwerpen: Van Dale Lexicografie).

52. Timmers, Corriejanne (1993), *Faxen faxte gefaxt. De juiste spelling van ruim 700 aan het Engels ontleende werkwoorden* (*Faxen faxte gefaxt*. The Correct Spelling of Some 700 Verbs Borrowed from English) (Apeldoorn: Auctor).

Timmers discusses the conjugation of foreign verbs, introducing her topic by a description of linguistic change, the spelling of verbs, the reliability and inconsistency of dictionaries, and popular attitudes to verbal inflexion.

53. VAN DALE = GEERTS, G. and H. HEESTERMANS (eds.) ([12]1995), *Van Dale Groot woordenboek der Nederlandse taal* (Van Dale's Dictionary of Dutch). (Utrecht/Antwerpen: Van Dale Lexicografie)

The dictionary describes present-day Dutch and its history, dealing with spelling, grammatical, and stylistic features, usages and etymology of words and combinations. It includes jargon and cant, dialects, archaic and obsolete words as well as neologisms, prefixes and suffixes, various types of names—and loanwords and calques (including information on form and meaning in the donor language and the ultimate source).

54. VOOYS, C. G. N. DE (1925), 'Engelse invloed op het Nederlands' (English Influence on Dutch), in *Verzamelde taalkundige opstellen* (Collected Linguistic Papers), 2: 71–119. (Groningen / The Hague: J. B. Wolters). (A revised version of the article (1914) 'Hoe zijn anglicismen te beschouwen?', *De Nieuwe Taalgids* 7: 124–31, 161–81, 225–35.)

The article looks at the status of anglicisms in Dutch concentrating on aspects of cultural history, in particular when and how English and Dutch came into contact and what social classes were affected.

55. —— (1946–56), 'Engelse invloed op het Nederlands' (English Influence on Dutch).

Eight small articles published 1946–56 collect new evidence of English influence on Dutch, the last one published postumously, all in *De Nieuwe Taalgids*, 39 (1946), 145–9; 40 (1947), 172–3; 41 (1948), 175–6; 42 (1949), 72–3; 43 (1950), 93–6; 46 (1953), 82–5; 47 (1954), 285–7; 49 (1956), 3–9.

56. —— (1951), *Engelse invloed op de Nederlandse woordvoorraad* (Verhandelingen der Koninklijke Nederlandse Akademie van Wetenschappen, Afd. Letterkunde, Nieuwe Reeks, Deel 57, no. 5; Amsterdam: North-Holland).

57. VRIES, J. DE (1971), *Nederlands etymologisch woordenboek* (Leiden: Brill).

58. *Woordenlijst van de Nederlandse taal (Het groene Boekje)* ([8]1997), (Word List of Dutch (The Green Book)). Collected on behalf of the Belgian and Dutch governments. (The Hague: SDU Uitg.).

This spelling dictionary is continuously updated; it includes (36–43) guidelines on how to spell foreign words, with special attention given to English loans. The indexes list some 110,000 words (including compounds and derivatives); there is no separate index for anglicisms.

59. ZAALBERG, C. A. (1975), *Taaltrouw* (Culemborg: Tjeenk Willink Noorduijn).

60. ZANDVOORT, R. W. (1964), *English in the Netherlands: A Study in Linguistic Infiltration* (Groningen: Wolters).

Finnish (Keith Battarbee)

(see also *25)

1. LESKINEN, H. (1981), 'Havaintoja englantilaisperäisten lainasanojen taivutuksesta' (Observations on the Inflection of English Loanwords), *Virittäjä*, 317–26.

2. OREŠNIK, BRIGITTA (1982), 'On the Adaptation of English Loanwords into Finnish', in *Filipović (ed.), 180–213.

3. PULKKINEN, P. (1984), *Lokarista sponsoriin: englantilaisia lainoja suomen kielessä* (From *lokari* to *sponsori*: English Loanwords in the Finnish Language) (Helsinki).

4. SAJAVAARA, K. (1986), 'Aspects of English Influence on Finnish', in *Viereck and Bald (eds.), 65–77.

The author gives a sketch of the history of Finnish language contacts (which explains why anglicisms are sometimes difficult to distinguish from borrowings from (or through) other Germanic languages) and then reports on an 'anglicism project' intended to 'study the impact of English on the Finnish language and Finnish culture'; this included a great number of empirical tests on competences and attitudes and was completed in 1980.

5. —— (1991), 'English in Finnish: Television Subtitles', in *Ivir and Kalogjera (eds.), 381–90.

6. SAJAVAARA, K., J. LEHTONEN, H. LESKINEN, P. PULKKINEN, A. RÄSÄNEN, and T. HIRVONEN (1978), *The Anglicism Project: Background and Methods* (Occasional papers, 2; Jyväskylä).

French (John Humbley)

(see also *37, *53, *54, *55, *60, *75, *77)

Recherches en linguistique étrangère (Besançon: Université de Franche-Comté) *TT* = *Terminologie et traduction*

1. *Actes du colloque sur les anglicismes et leur traitement lexicographique* (1994) (Montréal: Gouvernement du Québec).

This conference was called by Québec linguists and lexicographers who were concerned by the phenomenon of anglicisms which had been replaced in Québec coming through the 'back door' in the form of entries in dictionaries, those published in France in particular. The theme of the conference was thus how to present linguistic reality objectively in dictionaries without inciting the use of anglicisms.

It contains a most complete bibliography on anglicisms and borrowings from English in both European and North American French.

2. AGRON, PIERRE (1971), 'Le Comité d'étude des termes techniques français et les langues des spécialités', *La Banque des mots*, 1: 67–75.

The committee's aim was to maintain and to improve the clarity and the precision of technical languages. Language planning is judged to be useful because language contact is intensifying and, in consequence, many new words are introduced into the French language. Mass media play an important role in this because they popularize technical terms.

3. —— (1977), 'C'est un métier que fabriquer des mots', *Lebende Sprachen*, 22: 3–8.

4. —— (1991), 'La Destruction par les mots', *TT* 1: 235–59.

History of the 'Comité d'étude des termes techniques français', one of the oldest terminology groups, by its principal promoter; neologisms created to replace English loans, use of Greco-Latin roots; annex of the Committee's records. The author, the moving force behind the Comité d'étude des termes techniques français, provides a historical outline of his committee and its work, and gives some examples of anglicisms and their French substitutes.

5. Améro, Justin (1879), *L'Anglomanie dans le français et les barbarismes anglais usités en France* (Paris).

6. Application (1982), *Rencontre internationale sur l'application des législations linguistiques dans les pays francophones 10–11 mai 1982* (Paris).

7. Ashley, Leonard R. N. (1989), 'Franglais and Finance: Managing the Vocabulary of Money', *Geolinguistics*, 15: 23–56.

8. Bachmann, Hans (1916), 'Das englische Sprachgut in den Romanen Jules Vernes', D.Phil. thesis (Greifswald).

9. Bäcker, Notburga (1975), *Probleme des inneren Lehnguts: Dargestellt an den Anglizismen der französischen Sportsprache* (Tübingen: Narr).

This theoretical demonstration of the classification of borrowings according to criteria which go back to Hermann Paul and used in historical German linguistics is applied to a corpus of anglicisms in the field of sports and French.

10. Baggioni, Daniel (1974), 'Dirigisme linguistique et néologie', *Langages*, 36 ('La néologie lexicale'): 53–66.

Baggioni presents newspaper articles that deal with the linguistic laws enacted on 9 January 1972 and 18 January 1973. He examines their metalinguistic implications, how the laws were reformulated and what attitude is conveyed.

11. Ball, R. V. (1990), 'Lexical Innovation in Present-Day French: le français branché', *French Cultural Studies*, 1: 21–35.

12. Banks, David (1992), 'L'Habit emprunté ne fait pas le moine étranger', in *Actes de la troisième journée E.R.L.A.-G.L.A.T.: Lexiques spécialisés et didactique des langues, U.B.O-E.N.S.T. de Bretagne* (Brest), 23–32.

A study of fifty-six 'false anglicisms' with typology, which does not replace N. Spence's account (1989).

13. Barbier, Paul (1921), 'Loanwords from English in Eighteenth-century French', *Modern Language Review*, 16: 138–49, 252–64.

Barbier shows that many anglicisms entered the French language at an earlier date than M. Bonnaffé states in his *Dictionnaire des Anglicisms* (1920). Reasons for the substantial number of anglicisms borrowed in the eighteenth century are the revocation of the Edict of Nantes (1685) and the extreme French conservatism of the second half of the seventeenth century with respect to neology.

14. —— (1921/1923), *English Influence on the French Vocabulary* (Oxford: OUP).

15. —— (1923), 'Some Notes on English Influence in the Vocabulary of Written French', *Modern Languages*, 5: 139–46, 175–82.

16. BAUER, ROLAND (1990), 'Anglizismen im Französischen: am Beispiel fachsprachlicher Akronyme aus Werbetexten französischer EDV-Firmen', *Fachsprache*, 12: 36–49 (with English summary).

Comparison of acronyms and abbreviations actually used in French computer literature and those officially recommended. Most are not translated, a procedure which is interpreted as representing a more international attitude on the part of French writers of computer literature.

17. —— (1991), 'Parlons a bit du *bit*: Les Acronymes dans le français de l'informatique', *TT* 1: 87–100.

This and the preceding article present the results of a survey of initialisms and acronyms in six issues of a French computer magazine (1989–90). Fifty-six per cent of the acronyms have a French equivalent, but many English acronyms are used without translation.

18. BAUM, RICHARD (1983), 'Zum Problem der Norm im Französischen der Gegenwart', in Hausmann (ed.), 366–410 (first published in H. Stimm (ed.) (1976), *Aufsätze zur Sprachwissenschaft* (Wiesbaden), 53–89).

Baum wants to explain why the norm of the French language is in a state of crisis. Since the codification of the language in the seventeenth century its further development has been disregarded. The traditional norm can no longer be applied to the contemporary language. To introduce a new norm, it would be necessary to change speakers' linguistic attitudes.

19. BÉCHEREL, DANIEL (1981), 'A propos des solutions de remplacement des anglicismes', *La Linguistique*, 17: 119–31.

20. BECKER, KARLHEINZ (1970), *Sportanglizismen im modernen*

Französisch (aufgrund von Fachzeitschriften der Jahre 1965–1967) (Meisenheim a. Glan: Hain).

Becker examines anglicisms in the terminology of sports in present-day French, including the impact on phonetics, spelling, morphology, lexis, semantics, and style.

21. Behrens, Dietrich (1927), *Über englisches Sprachgut im Französischen* (Gießener Beiträge, Zusatzheft 4; Gießen: Universität).

Behrens examines England's cultural influence on French vocabulary to the end of the nineteenth century, arranged according to domains (e.g. trade, army, industry, sport).

22. Beinke, Christiane (1990), *Der Mythos franglais. Zur Frage der Akzeptanz von Angloamerikanismen im zeitgenössischen Französischen—mit einem kurzen Ausblick auf die Anglizismen-Diskussion in Dänemark* (Europäische Hochschulschriften: Reihe 13, Französische Sprache und Literatur, Bd. 151; Frankfurt: Peter Lang). 380 pp. (D.Phil. thesis, Münster University, 1988).

This thesis is particulary well documented and gives information not previously available in one volume on the debate on anglicisms in France and the organizations created to combat them. The extra-linguistic context is also examined, inevitably in a superficial way. A comparison with the situation in Denmark is given in an annex.

23. Béjoint, Henri (1978), 'Les nouveaux américanismes', *Confluents*, 2: 65–76.

24. Bement, N. S. (1956), 'Anglicisms in a French Magazine', *The French Review*, 19: 234–41.

25. Bengtsson, Sverker (1968), *La Défense organisée de la langue française* (Uppsala: Almqvist and Wiksell).

Bengtsson critically examines the different institutions which deal with the regulation of the French language. He also looks at the changes regarding the traditional norm of French.

26. Bertaut, Jules (1918), 'L'Anglicisme en France sous la Restauration', *Revue de Paris*, 25 (9): 153–83.

27. Bessé, Bruno de (1982), *Termes techniques nouveaux: Termes, officiellement recommandés par le gouvernement français* (Paris).

28. —— (1990), 'L'Etat terminologue: Peut mieux faire', *TT* 1: 87–100.

A critical appraisal of the work of the French Commissions ministérielles de terminologie, which the author finds insufficient both in number of terms treated, and from the point of view of methodology, which he finds vacillating and tinged with purism. He suggests greater cooperation with specialists.

29. BIZET, ANGE (1992), 'Etude de néologie: Création d'un nouveau modèle lexical en français: Pin's', *La Banque des mots*, 44: 39–44.

30. BOLY, JOSEPH (1974, [2]1979), *Chasse aux anglicismes: Petit glossaire franglais-français* (Brussels).

31. BONNAFFÉ, EDOUARD (1920), *Dictionnaire étymologique et historique des anglicismes* (Paris: Delagrave).

First scientific dictionary of anglicisms in French.

32. —— (1922), 'Anglicismes et mots d'influence anglaise', *French Quarterly*, 4: 164–71.

33. BONVENISTE, EMILE (1947), 'Deux mots anglais en français moderne', *Le Français moderne*, 15: 1–4.

34. BRINK-WEHRLI, VERENA (1961), 'Englische Mode- und Gesellschaftsausdrücke im Französischen (19. Jh.)', D.Phil. thesis (Zurich).

35. BRÜCH, JOSEF (1941), *Die Anglomanie in Frankreich* (Stuttgart and Berlin: Kohlhammer).

Brüch examines the social and political relations between France and England mainly in the eighteenth and nineteenth centuries. Anglicisms are mentioned but not examined more closely.

36. BRUNOT, FERDINAND (1969), *Histoire de la langue française des origines à nos jours* (Paris: A. Colin).

Detailed history of the French language in thirteen volumes up to the end of the nineteenth century, placing borrowings from English in the context of the development of the French language; recent edition 1969. Continued by Antoine, Martin (1985) for the time after 1880.

37. BUTTERWORTH, JOAN (1980), 'Attitudes to Franglais in Orleans 1969', in *Nelde, 125–30.

38. Cartier, Alice (1977), 'Connaissance et usage d'anglicismes par des français de Paris', *La Linguistique*, 13: 55–84.

On the basis of an opinion poll on anglicisms conducted in Paris between 1972 and 1974 Cartier tries to find out how social factors determine their acceptance. She states that it depends on the social level of the speakers and their knowledge of English rather than on age or sex.

39. —— (1978), 'Compréhension, compétence et performance d'anglicismes en français', in W. U. Dressler and W. Meid (eds.), *Proceedings of the Twelfth International Congress of Linguists* (Innsbruck: Universität), 252–7.

40. Cassen, Bernard (1979), 'La langue anglaise comme véhicule de l'impérialisme culturel', *Encrages*, 1: 8–13.

41. Causseron, Henri (1895), 'A List of English Words Used by French Writers', *Notes and Queries*, 10: 106–15.

42. Chansou, Michel (1990), 'Termes de la finance et de la bourse: Essai d'organisation conceptuelle d'une terminologie', *La Banque des mots* (numéro spécial), 35–48.

Four terms scheduled for official replacement (*trader, broker, market-maker* and *fixing*) are examined and alternative criteria for the choice of native equivalents and implementation techniques are suggested.

43. Christmann, Hans Helmut (1983), 'Das Französische der Gegenwart: Zu seiner Norm und seiner "Défense"', in Hausmann (ed.), 411–40.

Christmann states that some kind of norm still exists in contemporary French. These norms depend on the diastratic, diatopic, and diachronic dimensions. According to Christmann the classic norm cannot be defended by law—though the public opinion does not resist linguistic laws—because the obedience to these laws is difficult to monitor.

44. Clément, Pascal (1981), 'Rapport fait au nom de la Commission d'enquête sur la langue française', *Assemblée Nationale No. 2311* (Journal Officiel du 15.5.1981).

45. Colpron, Gilles (1982), *Dictionnaire des anglicismes* (Montréal).

46. Commission générale de la langue française (1989), *L'Avenir de la langue française, 2ème recontre internationale sur l'application de législations linguistiques dans les pays francophones, 7–8 juin 1985 Bruxelles* (Paris: La Documentation française).

47. Corbeil, Jean-Claude (1971), 'Aspects du problème néologique', *La Banque des mots*, 2: 123–36.

Corbeil examines how neologisms are formed and gives examples for each category. English loanwords are discussed in brief. The author condemns the authority of dictionaries and the French conservative attitude towards neologisms.

48. Coutier, Martine (1995), 'Boutons l'anglais hors de France—présentation critique du *Dictionnaire des termes officiels 1994*', *Recherches en linguistique étrangère*, 18: 15–40.

49. Cypionka, Marion (1994), *Französische 'Pseudoanglizismen'. Lehnformationen zwischen Entlehnung, Wortbildung, Form- und Bedeutungswandel* (Tübingen: Narr). (Review: Görlach, *IJL* 9 (1996), 79–80).

This 1992 Düsseldorf dissertation is devoted to the integration of English elements into French vocabulary with a stress on the creative processes, in particular 'pseudo-borrowing'. The author discusses the socio-political and attitudinal background and general linguistic aspects of borrowing, before she devotes her attention to controversial specimens selected from dictionaries and monographs, in particular Höfler's and Rey-Debove and Gagnon's dictionaries of anglicisms. She classifies her material under the headings 'hybrid compounds' (136–60, type *auto-coat*, 13 items), 'derivation' (161–84, type *bluesman*, 13 items), 'clipping' (185–96, type *scotch*, 6 items), 'semantic shift' (197–210, type *brushing*, 7 items), 'morphological change' (211–14, 2 items), 'graphic-phonetic anglicization' (215–17, *rallye-paper* only), 'names' (218–20, type *Browning*, 3 items). These categories are further discussed in her suggested typology (221–71, with more examples) and followed by a summary and comprehensive bibliography, and a list of items treated.

50. Daguet, Dominique (1984), *Langue Française à l'épreuve* (Troyes: Líbrairie bleue).

Daguet expresses her negative attitude towards loanwords. She believes that French cannot develop according to its proper rules if it accepts too many loanwords. She fears that French might become a product of Anglo-Saxon culture. Loanwords must therefore be replaced by French equivalents or, if necessary, by French neologisms.

51. DARBELNET, JEAN (1976), *Le Français en contact avec l'anglais en Amérique du Nord* (Québec: Presses de l'Univ. Laval).

The book consists of several articles published between 1963 and 1970. They deal with bilingualism, especially in Canada. Darbelnet underlines that the French Canadians are responsible for their own language and that the government has to furnish the instruments to support it.

52. DELAPORTE, VINCENT (1976), 'La Loi relative à l'emploi de la langue française', *Revue critique de droit international privé*, 65: 447–76.

53. Délégation générale à la langue française (1994), *Dictionnaire des termes officiels* (Paris: La Documentation française).

This was, in 1997, the definite version of the terms officially adopted by the Commissions ministérielles de terminologie over the preceding twenty years or so. At the time of writing a new version was in preparation.

54. DELISLE, JEAN (1988), 'Les Anglicismes insidieux', in Pergnier (ed.), 147–58.

55. DELOFFRE, FRÉDÉRIC (1991), 'Français et anglais', *Revue des deux mondes*, 69–78.

56. DENIAU, XAVIER (1983), *La Francophonie* (Paris: Pr. univ. de France).

Deniau defines francophony, describes its structures and surveys linguistic laws concerning francophony. He also discusses the distribution of English in the French-speaking communities.

57. DEPECKER, LOÏC and GINA MAMAVI (eds.) (1997), *La Mesure des mots: Cinq études d'implantation terminologique* (Publications de l'université de Rouen), 528 pp.

Publication of the reports on the actual usage of terms officially promoted in France, which was first presented in *Terminologies nouvelles*, 12 (1993). The main subject fields covered are: the media (M. Chansou), computer data processing (D. Gouadec), biotechnology and genetic engineering (L. Guespin), remote sensing (J.-L. Fossat, J. Rouges-Martinez), medicine (Ph. Thoiron). The reports underline methods used to obtain measures of implementation, and focus on both substitute terms which are adopted and borrowings which remain.

58. DJIAN, JEAN-MICHEL (1996), 'Vive le français!', special issue of *Le Monde de l'éducation*, July–August.

A selection of articles and interviews on French and how it is faring in competition with English, in Europe and the rest of the world.

59. DOPPAGNE, ALBERT (1979, [2]1980), *Pour une écologie de la langue française avec un lexique de termes anglais utilisés dans la vie courante à Bruxelles: Ouvrage couronné par l'Académie Française* (Brussels).

60. —— and MICHÈLE LENOBLE-PINSON (1982), *Le Français à la sauce anglaise. Lexique des termes anglais et américains relevés en une année dans un grand quotidien bruxellois* (Brussels: Commission française de la culture de l'agglomération bruxelloise).

61. DROZDALE, ELIZABETH J. (1988), 'Anglicisation du français dans la presse: Informer sans déformer', in Pergnier (ed.), 131–45.

62. DUBOIS, JEAN *et al.* (1960), 'Le Mouvement général du vocabulaire français de 1949 à 1960 d'après un dictionnaire d'usage', *Le Français moderne*, 28: 86–106, 196–210.

63. —— and CLAUDE DUBOIS (1971), *Introduction à la lexicographie: Le Dictionnaire* (Paris: Larousse).

The authors describe how a dictionary is compiled and how the French lexicon developed; the influence of English is judged as marginal.

64. ELIADE, IRINA (1962), 'Rezistenţa împotriva noului val de anglicisme în limba franceză', *Revista de filologie romanică şi germanică*, 6: 271–89.

A well-documented presentation of the different periods of English influence upon French vocabulary. In spite of the puristic attitude advocated by many writers and linguists, more and more anglicisms have penetrated the French language since the eighteenth century. The first waves were characteristic of specific terminologies. Twentieth-century borrowings (comprising anglicisms and americanisms) are no longer restricted to specialized terminologies, occurring in every day parlance (especially after World War II).

65. ETIEMBLE, RENÉ (1952), 'De la prose française au sabir atlantique', *Les Temps modernes* (published also in René Etiemble (1955), *Hygiène des lettres* (Vol. II; Paris), 23–49).

Etiemble complains about the influence of English on French and considers the political effects. He wants the French government to regulate the adaptation of foreign words. A correspondence between Etiemble and M. Abraham about 'français élémentaire/basic français' is reprinted at the end.

66. —— (1959–62), *Le Babélien*, 3 vol. Centre de documentation universitaire.

67. —— (1964, [2]1973), *Parlez-vous franglais?* (Paris: Gallimard).

Etiemble, in a satirical vein, provides a complete grammar of 'Franglais'. He tries to explain why French speakers use anglicisms and shows how they can be avoided.

68. —— (1966), *Le Jargon des sciences* (Paris: Hermann).

Etiemble examines the development of technical terminology and syntax in various sciences since 1945. He claims that loanwords should be adapted and shows that this has been achieved for Arabic. He denies the usefulness of an international *lingua franca*. Once more he underlines the danger of English and American influence and asks the state to intervene. The 1996 edition (slightly revised) appeared under the title *Au secours, Athéna! Le Jargon des sciences* (Paris: Hermann).

69. FANTAPIÉ, ALAIN and MARCEL BRULÉ (1984), *Dictionnaire des néologismes officiels: Tous les mots nouveaux. Avec en annexe l'ensemble des textes législatifs et réglementaires sur la langue française* (Paris).

70. FEYRY, MONIQUE (1972), 'Les mots anglais dans les dictionnaires de langue française', *La Banque des mots*, 3: 17–34.

71. —— (1973*a*), 'Les Commissions ministérielles de terminologie: Observations générales', *La Banque des mots*, 5: 47–74.

72. —— (1973*b*), 'L'anglomanie dans les marques de fabrique et les raisons sociales françaises', *La Banque des mots*, 6: 123–32.

73. Forgue, Guy Jean (1980), 'Le "Franglais" dans *Le Monde*', in *Nelde, 69–74.

74. —— (1986), 'English Loan Words in French Today', *Journal of English Linguistics*, 19: 285–94.

75. —— (1988), 'Le "Franglais" dans *Le Monde*. Essai d'analyse quantifiée de contenu (Année 1977)', *Actes du II° colloque du G.E.P.E., Strasbourg 1986*, 64–75.

76. Frey, Robert (1943), 'Das englische Lehnwort im modernsten Französisch (nach Zeitungsexzerpten von 1920–1940)', D.Phil. thesis (Zürich).

77. Fugger, Bernd (1980*a*), 'Die Einstellung der Franzosen zur französischen Sprachpolitik', in Helmut Stimm (ed.), *Zur Geschichte des gesprochenen Französisch und zur Sprachlenkung im Gegenwartsfranzösisch* (Wiesbaden: Steiner), 58–78.

78. —— (1980*b*), 'Les Français et les arrêtés ministériels: Etude sur l'impact de la loi linguistique dans l'est de la France', *La Banque des mots*, 18: 158–70.

79. —— (1982), 'Neologismus und Wortbildung: Tendenzen bei der Herausbildung einer neuen französischen Fachsprache der Medizin', in P. Wunderli and W. Müller (eds.), *Romania historica et Romania hodierna* (Frankfurt), 283–97.

80. —— (1983), 'Sprachentwicklung—Sprachbeeinflussung—Sprachbewußtsein: Eine soziolinguistische Untersuchung zur französischen Sprachpolitik', *Fachsprache*, 5: 128–37.

81. Galliot, Marcel (1955), *Essai sur la langue de la réclame contemporaine* (Toulouse: Edouard Privat).

First postwar study of French advertising language, showing the important role that English was already playing.

82. Gebhardt, Karl (1975), 'Gallizismen im Englischen, Anglizismen im Französischen: Ein statistischer Vergleich', *ZRP* 91: 292–309.

The author contrasts the French impact on English and the English influence on French right from the beginning. After sketching the history of loanwords from French, and the research devoted to their description, he provides a statistical analysis of the 22,556 gallicisms thus classified in the *Chronological English*

Dictionary (1970). Although critical of his data base, he fails to discuss whether the *CED*'s etymologies correlate with what was felt to be French by English users. His analysis of English words in French is made on the basis of entries in *Le Grand Robert* (1951–64) and *Supplément* (1970). He found a total of 1254 anglicisms (= 2,1 per cent of the total lexis) showing a marked increase from 1700 onward: eighteenth century/123 items, nineteenth/444, twentieth/578. The English language has replaced Italian as the main donor, now reducing French itself to a *langue emprunteuse*.

83. GECKELER, HORST (1982), '*Glanures lexicales franco-anglo-françaises*: Die Rückwanderwörter als möglicher Faktor der Moderation in der Polemik um das "franglais"', in K. R. Jankowsky and E. S. Dick (eds.), *Festschrift für Karl Schneider: Zum 70. Geburtstag am 18. April 1982* (Amsterdam: Benjamins), 187–203.

84. GENEVOIX, MAURICE (1973), 'L'Académie Française et les commissions de terminologie', *La Banque des mots*, 5: 3–8.

85. GEORGE, K. E. M. (1976), 'Anglicisms in Contemporary French', *Modern Languages*, 57: 6–11, 63–8.

86. *GEPE* (1986), *Actes du deuxième colloque due G.E.P.E.: Langue française langue anglaise: Contacts et conflits* (Université des Sciences humaines de Strasbourg).

This conference explored contacts and conflicts caused by the use of English in France, as revealed in the press and other corpora, and discussed means of defining a language policy for France and for Europe.

87. GESNER, EDWARD (1997), 'Les Anglicismes en français de France: Éléments de morphosyntaxe ou le *Parlez-vous franglais?* d'Etiemble revue, corrigé er supergénialement augmenté', in Lapierre, Oore and Runte (eds.), *Mélanges linguistiques offerts à Rostislav Kocourek*, 327–33.

88. GILBERT, PIERRE (1971), *Dictionnaire des mots nouveaux* (Paris: Le Robert).

89. —— (1980), *Dictionnaire des mots contemporains* (Paris: Le Robert).

90. GOBARD, HENRI (1976), *L'Aliénation linguistique: Analyse tétraglossique* (Paris).

91. —— (1979), *La Guerre culturelle: Logique du désastre* (Paris).

92. GOOSSE, ANDRÉ (1975), *La néologie française aujourd'hui: Observations et réflexions* (Paris: Conseil international de la langue française).

93. —— (1984), 'Influence de l'anglais sur le français de Belgique', *Cahiers de l'Institut de linguistique de Louvain*, 9 (1–2): 27–49.

94. GOSSEN, CARL THEODOR (1980), 'Wie gefährlich ist "franglais"?', in Gerhard Schmidt and Manfred Tietz (eds.), *Stimmen der Romania: Festschrift für W. Theodor Elwert* (Wiesbaden: Steiner), 561–70.

95. GOUDAILLER, JEAN-PIERRE (1977), 'A nouveau les puristes contre la langue', *La Linguistique*, 13: 85–98.

96. —— (1982), 'Sprache und Macht: Wie ein Gesetz in Frankreich die Sprache reinigen will', *Dialect*, 6: 28–51.

97. —— (1986), 'Pour ou contre la langue: Vingt ans de planification linguistique en France', *Dilbilim* (Revue du département de français de la Faculté des Lettres de l'Université d'Istanbul), 7: 101–16.

98. —— (1987), 'De la nécessité des enquêtes linguistiques pour le travail des commissions de terminologie', *Meta*, 32 (3): 361–5.

99. GOURMONT, RÉMY DE (1899, [13]1923, repr. 1955), *Esthétique de la langue française* (Paris: Société du Mercure de France).

Some chapters of the book deal with the influence of modern foreign languages, especially English, on French. Gourmont complains about the lack of adaptation of foreign words and gives several examples of possible adaptation procedures. To him the influence of a foreign language is a threat to the purity of speech and mind and to the logic of French. He proposes the foundation of an institution charged with the creation of new French words.

100. GRAND COMBE, FÉLIX DE (1954), 'De l'anglomanie en français', *Le Français moderne*, 22: 187–200, 267–76.

101. GRIGG, PETER (1997), 'Toubon or Not Toubon: The Influence of the English Language in Contemporary France', *English Studies*, 78: 368–84.

102. GRITTI, JULES (1985), 'Vocabulaire des sports, les anglicismes', in Martin Antoine (ed.), *Histoire de la langue française 1880–1914*, 175–91.

103. Groupe d'études sur le plurilinguisme européen (1984), *GEPE 1984. Actes du premier colloque du G.E.P.E.: L'anglais: Langue étrangère ou langue seconde?* (Université des Sciences humaines de Strasbourg).

This conference dealt with the status of English in France, which was perceived as passing from that of a foreign to a second language.

104. GUILBERT, LOUIS (1959), 'Anglomanie et vocabulaire technique', *Le Français moderne*, 27: 272–95.

105. —— (1975), *La Créativité lexicale* (Paris: Larousse).

Guilbert gives detailed information about French word-formation. The influence of English on French only concerns borrowings and the relation 'déterminant—déterminé', arguing that in French the Latin-based form of compounds and English syntax are mixed (as in *mini-jupe*).

106. GUILLERMOU, ALAIN (1959), 'Le Purisme est plus qu'une sottise', *Vie et Langage*, 454.

107. GUIRAUD, PIERRE (1965), *Les Mots étrangers.* (*Que sais-je?*, Paris: PUF, N° 1166).

Guiraud tries to find out the origin of borrowed words, how they came to France and what circumstances facilitated the borrowing. The last chapter deals with the integration of foreign words.

108. HAENSCH, GÜNTHER (1968), 'Die Aussprache englischer Wörter im Französischen', *Idioma*, 5–6: 224–8.

109. HAGÈGE, CLAUDE (1987), *Le Français et les siècles* (Paris: Odile Jacob).

Hagège describes the French puristic tradition, which, according to him, is not in line with the linguistic facts. He analyses the influence of American English and the reactions to this. In a second part he tries to find out why English became the most important world language rather than French.

110. HANON, SUZANNE (1970), 'Anglicismes en français contemporain: Méthodes et problèmes', unpublished Ph.D. thesis (Aarhus University).

111. HAUSMANN, FRANZ JOSEF (ed.) (1983), *Die französische Sprache von heute* (Wege der Forschung, 496; Darmstadt: Wissenschaftliche Buchgesellschaft).

The book contains several articles published between 1877 and 1982 focussing on a synchronic description of French.

112. —— (1986), 'The Influence of the English Language on French', in *Viereck and Bald (eds.), 79–105.

Hausmann gives an account of anglicisms in French texts and dictionaries before he turns to attitudes after 1945 and the importance of the French Language Law of 1975; he includes a list of suggested replacements and another of 105 loanwords which have apparently survived the persecution. Finally, there is a short contrastive sketch of how Canadian French is affected by influences from English.

113. HÉBERT, PIERRE (1983), *Répertoire d'anglicismes* (Montréal).

114. HENRY, FRANÇOISE (1990), 'Traitement de deux mots empruntés à l'anglais: *Canopée et groupie*', in *Dictionnairique et lexicographie* (Autour d'un dictionnaire: Le 'Trésor de la Langue Française: Témoignages d'atelier et voies nouvelles') (Paris: Didier Erudition), 1: 117–40.

How to deal with anglicisms in a large French general language dictionary, based on a technical term (*canopy*), and a modish but widespread word (*groupie*).

115. HÖFLER, MANFRED (1970), 'Beiträge zu den Anglizismen im Französischen', *ZRP*, 86: 324–39.

116. —— (1980), 'Methodologische Überlegungen zu einem neuen Historischen Wörterbuch der Anglizismen im Französischen', in R. Werner (ed.), *Sprachkontakte. Zur gegenseitigen Beeinflussung romanischer und nicht-romanischer Sprachen* (Tübingen: Narr), 69–86.

117. —— (1982), *Dictionnaire des anglicismes* (Paris: Larousse).

118. HÖFLER, MANFRED (1986), 'Zur Verwendung von *anglicisme* als Indiz puristischer Haltung im *Petit Robert*', *Zeitschrift für französische Sprache und Literatur*, 86: 334–8.

119. —— (1989), 'Le Traitement des emprunts par substitution lexematique dans la lexicographie historique française', *Travaux de linguistique et de philologie*, 27: 115–25.

120. HOPE, THOMAS (1971), *Lexical Borrowing in the Romance Languages: A Critical Study of Italianisms in French and Gallicisms in Italian from 1100 to 1900* (Oxford: Blackwell), 755 pp.

121. HUBER, HERBERT and M. CHEVAL (1997), 'Anglicismes à la mode. Une étude comparative (F-D)', *Lebende Sprachen*, 42: 115–18.

122. HUMBLEY, J. (1974*a*), 'Vers une théorie de l'emprunt linguistique', *Cahiers de lexicologie*, 25: 46–70.

Humbley applies Haugen's 1951 typology of borrowing to anglicisms in French.

123. —— (1974*b*), 'L'Influence anglo-saxonne dans la presse française 1959–1969', unpublished Ph.D. thesis (available from the Bibliothèque de la Sorbonne, Bibliothèque Paris XIII).

Recent anglicisms (direct and indirect loans not in the 1967 *Petit Robert* dictionary) were collected from two Paris dailies and two weeklies of the first two quarters of 1959 and of 1969 and arranged according to subject fields. It is shown that many English words present in 1959 had disappeared by 1969. However, a sharp increase in advertising led to a general higher proportion of anglicisms in general. The second volume is devoted to the anglicisms presented in context.

124. —— (1986), 'Les Anglicismes dans le Dictionnaire critique et dans le Suplément', in *Autour de Féraud: La Lexicographie en France de 1762 à 1835. Actes du Colloque international du Groupe d'études en histoire de la langue française, Ecole Normale Supérieure de Jeunes Filles* (Paris), 147–55.

125. —— (1987), 'L'Emprunt sémantique dans la terminologie de l'informatique', *Meta*, 32: 321–5.

Though direct loans and radical word coinages attract most attention with regard to the English element in French computer terminology, the numerical importance and the facility of adaptation of semantic loans is often overlooked. Such disguised loans are often further facilitated for French by the use in English of terms based on Greek and Latin.

126. —— (1988*a*), 'La Traduction dans la terminologie informatique en français et en allemand', in *Actes du II° colloque du Groupe d'Etudes sur le plurilinguisme européen* (Strasbourg 1986), 6–14.

127. —— (1988*b*), 'Comment le français et l'allemand aménagent la terminologie de l'informatique', *La Banque des Mots* (numéro spécial CTN) (CILF), 85–148.

128. —— (1990*a*), 'Le Purisme dans les dictionnaires de l'informatique grand public', *Cahiers de lexicologie*, 56–7: 241–53.

A survey of French popular science computer dictionaries and a comparison with actual usage in computer magazines suggests that dictionaries are reluctant to admit anglicisms that are quite current in the press.

129. —— (1990*b*), 'Semantic Convergence of English Borrowings in Western European Languages', in *Filipović and Bratanić, 82–7.

130. —— (1997), 'Language and Terminology Planning in National Monolingual Environments, with Special Emphasis on the Francophone Experience', in Budin Wright, *Handbook of Terminology Management*, vol. 1 (Amsterdam and Philadelphia: Benjamins), 261–77.

An account of the workings of one Commission ministérielle de terminologie (transport) in the early 1990s, in the context of official terminology policy since World War II.

131. —— and Liselotte Biedermann-Pasques (1995), 'Réception de mots anglais dans les journaux français: Proposition d'harmonisation graphique des mots d'emprunt anglais', *Langue française*, 108: 57–65.

132. Jastrab de Saint-Robert, Marie-Josée (1987), 'Les Syntagmes nominaux complexes en anglais et en français. Eléments de réflexion', *Meta*, 32: 260–6.

133. Jinemo Barrerea, Pilar (1991), 'Apuntes sobre la traducción de los neologismos franceses: La Importancia de saber inglés', *TT* 1: 261–7.

Criticism of official terms replacing anglicisms, which the author considers unenlightening, especially for foreign users of French.

134. JOBERT, MICHEL (1974), *Mémoires d'avenir* (Paris).

135. JOHNSON, MICHELINE (1986), *Les Mots anglais dans un magazine des jeunes (Hit magazine 1972–1979)* (Heidelberger Beiträge zur Romanistik, 18; Frankfurt/M.: Peter Lang).

136. KERVIGAN, AURÈLE (1865), *L'Anglais à Paris: Histoire humoristique de son introduction dans notre langue et dans nos mœurs* (Paris).

137. KINEC'HDU, TANGUY (1984), *Avatars du français* (Paris).

138. KINGSTON, MILES (1981), *Let's parler Franglais* (London).

139. KUTTNER, MAX (1926), 'Anglomanie im heutigen Französisch', *Zeitschrift für französische Sprache und Literatur*, 48: 446–65.

140. LAURIAN, ANNE-MARIE (1985), 'Vocabulaire des techniques', in Martin Antoine (ed.), *Histoire de la langue française* (Paris: Ed. du Centre Nationale de la Recherche Scientifique), 157–73.

141. LE CORNEC, JACQUES (1981), *Quand le français perd son latin: Nouvelle défense et illustration* (Paris).

142. LEDERER, MARIANNE (1988), 'Les Fausses traductions, sources de contamination du français', in Pergnier (ed.), 119–29.

143. LE GUILLY-WALLIS, ANNE (1991), 'Etude de cas: L'Impact des arrêtés de terminologie sur l'informaticien français', *TT* 1: 117–42.

A survey of French computer experts reveals that despite negative reactions to Ministerial Commissions in replacing anglicisms in the field, the replacements are used to a significant degree.

144. LENOBLE-PINSON, MICHÈLE (1991), *Anglicismes et substituts français, l'esprit des mots.* (Brussels: Duculot, Paris, Louvain-la-Neuve).

List of common anglicisms and proposed substitutes elaborated by the Atelier de vocabulaire de Bruxelles.

145. LE PRAT, GUY (1980), *Dictionnaire de franglais: Plus de 850 mots et locutions de langue anglaise couramment utilisés dans les médias, la conversation ou la correspondance française d'aujourd'hui et leur traduction en français* (Paris: Guy le Prat).

More than 850 English loanwords are included, but technical terms are not taken into account. Only the French translation is provided.

146. LERAT, PIERRE (1987*a*), 'Le Traitement des emprunts en terminographie et en néographie', *Les Cahiers de lexicologie*, 50: 137–44.

147. —— (1987*b*), 'L'Acceptabilité des mots', *Etudes de linguistique appliquée*, 67: 7–34.

148. *Loi* (1975), *La Loi relative à l'emploi de la langue française* (Paris: La Documentation française).

149. LOUBENS, DIDIER (1882), *Recueil de mots français tirés des langues étrangères* (Paris).

150. MACKENZIE, FRASER (1939), *Les Relations de l'Angleterre et de la France d'après le vocabulaire*, 1: *Les Infiltrations de la langue et de l'esprit anglais: Anglicismes français* (Paris: Droz), 335–53.

151. MARCELLESI, CHRISTIANE (1973), 'Le Langage des techniciens de l'informatique', *Langue française*, 17: 59–71.

Marcellesi shows that the very numerous English words used by computer operators at the beginning of the 1970s had almost completely disappeared by 1973.

152. MARESCHAL, GÉNEVIÈRE (1988), 'Contribution à l'étude comparée de l'anglicisation en Europe francophone et au Québec', in Pergnier (ed.), 67–78.

153. —— (1992), 'L'Influence comparée de l'anglais sur le français dans différentes aires géographiques francophones', *Revue de l'association canadienne de linguistique appliquée*, 14 (2): 107–20.

154. MARMIN, MICHEL (1979), *Destin du français: Identité et langage. Propos tétraglossiques* (Lausanne).

155. MARTINET, ANDRÉ (1977), 'La Prononciation française des mots d'origine étrangère: Phonologie et société', *Studia Phonetica*, 13: 79–88.

156. MATZEN, RAYMOND (1988), 'Le Franglais en Alsace et les anglicismes alsaciens', in Gilbert-Lucien Salmon (ed.), *Variété et variantes du français des villes: Etats de l'est de la France: Alsace-Lorraine—Lyonnais—Franche-Comté—Belgique* (Paris: Champion-Slatkine), 127–37.

157. *Médias et langage* (1979–) (most recent issue 19/20, 1984) (Paris).

158. MESSNER, DIETER (1977), *Einführung in die Geschichte des französischen Wortschatzes* (Darmstadt: Wissenschaftliche Buchgesellschaft).

159. MØLLER, BERNT (1989), 'Udviklingstentendenser i orddannelsen i teknisk frank i informatikterminologisk belysning' (Tendencies in Word Formation in Technical French Illustrated by Computer Terminology), *Hermes* (Handelshsøjskolen i Aarhus), 3: 51–73.

Accounts for present-day trends in technical French word-formation, illustrated by the field of computer technology; the author also evaluates the proportion of English borrowings and their influence on French models.

160. MOREY, PHILIP (1981), 'The Treatment of English Words in Queneau', *MLR* 76 (4): 823–38.

161. MORGENROTH, KLAUS (1993), 'Doublets franco-anglais en langue de spécialité économique et informatique: *Joystick ou mance à balai*?' *Zielsprache Französisch*, 4: 219–25.

162. MORTUREUX, MARIE-FRANÇOISE (1987), 'Les Résistances à la néologie terminologique: Système lexical et facteurs socio-culturels', *Meta*, 32: 250–4.

163. MOSSÉ, FERNAND (1923), 'Essai sur l'anglicisme', *Les Langues modernes*, 21: 519–35.

164. MÜLLER, BODO (1975), *Das Französische der Gegenwart* (Heidelberg: Winter).

165. —— (1983), 'Phonologie und Purismus', in Hausmann (ed.), 337–44 (first published 1975).

Müller claims that [ŋ] belongs to the phonematic system of French. It occurs occasionally as a product of assimilation and habitually after nasal vowel before [g] and [k]. It is not a consequence of the anglicisms on [iŋ] borrowed since the nineteenth century, but rather a basis for this borrowing.

166. NAKOS, DOROTHY (1991), 'Les Syntagmes terminologiques

dans le domaine de l'informatique (Etude comparée de l'anglais et du français)', *Contrastes*, 20–21: 31–7.

French and Canadian standardized computer-field terminology is analysed in terms of key-words, joining words, paradigms. European French is claimed to accept more loans from English than Canadian French.

167. Nüssler, Otto (1979), 'Das Sprachreinigungsgesetz', in *Braun, 186–98.

168. Nymansson, Karin (1995), 'Le Genre grammatical des anglicismes contemporains en français', *Les Cahiers de lexicologie*, 66: 95–113.

169. O'Neil, Charmian (1986), 'L'Anglais dans la presse quotidienne régionale de ix départements', *GEPE 1986*.

170. Orr, John (1935), 'Les Anglicismes du vocabulaire sportif', *Le Français moderne*, 3: 239–311.

171. Pagani, Robert (1979), 'Face aux anglicismes', *Interprète*, 3–4: 11–14.

172. Pergnier, Maurice (ed.) (1988), *Le Français en contact avec l'anglais. En hommage à Jean Darbelnet* (Paris: Didier-Erudition).

Important collection of articles which are separately listed in this bibliography.

173. —— (1989*a*), *Les Anglicismes*. Paris: Presses Universitaires de France.

174. —— (1989*b*), *Les Anglicismes, danger ou enrichissement pour la langue française?* (Collection Linguistique Nouvelle) (Paris: Presses Universitaires de France).

175. Petiot, Geneviève (1987), 'Le Cinéma américain et langue française', *Meta*, 32 (2): 299–305.

176. Petiot, Georges and Geneviève (1982), *Le Robert des sports: Dictionnaire de la langue des sports* (Paris: Le Robert).

A dictionary of sports vocabulary giving first attestations and evidence of replacements of English borrowings.

177. Pickup, Ian (1988), 'Anglicisms in the French Sporting Press', *Modern Languages*, 69: 218–25.

178. Picone, Michael David (1988), 'De l'anglicisme et de la dynamique de la langue française', D.Phil. thesis (Lille: Atelier national de reproduction des thèses, Université de Lille; also available on microfiche), 405 pp.

This thesis claims that the trend towards synthetic compound nouns in French (no preposition, modifier preceding the head noun) is in fact inherent in the language, and that the English influence merely reinforces existing tendencies. The original corpus is large and varied and includes much advertising and contemporary press material. The discussion focuses on semantic and category change of borrowed words and compares the terms proposed by the Ministerial Commissions and those actually found in the corpus. (Printed version 1996).

179. —— (1991), 'The Phonology of the Velar Nasal in Contemporary Metropolitan French', *The SECOL Review*, 15: 121–45.

180. —— (1992), 'Le Français face à l'anglais: Aspects linguistiques', *Cahier de l'Association internationale des études françaises*, 44: 9–23.

181. —— (1996), *Anglicisms, Neologisms and Dynamic French* (Amsterdam/Philadelphia: Benjamins), 462 pp.

A major work on French neology and the role of anglicisms. The thrust of the argument is that English borrowings only confirm existing tendencies in French synthetic word-formation patterns. (Based on Picone 1988, review: Görlach, *IJL*).

182. Quemada, Bernard (1978), 'Technique et langage', in E. Gille (ed.), *Histoire des techniques* (Paris: Pléiade), 1146–240.

183. —— (1983/84), 'Les Réformes du français', in I. Fodor, Bernard Quemada and Claude Hagège (eds.), *La Réform des langues, histoire et avenir* (Hamburg: Buske), III: 79–117.

184. Retman, Roman (1978), 'L'Adaptation phonétique des emprunts à l'anglais en français', *La Linguistique*, 14 (1): 111–24.

185. Rey-Debove, Josette (1973), 'La Sémiotique de l'emprunt lexical', *Travaux de linguistique et de littérature*, 11: 109–23.

186. —— and GILBERTE GAGNON (1980), *Dictionnaire des anglicismes: Les Mots anglais et américains en français* (Paris: Robert).

The dictionary lists more than 2700 words borrowed from British or American English and used in France. Each entry consists of date of first attestation, meaning, quotations, and etymology. There is a useful introduction about loanwords in general.

187. —— (1987), 'Effet des anglicismes lexicaux sur le système du français', *Cahiers de lexicologie*, 51: 257–65.

Rey-Debove argues that the borrowing of English blends creates confusions in learned scientific morphology in French and is thus the most pernicious form of loan.

188. RINT (Réseau international de néologie et de terminologie) (1994), 'Séminaire implantation des termes officiels', *Terminologies nouvelles*, 12 (Implantation des termes officiels: Actes du séminaire, Rouen, Décembre 1993) (Brussels).

Proceedings of a seminar held for official terminology bodies of French-speaking countries aimed at evaluating the implementation of official terminology, especially in France and Québec. The vocabulary of certain subject fields is examined in detail: computer technology, medicine, audio-visual media, remote sensing, and the presence of official terms or their anglicism equivalents in dictionaries. Methodology is an important issue: how can implementation be gauged? One answer is a sociolinguistic study of language usage in the workplace.

189. ROBERT, PAUL and REY ALAIN, ([2]1987), *Le Grand Robert de la langue française* (6 vols., Paris: Le Robert).

190. ROHR, RUPPRECHT (1964), 'Zu den englischen Wörtern in einem französischen Gebrauchswörterbuch', in D. Riesner and H. Gneuss (eds.), *Festschrift für Walter Hübner* (Berlin: E. Schmidt), 61–76.

Rohr surveys the history of research on anglicisms in French before he turns to a quantificational analysis of the data collected in Behrens (1927), and to the material contained in two editions of the *Petit Larousse* of 1910 and 1956, concentrating on the pronunciation of words with various problematic vowels and consonants and those ending in *-er* and *-ing*, including remarks on their morphological integration.

191. ROTHWELL, W. (1979), 'Anglo-French Lexical Contacts, Old and New', *The Modern Language Review*, 74: 287–96.

192. ROUDET, LÉONCE (1908), 'Remarques sur la phonétique des mots français d'emprunt', *Revue de philologie française*, 22: 241–67.

193. SANDERS, CAROL (ed.) (1993), *French Today: Language in its Social Context* (Cambridge: Cambridge University Press).

194. SAUVAGEOT, AURÉLIEN (1959), 'Dirigisme et purisme: Pour un dirigisme linguistique: Qui fait la loi? Qui dit la loi?', *Vie et langage*, 200–3, 261–4, 315–17.

195. —— (1960), 'Le Langage et la pensée', *Vie et langage*, 76–9, 269–72, 329–32, 383–6, 536–9.

196. —— (1961), 'Comment agir sur la langue française?', *Vie et langage*, 399–404.

197. —— (1966), 'La Langue française et les nécessités de l'expression scientifique et technique', *Vie et langage*, 576–82, 630–7.

198. SAUVY, ALFRED (1963*a*), 'Destruction et rénovation de la langue française', *Revue de Paris*, 70: 12–23.

199. —— (1963*b*), 'Menaces sur la langue française', *Revue de Paris*, 70: 37–47.

200. SCHAFROTH, ELMAR (1996), '*Zapping*/*Zapper*: Zur Eigendynamik eines Anglizismus im Französischen', *Französisch Heute*, 27: 19–28.

201. SCHAPIRA, CHARLOTTE (1987), 'Comment rendre en français les termes anglais dérivés et composés à la fois?', *Meta*, 32: 342–6.

202. SCHERER, MATTHIAS (1923), *Englisches Sprachgut in der französischen Tagespresse der Gegenwart* (Gießen: Universität).

203. SCHMITT, CHRISTIAN (1977), 'Zur Kodifizierung der neufranzösischen Wirtschaftssprache', in *Imago linguae: Festschrift für Fritz Paepcke* (München: Fink), 511–32.

204. —— (1979), 'Sprachplanung und Sprachlenkung im Französischen der Gegenwart', in Eckhard Rattunde (ed.), *Sprachnorm(en) im Fremdsprachenunterricht* (Frankfurt/M.: Diesterweg), 7–44.

205. ——(1998), 'Die Rolle von Fachsprachen im Kontakt von Einzelsprachen II: English—Französisch im 20. Jahrhundert', in Lothar Hoffmann *et al.* (eds.), *Fachsprachen: Languages for Special Purposes* (Berlin: de Gruyter), 771–84.

206. Schmitt, H. J. (1980), 'Deux mots français ressuscités par l'influence de l'anglais: *Créatif et crédible*', *Cahiers de lexicologie*, 36: 80–94.

207. ——(1982), 'Die semantische Motivation lexikalischer Entlehnungen—Untersuchungen an Anglizismen im Französischen', *Sprachen in Kontakt* (Tübingen: Narr), 77–95.

208. Schütz, Armin (1968), *Die sprachliche Aufnahme und stilistische Wirkung des Anglizismus im Französischen, aufgezeigt an der Reklamesprache (1962–1964)* (Meisenheim a. Glan: Hain).

209. Schweikard, Wolfgang (1998), 'Englisch und Romanisch', in Günter Holtus *et al.* (eds.), *Lexikon der Romanischen Linguistik 7* (Berlin: de Gruyter), 184–230.

210. Seewald, Uta (1992), 'Besonderheiten der Wortbildung im französischen Wortschatz der Datenverarbeitung', *Fachsprache*, 14: 2–13.

211. Seibold, Hans (1974), 'Der Einfluß des Englischen auf die französische Sportsprache der Gegenwart', unpublished D.Phil. thesis (Erlangen).

212. Söll, Ludwig (1968), '*Shampooing* und die Integration des Suffixes *-ing*', in Helmut Stimm and J. Wilhelm (eds.), *Verba et vocabula: Festschrift Ernst Gamillscheg* (München: Fink), 565–78.

213. Sommant, Micheline (1996), 'Les Termes de langue anglaise et l'usage des formes contractées (sigles et mots-valises) dans le langage des multimédias (informatique, audiovisuel et télécommunications)', *6èmes Journées de l'ERLA-GLAT* (Brest), 179–90.

214. Spence, Nicol C. W. (1976), 'Le Problème du franglais', in N. C. W. Spence, *Le Français contemporain* (München: Fink), 75–103.

215. ——(1989), 'Qu'est-ce que c'est qu'un anglicisme?', *Revue de linguistique romane*, 53: 323–34.

216. SPENCE, NICOL C. W. (1991), 'Les Mots français en -ING', *Le Français moderne*, 59: 188–213.

After listing the some 450 anglicisms ending in *-ing*, Spence comprehensively reviews literature on the subject and identifies the fields where these forms are particularly current. He analyses the semantic evolution of these words, whether genuine loans or 'false anglicisms', and examines the success of attempts to replace this category of anglicism.

217. STEFENELLI, ARNULF (1981), *Geschichte des französischen Kernwortschatzes* (Berlin: E. Schmidt).

218. STUART, MALCOLM (1985), 'Langage musical et langue étrangère: Incursions de l'anglais parlé sur les ondes de France-Musique', *Actes du Colloque du G.E.P.E., Strasbourg 1984*, 161–7.

219. *Termes* (1972), *Termes techniques français: Essai d'orientation de la terminologie* (Paris).

220. THIBAU, JACQUES (1980), *La France colonisée* (Paris).

221. THODY, PHILIP (1995), *Le Franglais. Forbidden English. Forbidden American: Law, Politics and Language in Contemporary France. A Study in Loan Words and National Identity* (London: Athlone), 300 pp.

A selective dictionary of anglicisms preceded by a lengthy introduction which charts the life and death of the various combats largely in the press and parliament against franglais, and explains the arguments used. This introduction is more than a chronicle of events; it seeks to explain why the French have reacted more strongly against anglicisms than other Europeans, and how this is indicative of the French attitude to the outside world. The political nature of this reaction is demonstrated by the contention that franglais is actually quite rare in normal discourse, written or spoken. The dictionary part is arranged thematically aiming at the least specialized of borrowings. It contains some three hundred anglicisms with attestations from primary and secondary sources, an evaluation of actual usage, and other comments. The work is well documented, although the conclusions are sometimes tendentious. A third part gives French expressions used in English.

222. Thogmartin, Clyde (1984), 'Some "English" Words in French', *The French Review*, 57: 447–555.

223. Tournier, Jean (1988), 'Parlez-vous médiais?', *Bulletin de Linguistique Appliquée et Générale*, 14: 25–33.

224. —— (1998), *Les mots anglais du français* (Collection le français retrouvé) (Paris), 623 pp.

This most important recent dictionary devoted to anglicisms in French comprises 3610 headwords arranged in seven sections within which items are listed alphabetically in subsections: 1 'Sports et loisirs' (25–96 = 13.62%), 2 'Sciences humaines' (97–197 = 18.91%), 3 'Sciences juridiques, politiques et économiques' (198–240 = 7.91%), 4 'Sciences et techniques' (241–425 = 34.18%), 5 'Les arts' (426–72 = 8.27%), 6 'La vie quotidienne' (473–550 = 12.98%) and 7 'Divers' (551–77 = 4.09%). The coverage is remarkably complete, including words in all stages of integration, internationalisms of neo-classical basis and a few calques drawn from general lexis as well as specialized registers, archaisms and pseudo-anglicisms. Individual entries include information on pronunciation, dates, etymology, and suggested replacements.

225. Trescases, Pierre (1979), 'Les Anglo-américanismes du *Petit Larousse illustré* 1979', *The French Review*, 53(1): 68–74.

226. —— (1982), *Le Franglais vingt ans après* (Montréal).

Trescases gives a short linguistic introduction to the subject, but he mainly presents different attitudes towards 'franglais'. His statements are based on relevant texts written between 1976 and 1978 and dealing with this subject.

227. —— (1983), 'Aspects du mouvement d'emprunt à l'anglais reflétés par trois dictionnaires de néologismes', *Cahiers de lexicologie*, 42: 86–101.

228. —— (1987), 'Phonétisation automatique du français at aménagement phonético-graphique des emprunts à l'anglais', *Meta*, 32 (2): 230–9.

229. Truchot, Claude (ed.) (1986), *Langue française–langue anglaise: Contacts et conflits. Actes du deuxième colloque du GEPE* (Strasbourg).

230. TRUCHOT, CLAUDE (1994), 'La France, l'anglais, le français et l'Europe', in *Sociolinguistica*, 8: 15–25.

231. ULLMANN, STEPHEN (1941), 'The Rhythm of English Infiltration into Classical French', *Modern Languages*, 12: 55–8.

232. —— (1947), 'Anglicisms in French: Notes on their Chronology, Range, and Reception', *PMLA* 62: 1153–77.

233. —— (1950), 'The Stylistic Role of Anglicisms in Vigny', *French Studies*, 4: 1–15.

234. —— (1957), 'Anglicismes patents et anglicismes latents', *Vie et langage*, 172–7.

235. VANDAELE, HILAIRE (1902), *Le Néologisme exotique: Les Emprunts anglais dans le français actuel* (Discours) (Besançon).

236. VOIROL, MICHEL (1989), *Anglicismes et anglomanie*. Les Guides du Centre de formation et de perfectionnement des journalistes.

237. WALKER, DOUGLAS C. (1982), 'On a Phonological Innovation in French', *Journal of the Phonetic Association*, 12: 72–7.

238. WALTER, HENRIETTE (1976), *La Dynamique des phonèmes dans le lexique français contemporain* (Paris).

239. —— (1983), 'La Nasale vélaire /ŋ/: Un Phonème du français?', *Langue française*, 60: 14–29.

240. —— and GÉRARD WALTER (1991), *Dictionnaire des mots d'origine étrangère* (Références Larousse: Langue française; Paris: Larousse).

241. —— (1997), *L'Aventure des mots français venus d'ailleurs* (Paris: Robert Laffont).

A popular but reliable study of words incorporated into French from other languages. One chapter on English, containing an interesting glossary of anglicisms which have resisted replacement, and a section on loanwords from other languages transmitted via English. The author also points out the many English borrowings considered well on the way to integration in Etiemble's day, which are now felt to be hopelessly out of date.

242. WARTBURG, WALTHER VON (1967), *Französisches Etymologisches Wörterbuch*, Vol. 18: *Anglizismen* (Basel: Zbinden).

243. WEXLER, PETER (1955), *La Formation du vocabulaire des chemins de fer en France 1778–1842* (Genève: Droz).

244. WOLF, LOTHAR (1977), 'Französische Sprachpolitik der Gegenwart: ein Sprachgesetz gegen die Anglomanie', in J. Hampel and R. Sussmann (eds.), *Lernziel Europa. Ein Werkstattbericht* (Politische Studien Sonderheft 3; München), 45–68.

245. ZANOLA, MARIA TERESA (1991), 'L'Emprunt lcxical anglais dans le français contemporain: Analyse d'un corpus de presse (1982–1989)', *Quaderni del Centro di linguistica dell'Università cattolica* (Brescia), 3: 96.

The corpus is made up of anglicisms (presented in an appendix) in three Paris dailies and four weeklies. The occurrence of anglicisms diminishes over the period. Certain sectors and certain media are shown to be particularly permeable, especially those open to international tendencies. The account includes a history of official organizations set up to fight anglicisms.

246. ZWANENBURG, WIECHER (1987), 'Le Statut formation des mots savants en français et en anglais', *Meta*, 32 (2): 223–9.

German (Manfred Görlach and Ulrich Busse)

(see also *25, *45, *53, *54, *55, *60, *77, *80, *85)

1. ARNOLD, ROBERT F. (1904), 'Die englischen Lehn- und Fremdwörter im gegenwärtigen Neuhochdeutsch', *Zeitschrift für die österreichischen Gymnasien*, 55: 97–114.

A temperate statement, mostly a listing of those English words which in the author's opinion had become current in the German language of his time.

2. AUGST, GERHARD (1987), 'Zur graphemischen Bezeichnung der Vokalquantität bei Fremdwörtern', in Hermann Zabel (ed.), *Fremdwortorthographie. Beiträge zu historischen und aktuellen Fragestellungen* (RGL 79; Tübingen: Niemeyer), 94–110.

3. —— (1989), 'Ein Pin-up-Girl an der Pinnwand? Zur orthographischen Integration des englischen Geminatenwechsels', in Peter Eisenberg and Hartmut Günther (eds.), *Schriftsystem und Orthographie* (Tübingen: Niemeyer), 1–9.

4. —— (1992), 'Die orthographische Integration von zusammengesetzten Anglizismen', *Sprachwissenschaft*, 17: 45–61.

The articles concentrate on various problems linked with the foreign principles of spelling and pronunciation of anglicisms and their effects upon the German system, e.g. vowel quantity, single vs. double consonants, the spelling of compounds and multiword units, etc.

5. BARTH, MAX (1957), 'Englisches im Deutschen', *Muttersprache*, 67: 143–5, 186–8.

6. BENNETT, JOHN F. (1979), 'The Influence of English on the German Vocabulary 1800–1850', unpublished Ph.D. thesis (Oxford).

This thesis summarizes the English influence on German in the first half of the nineteenth century, based on the entries in the *Deutsches Fremdwörterbuch* (Berlin: de Gruyter) of the Institut für deutsche Sprache, Mannheim.

7. BERNS, MARGIE (1988), 'The Cultural and Linguistic Context of English in West Germany', *World Englishes*, 7: 37–49.

The spread and nativization of English borrowings in German, its forms and functions are analysed in a sociolinguistic framework; not quite reliable.

8. BUCK, TIMOTHY (1971), 'Pseudoenglisches im heutigen Deutsch', in *German into English, II* (Göttingen: Vandenhoeck and Ruprecht), 86–7.

9. —— (1974), '"Selfmade-Englisch [*sic*]"—Semantic Peculiarities of English Loan-Material in Contemporary German', *Forum for Modern Language Studies*, 10: 130–46.

The author points out that many English loanwords have developed new meanings beyond their English etymons, which makes them pseudo-loans; in some cases German retains usages obsolete in present-day English.

10. BUNGERT, HANS (1963), 'Zum Einfluss des Englischen auf die deutsche Sprache seit dem Ende des zweiten Weltkrieges', *JEGPh* 62: 703–17.

Material collected from newspapers, periodicals, and advertisements from 1960–1962 and a novel, arranged in subject groups; processes of assimilation, pronunciation, spelling, and syntactic influences are discussed.

11. BUSSE, ULRICH (1992), 'Doppelformen von Anglizismen im Rechtschreib-Duden', in Karl Hyldgaard-Jensen and Arne Zettersten (eds.), *Symposium on Lexicography V. Proceedings of the Fifth International Symposium on Lexicography May 3–5, 1990 at the University of Copenhagen* (Lexicographica, Series Major 43; Tübingen: Niemeyer), 341–71.

The treatment of spelling variants (entries beginning with C-, K-, or Z-) in the leading German spelling dictionary casts light on the principles of orthographic integration of selected anglicisms.

12. —— (1993), *Anglizismen im Duden. Eine Untersuchung zur Darstellung englischen Wortguts in den Ausgaben des Rechtschreibdudens von 1880–1986* (RGL 139; Tübingen: Niemeyer), 328 pp. (Reviews: Görlach, *IJL* 8 (1995), 79–80; Posthumus, *Trefwoord* 8 (1994), 40–3; *Year's Work in English Studies* 55 (1994), 693; Yeandle, *Germanistik* 36 (1995), 76–7.)

This book, based on a D.Phil. thesis, is the most thorough study of the lexicographical treatment of anglicisms in the leading

German spelling dictionary to date. Busse analyses (often on the basis of sections of the complete dictionary) the number of entries marked 'from English', their chronological development and representation according to twenty domains, the time-lag between their first attestation in texts and inclusion in a Duden, the difference between 'Eastern' and 'Western' editions after 1947, the problematic distinction between BrE and AmE, and discusses grammatical problems (gender assignment and pluralization) and spelling variants. A comprehensive compilation (224–311) lists the first occurrences of all anglicisms in the nineteen editions analysed, and the first *omissions* of items from earlier editions (cf. Langner 1995).

13. BUSSE, ULRICH (1994*a*), 'Das *Anglizismen-Wörterbuch* und seine Benutzer', *Fremdsprachen Lehren und Lernen*, 23: 175–91.

From the viewpoint of the dictionary-maker the author discusses the objectives, the scope, content, and the structure of the dictionary in respect to envisaged readers; he concludes that the dictionary is primarily academically oriented but also tries to cater for users interested in questions of language change. A modified English version is printed in 'A Dictionary of Anglicisms—an Outline of its History, Content and Objectives', *Suvremena Lingvistica*, 41/42 (= Festschrift for Rudolf Filipović), 103–14.

14. —— (1994*b*), 'Anglizismen im Einheitsduden', in Karl Hyldgaard-Jensen and Viggo Hjørnager Pedersen (eds.), *Symposium on Lexicography VI: Proceedings of the Sixth International Symposium on Lexicography May 7–9, 1992 at the University of Copenhagen*. (Lexicographica, Series Maior 57; Tübingen: Niemeyer), 183–206.

The article continues the one of 1993 investigating the lexicographical treatment of anglicisms in the 'unified' Duden after the separation into 'Eastern' and 'Western' editions had come to an end.

15. —— (1994*c*), '"Wenn die Kötterin mit dem Baddibuilder . . . ". Ergebnisse einer Informantenbefragung zur Aussprache englischer Wörter im Deutschen', in Dieter W. Halwachs and Irmgard Stütz (eds.), *Sprache—Sprechen—Handeln. Akten des 28. Linguistischen Kolloquiums, Graz 1993* (LA 320; Tübingen: Niemeyer), I: 23–30.

A questionnaire is used to test the pronunciation of four groups of anglicisms on a non-representative group of informants: anglicisms with <u> such as *Butler*, *Cutter*, those beginning with <st> (*Straps*, *Steak*, etc.), or <j> (*Jazz*, *Jumbo-jet*), and those with BrE [ɒ] pronunciation (*bodybuilder*, *Common Sense*).

16. —— (1995), 'Drinks und Dinks—Correctness auf gut Deutsch', in Bernd Polster (ed.), *Westwind. Die Amerikanisierung Europas* (Köln: DuMont), 140–7.

A brief history of German borrowing from English outlining the critical, at times hostile, puristic reactions in the late nineteenth and early twentieth centuries is followed by a sketch of the lexicographical treatment and modern usage of anglicisms in the domains of media and languages for special purposes, e.g. advertising, youth slang, etc. Major periods of twentieth-century usage are highlighted by means of keywords typical of a decade. A short chronological glossary (by the editor) from 1945 to the mid-1990s is appended (148–50).

17. —— (1996), 'Probleme der Aussprache englischer Wörter im Deutschen und ihre Behandlung im *Anglizismen-Wörterbuch*', in Arne Zettersten and Viggo Hjørnager Pedersen (eds.), *Symposium on Lexicography VII.* (Lexikographica, Series Maior 76; Tübingen: Niemeyer), 83–92.

18. —— (1998), 'A Dictionary of Anglicisms. An Outline of its History, Content and Objectives', in *Suvremana Lingvistika. Festschrift für Rudolf Filipović*, 41/42: 103–14.

19. —— (1999), 'Keine Bedrohung durch Anglizismen', *Der Sprachdienst*, 43: 18–20.

20. Carstensen, Broder (1965), *Englische Einflüsse auf die deutsche Sprache nach 1945* (Beihefte zum Jahrbuch für Amerikastudien 13; Heidelberg: Winter), 296 pp. (Reviews: Eggers, *Jahrbuch für Amerikastudien*, 12 (1967), 291–6; Höfler, *Zeitschrift für Romanische Philologie*, 84 (1968), 154–9; Lehnert, *ZAA* 15 (1967), 71–4; Stanforth, *Zeitschrift für Mundartforschung*, 33 (1966), 346–9; Urbanová, *Muttersprache*, 76 (1966), 177–81; Zandvoort, *English Studies*, 47 (1966), 79–81.)

Carstensen provides an analysis of the English influence on the German language after 1945 based on West German newspapers and magazines and *Der Spiegel*, which is considered to introduce the greatest number of Americanisms into the German language.

This analysis covers English influence on German spelling, morphology, loan syntax, and its influence on the vocabulary. Words taken over before 1945 are also treated if obvious semantic changes have taken place.

21. Carstensen, Broder (1971), *Spiegel-Wörter—Spiegel-Worte. Zur Sprache eines deutschen Nachrichtenmagazins* (Munich: Hueber), 140 pp.

Basing his study on a corpus of citations from 1962 to 1971, Carstensen characterizes the linguistic peculiarities of the German news magazine *Der Spiegel*. A theoretical introduction is followed by selected examples illustrating foreign lexical influences, esp. anglicisms, puns, allusions, and also some observations on morphology, syntax, and style.

22. —— (1973/74), 'Englisches im Deutschen: Zum Einfluß der englischen Sprache auf das heutige Deutsch', *Paderborner Studien*, 3: 5–15.

23. —— (1979*a*), 'Morphologische Eigenwege des Deutschen bei der Übernahme englischen Wortmaterials', *AAA* 4: 155–70.

The article describes the various morphological changes at work in integration of anglicisms. The categories discussed are clippings, blends, conversions, and inflectional changes (plural or infinitive formation). Carstensen categorizes individual lexemes, compounds, and phraseological units on the basis of a great number of examples.

24. —— (1979*b*), 'The Influence of English on German—Syntactic Problems', *Studia Anglica Posnaniensia*, 11: 65–77.

25. —— (1980*a*), 'Semantische Scheinentlehnungen des Deutschen aus dem Englischen', in Viereck (ed.), 77–100.

Carstensen discusses semantic pseudo-loans in German which he defines as English borrowings in their original form with new meanings lacking an apparent English model; he admits that evidence is sometimes difficult to provide due to differences in usage between AmE and BrE and insufficient dictionary documentation.

26. —— (1980*b*), 'Der Einfluß des Englischen auf das Deutsche—Grammatische Probleme', *AAA* 5: 37–63.

27. —— (1980*c*), 'Das Genus englischer Fremd- und Lehnwörter im Deutschen', in Viereck (ed.), 37–75.

Carstensen treats the manifold problems of noun gender assignment to English loanwords in present-day German on the basis of dictionaries, informants, examples of printed texts, and data from previous research. He attempts to analyse the relevant factors, discarding the hypothesis that older loans do not waver in their gender attribution; he concludes that dictionary evidence is often at odds with the data provided by informants.

28. —— (1981*a*), 'Lexikalische Scheinentlehnungen des Deutschen aus dem Englischen', in Wolfgang Kühlwein *et al.* (eds.), *Kontrastive Linguistik und Übersetzungswissenschaft—Akten des Internationalen Kolloquiums Trier/Saarbrücken vom 25.–30.9.1978* (Munich: Fink), 175–82.

Carstensen lists the most important lexical pseudo-loans, e.g. *Show-master, Dressman, Pullunder, Highboard*, and a few others.

29. —— (1981*b*), 'Zur Deklination aus dem Englischen entlehnter Substantive im Deutschen', in Jürgen Esser and Axel Hübler (eds.), *Forms and Functions. Festschrift Vilém Fried* (TBL 149; Tübingen: Narr), 103–22.

By referring to grammars, dictionaries, a corpus, and informants Carstensen tries to explain how English nouns are incorporated into German declension patterns; this process can often be interpreted as a sign of growing integration.

30. —— (1982*a*), 'Eine neue Bedeutung von *Bank*', *Deutsche Sprache*, 10: 366–76.

31. —— (1982*b*), '"Babys" oder "Babies"? Zum Plural englischer Wörter im Deutschen', *Muttersprache*, 92: 200–15.

32. —— (1983), 'English Elements in the German Language—their Treatment and Compilation in a Dictionary of Anglicisms', *Germanistische Linguistik*, 82 (5–6): 13–34.

33. —— (1984), 'Wieder: Die Engländerei in der deutschen Sprache', in *Die deutsche Sprache der Gegenwart* (Göttingen: Vandenhoeck and Ruprecht), 43–57.

Carstensen discusses whether the majority of anglicisms in current German is found in the common core or in the technical language and how far English 'damages' written and spoken German or, rather, has positive side effects.

34. CARSTENSEN, BRODER (1986), '*Best-*, *Long-*, *Steady-* und andere *-Seller* im Deutschen', in Brigitte Narr and Hartwig Wittje (eds.), *Spracherwerb und Mehrsprachigkeit. Festschrift für Els Oksaar* (Tübingen: Narr), 181–98.

35. —— (1987), 'Der englische Einfluß auf die deutsche Sprache', in Adolf M. Birke and Kurt Kluxen (eds.), *Die europäische Herausforderung. England und Deutschland in Europa* (Munich: Saur), 93–107.

36. —— (1988), 'Loan-Translation: Theoretical and Practical Issues', *Folia Linguistica*, 22: 85–92.

37. —— and ULRICH BUSSE (1993–1996), *Anglizismen-Wörterbuch. Der Einfluß des Englischen auf den deutschen Wortschatz nach 1945* (3 vols.; Berlin: de Gruyter), x + 236* + 1752 pp. (Reviews: Burgschmitt, *Anglistik*, 9 (1998); *Deutscher Forschungsdienst*, 11.1.1994, 14; Fröschl, *AAA* 20 (1995), 268–9; Gardt, *Anglia*, 114 (1996), 99–103; Göldenboog, *Deutschland*, 6 (1994), 38–9; Görlach, *IJL* 8 (1995), 77–8; Herbst, *ZAA* 42 (1994), 384–7; Hiltscher, *Praxis des neusprachlichen Unterrichts*, 42 (1995), 106–7; Müller, *Germanistik*, 35 (1994), 434; *Germanistik*, 36 (1995), 419–20; *Germanistik*, 37 (1996), 785–6; Pfeffer, *Beiträge zur Geschichte der deutschen Sprache und Literatur*, 119 (1997), 285–9; Russ, *MLR* 91 (1996), 1028–9; Stanforth, *Sprachreport*, 2 (1996), 5–6; *MLR* 92 (1997), 779–80.)

The *Dictionary of Anglicisms* is based on a corpus of 100,000 citations from German newspapers, periodicals, catalogues, advertisements, booklets, pamphlets, and from high and trivial literature, also including a few samples of spoken German, esp. from television and radio. It documents the 3,500 most common and current anglicisms in present-day German. The term *anglicism* is used as a generic term for Briticism, Americanism, Canadianism, etc. The main focus of the dictionary is on those anglicisms which have entered German after 1945. Older loans are included only if they exhibit changes in meaning or new meanings. The dictionary includes a large number of hybrids and calques (translations, creations, and semantic loans). A detailed introduction describes the problems connected with the lexicographic documentation of the complex material and gives reasons for their treatment. A comprehensive bibliography of ca. 1450 titles covers research (up to 1992) on the influence of the English language on German and on problems of transference linguistics in general.

38. —— and HANS GALINSKY (^{3}1975), *Amerikanismen der deutschen Gegenwartssprache—Entlehnungsvorgänge und ihre stilistischen Aspekte* (Heidelberg: Winter), 86 pp.

The first part (in German, by Carstensen) deals with the processes of borrowing. The data for this analysis were taken from twenty West German newspapers and magazines, among which *Der Spiegel* is considered to be the richest source for Americanisms. The second part (by Galinsky, in English) deals with stylistic aspects of linguistic borrowing. This analysis is based on German literary texts, travel books, scientific prose, and newspapers, which serve as sources for written language, and public addresses, public hearings, radio, and TV, and conversation as sources for spoken language. Galinsky concludes that the various stylistic uses not only affect the vocabulary but also the morphology and, more rarely, the syntax.

39. —— and PETER HENGSTENBERG (1983), 'Zur Rezeption von Anglizismen im Deutschen', *Germanistische Linguistik*, 82: 67–118.

The authors developed and tested a questionnaire with selected items on 682 informants to explain the factors influencing the comprehension of anglicisms. The analysis of the linguistic motives that led to incorrect interpretations indicates that the reception is determined by linguistic and non-linguistic factors, but primarily by the informants' knowledge of English and the modernity of the items in question.

40. CLYNE, MICHAEL G. (1973), 'Kommunikation und Kommunikationsbarrieren bei englischen Entlehnungen im heutigen Deutsch', *ZGL* 1: 163–77.

41. —— (1995), *The German Language in a Changing Europe* (Cambridge: Cambridge University Press), 260 pp.

In this revised study Clyne expands his former analysis of the German language in *Language Society in the German Speaking Countries* (1984) in the light of recent socio-political events. One of the book's eight chapters (ch. 8) gives a short summary of 'Recent Anglo-American Influence' on the German language.

42. DALCHER, PETER (1967), 'Der Einfluß des Englischen auf die Umgangssprache der deutschen Schweiz', *Schweizerdeutsches Wörterbuch—Schweizerisches Idiotikon. Bericht über das Jahr 1966* (Zurich: City Druck AG), 11–22.

43. —— (1986), 'Anglicisms in Swiss German: The Evaluation by Computer of a Survey Conducted in 1964/5', in *Viereck and Bald (eds.), 179–206.

A study based on a limited sociolinguistic (usage) survey of 1964/5, analysing frequencies of a small number of anglicisms according to subject areas and phonetic and morphological accommodation in ten Swiss towns.

44. DROSDOWSKI, GÜNTHER (ed.) ([2]1993–95), *Duden. Das große Wörterbuch der deutschen Sprache* (8 vols.; Mannheim, Leipzig, Wien, Zürich: Dudenverlag). (Review: Görlach, *IJL* 10 (1997), 156–7.)

This new edition is the most complete general dictionary of modern German, comprising some 200,000 items. Among these, anglicisms are extensively covered; entries include a great number of words relating to Anglo-Saxon culture (foreignisms), technical terms and words which are not German but can be found in present-day German newspapers. Information includes details on pronunciation (IPA, of the English original form), on inflection and meaning, with occasional quotations from literary or newspaper texts taken from the Duden text corpus. A greatly revised edition was recently published in ten volumes (4,800 pp., 1999).

45. —— *et al.* (eds.) ([21]1996), *Duden. Rechtschreibung der Deutschen Sprache* (Mannheim: Bibliographisches Institut).

This edition of the Duden orthographic dictionary marks all the changes that result from the new 1996 regulation of the German spelling system (including syllabification) in red print. As regards their syllabification, morpho-phonemic integration, spelling variants, etc. anglicisms are also affected by this change.

46. DUCKWORTH, DAVID (1964), 'Der Einfluß des Englischen auf den deutschen Wortschatz seit 1945', unpublished MA thesis (Manchester).

An MA thesis indebted to Zindler (1959) which, however, covers loans in technical languages, esp. in economics and military policy, giving particular emphasis to calques to show the various processes of assimilation. Detailed word histories are provided in a dictionary arranged according to subject areas grading the entries on a scale from foreign to integrated. The author adds citations from Dutch, Danish, and Swedish to illustrate how these languages have coped with the foreign word material. (cf. next entry).

47. —— (1979), 'Der Einfluß des Englischen auf den deutschen Wortschatz seit 1945', in *Braun (ed.), 212–45 (first in *ZdSpr* 26 (1970), 9–31).

An account of the methods and findings of a research project classifying forms of influence, distribution according to subject areas and problems of dating, with a few specimens interpreted in detail. A somewhat incoherent presentation.

48. Dunger, Hermann (1899), 'Wider die Engländerei in der deutschen Sprache', *Zeitschrift des Allgemeinen Deutschen Sprachvereins*, 14: 241–51.

An early document devoted to the increasing influence of English on German from a moderate purist's viewpoint, who mildly resents the encroachment of English on German and usually prefers German translations or renditions.

49. —— ([2]1909), *Engländerei in der deutschen Sprache* (Berlin: Verlag des ADSV F. Bergold), 99 pp. (repr. 1989, together with Dunger's *Wörterbuch von Verdeutschungen entbehrlicher Fremdwörter* (1882), introduction by W. Viereck (Hildesheim: Olms), 12* + 194 + 99 pp.). (Review: Görlach, *IJL* 9 (1996), 161).

A revised and enlarged version of his 1899 article. Despite considerable augmentation and inclusion of new subject areas Dunger does not claim to be exhaustive. One of the merits of his study is that it is the first entirely devoted to the new influence of English.

50. Engels, Barbara (1976), *Gebrauchsanstieg der lexikalischen und semantischen Amerikanismen in zwei Jahrgängen der 'Welt' (1954 und 1964). Eine vergleichende computer-linguistische Studie zur quantitativen Entwicklung amerikanischen Einflusses auf die deutsche*

Zeitungssprache (Mainzer Studien zur Amerikanistik 6; Frankfurt/M.: Lang), 265 pp.

A computer-based diachronic study comparing the frequencies of Americanisms of all 1954 issues of the daily *Die Welt* with those of 1964. This dissertation takes the study of Fink (1970) as a starting point. The author restricts the analysis of her corpus, which served as a basis for the computer retrieval program, to the Americanisms already listed by Fink.

51. Erämetsä, Erik (1955), *Englische Lehnprägungen in der deutschen Empfindsamkeit des 18. Jahrhunderts* (Annales Academiae Scientiarum Fennicae, Series B. 98.1; Helsinki: Akateeminen Kirjakauppa; Wiesbaden: Harrassowitz), 135 pp.

The monograph treats semantic loans and loan translations, which owe their existence to the dominance of English-inspired sentimentalism and its influence on the German literature of the eighteenth century, by providing detailed word studies.

52. Fink, Hermann (1970), *Amerikanismen im Wortschatz der deutschen Tagespresse, dargestellt am Beispiel dreier überregionaler Zeitungen (Süddeutsche Zeitung, Frankfurter Allgemeine Zeitung, Die Welt)* (Mainzer Amerikanistische Beiträge 11; Munich: Hueber), 215 pp. (Review: Viereck, *Jahrbuch für Amerikastudien*, 17 (1972), 254–7).

This study is a shortened version of the author's 1968 Mainz dissertation: the descriptive part of the book comprises only two of the fifteen domains, but the summaries and conclusion are printed in full. The author's main objectives are to reveal the extent of AmE influence on the German language after 1945 and to explore whether there are regional differences or varying frequencies of usage in different subject areas. As a corpus the author chose the weekend issues of two months in 1963 in three national newspapers: *Die Welt, FAZ,* and *Süddeutsche Zeitung*, which he considered representative of the northern, central, and southern parts of Germany—a corpus of an estimated seven million words. The main descriptive part of the thesis is organized in fifteen domains within which the loans are classified according to their state of assimilation. The exposition of the data is followed by an extensive summary and thorough analysis of the evidence.

53. —— (1975), '"Know-how" und "Hifi-Pionier": Zum Verständnis englischer Ausdrücke in der deutschen Werbesprache', *Muttersprache*, 85: 186–203.

The article reviews the results of an empirical study in which the reception and comprehension of thirty items were tested on a group of 195 persons. Their reactions are described taking into account social and educational factors.

54. —— (1977), '"Texas-Look" und "Party-Bluse": Assoziative Effekte von Englischem im Deutschen', *Wirkendes Wort*, 27: 394–402.

A questionnaire is used to test the associations and attitudes of 160 informants on a list of twenty current anglicisms, including direct loans and hybrids.

55. —— (1979), 'Ein "Starangebot"—Englisches im Versandhauskatalog', in *Braun (ed.), 339–59.

An analysis of English items in the widely known *Quelle* mail catalogue (ca. 1000 pages, circulation 7.5 million), concentrating on frequencies, blends, eccentric forms, gender attribution, spelling, and degrees of adaptation, German equivalents and the 'need' for borrowing, and the relation of the data to 'advertese'.

56. —— (1980), 'Zur Aussprache von Angloamerikanischem im Deutschen', in Viereck (ed.), 109–83.

This empirical study outlines the results of an interview of 184 informants mainly from southeastern Westfalia on the pronunciation of fifty-one anglicisms from the common core and the language of advertising. It includes older and more recent loans.

57. —— (1983), *Amerikanisch-englische und gesamtenglische Interferenzen der deutschen Allgemein- und Werbesprache im aktiven und passiven Sprachverhalten deutscher Grund-, Haupt- und Oberschüler.* (Europäische Hochschulschriften Reihe 14, Bd. 113; Frankfurt/M.: Lang), ix + 411 pp.

Fink analyses the pragma-, socio- and psycholinguistic factors governing attitudes towards anglicisms. A set of eighteen items from the standard and colloquial registers of German and including some pseudo-anglicisms is tested on a panel of almost a thousand German students (ranging from primary school to grammar school) by means of a questionnaire and standardized interviews. The bulk of the data was processed by computer. This systematic and extensive study offers insights into the sources of anglicisms, attitudes of speakers towards them and general educational and cross-cultural implications.

58. Fink, Hermann (1997), *Von* Kuh-Look *bis* Fit for Fun: *Anglizismen in der heutigen deutschen Allgemein- und Werbesprache* (Freiberger Beiträge 3; Frankfurt/M.: Lang), 228 pp.

Thousands of anglicisms are analysed on the basis of occurrences in journals, quality dailies, and tabloids of national currency, and advertisements. Fashionable coinages typical of advertising are described—and criticized. Methodologically weak and incoherent.

59. —— Liane Fijas, and Danielle Schons (eds.) (1997), *Anglizismen in der Sprache der Neuen Bundesländer. Eine Analyse zur Verwendung und Rezeption* (Freiberger Beiträge 4; Frankfurt/M.: Lang), 211 pp.

This is the first systematic attempt to describe the impact of English on the language of East Germany after 1989; the book permits one to contrast usage in the former GDR (as summarized in Lehnert 1990) and modern developments in West Germany. Some of these differences have survived the reunification of Germany.

60. —— and Victor Shakkovsky (2000), *Angloamerikanisches in der russischen Gesellschaft sowie Wirtschafts- und Allgemeinsprache.* (Freiberger Beiträge 6; Frankfurt/M.: Lang), 126 pp.

The slim volume has a chapter on the Americanization of Russia and Russian (by Shakkovsky, 5–50) summarizing attitudes in the Russian public in general and among linguists in particular, concentrating on recent changes after the political turnover, but quoting only very selective evidence. Fijas (51–118) contributes an empirical study of some 1,600 anglicisms documented in economic and journalistic registers—a praiseworthy attempt which calls out for more comprehensive documentation.

61. Fischer, Urs (1980), *Der Einfluß des Englischen auf den deutschen Wortschatz im Bereich von Essen und Trinken, dargestellt anhand schweizerischer Quellen* (Europäische Hochschulschriften Reihe 1, Bd. 372; Bern: Lang), 804 pp.

The author describes the influence of English on the Swiss-German vocabulary of eating and drinking in the twentieth century. The main part of this 1979 dissertation is organized as an alphabetical dictionary based on a large corpus of spoken and mainly written sources including advertisements, brand labels, recipes, menus, radio, and TV programmes up to 1976.

62. FRIMAN, KIRSTI (1977), *Zum angloamerikanischen Einfluss auf die heutige deutsche Werbesprache* (Studia Philologica Jyväskyläensia 9; Jyväskylä: University of Jyväskylä), 353 pp.

The author of this 1977 Finnish doctoral thesis on the lexical influence of English on the current German language of advertising covers morphological problems rather than syntactic or stylistic questions. The sources are 196 issues of German newspapers, periodicals, and catalogues between 1966 and 1973. One of the author's objectives is to find out how quickly new loans are included in standard dictionaries. Friman organizes her material according to subject areas and concludes that advertising is one of the domains where English influence is most intense. There is an appendix listing some one thousand anglicisms treated.

63. GALINSKY, HANS (1962), 'Stylistic Aspects of Linguistic Borrowing. A Stylistic View of American Elements in Modern German', in Carstensen and Galinsky ([3]1975), 35–72.

64. —— (1968), 'Der anglo-amerikanische Einfluß auf die deutsche Sprachentwicklung der beiden letzten Jahrzehnte. Versuch einer systematischen Übersicht', in Herbert E. Brekle and Leonhard Lipka (eds.), *Wortbildung, Syntax und Morphologie. Festschrift für Hans Marchand* (The Hague: Mouton), 67–81.

Galinsky takes account of the AmE/BrE influence on German lexis in different subject areas. He regards the languages for special purposes as mediators for anglicisms into colloquial German. Galinsky gives reasons for the growing American influence, not only on German but also on other European languages, including BrE, and delineates the consequences and attitudes. The article also covers questions of morphology, syntax, and style. The examples are mainly taken from the *Frankfurter Allgemeine Zeitung*.

65. —— (1980), 'American English post-1960 Neologisms in Contemporary German: Reception-lag Variables as a Neglected Aspect

of Linguistic Interference', in Viereck (ed.), 213–35 (identical to his 'American Neologisms in German', *American Speech*, 55: 243–63).

Galinsky analyses the time span that elapses between the coinage of a neologism in AmE and its reception and integration into the German language, covering post-1960 AmE neologisms. He adds a review of international writings on theoretical and practical neology and a chronologically ordered wordlist with citations and dictionary attestations.

66. GALINSKY, HANS (1991), 'Americanisms, Briticisms, Canadianisms, New Zealandisms, and Anglicisms in Contemporary German', in *Ivir and Kalogjera (eds.), 195–220.

The four items *cogeneration, snowmobile, kiwi*, and *quality of life* are used to analyse the speed of transference to distinguish English neologisms according to their ethnolectal origins and primary from inter-ethnolectal distribution areas in the English-speaking world and their respective status in German.

67. GANZ, PETER F. (1957), *Der Einfluß des Englischen auf den deutschen Wortschatz 1640–1815* (Berlin: E. Schmidt), 257 pp.

Ganz uses the background of the English-German linguistic and cultural relationships from 1640 to 1815 as mirrored in German lexis. He describes this influence by providing detailed word histories in form of a dictionary supplemented by attestations in lexicons and citations from primary sources, especially travel literature. The dictionary constitutes the second part of the book, the first being devoted to methodological questions. Although there is some overlap in the seventeenth century this monograph is intended to be a sequel to Palmer (1950), carrying on his work to the end of the eighteenth century.

68. GLAHN, RICHARD (2000), *Der Einfluß des Englischen auf gesprochene deutsche Gegenwartssprache, Eine Analyse öffentlich gesprochener Sprache am Beispiel 'Fernsehdeutsch'* (Frankfurt/M: Peter Lang), 211 pp.

Glahn listened to 25 items of various types (economy/politics, scientific, children's, music, series, and talkshows) as well as several sports reports and advertisements broadcast on German TV in 1998 (18 hours altogether), carefully noting down the form and meaning of anglicisms that he identified. The 629 items include a great number of translations and mixed compounds (with well-integrated early words), as well as product names. That *record, super, Start, Team, Sex*, and *Sport* are the most frequently listed items does not come as a surprise. Altogether the corpus is obviously too small, and the material accepted as 'anglicisms' too heterogeneous to allow further conclusions.

69. GÖRLACH, MANFRED (1994), 'Continental Pun-Dits.' *English Today*, 37: 50–2.

A short article illustrating that puns—normally considered bad style in German—are obviously becoming more acceptable when including English material.

70. GREGOR, BERND (1983), *Genuszuordnung. Das Genus englischer Lehnwörter im Deutschen* (LA 129; Tübingen: Niemeyer), 194 pp. (Review: Carstensen, *Anglia*, 103 (1985), 133–7).

This shortened version of a Munich dissertation deals with the problems of gender attribution of anglicisms in German. The author describes the factors and criteria and tries to give reasons for the assignment. His corpus is mainly based on the *Duden-Fremdwörterbuch.*

71. HEISS, INGRID (1987), 'Untersuchungen zu Anglizismen in der deutschen Gegenwartssprache in der DDR', unpublished D.Phil. thesis (Potsdam).

This thesis, together with that of Kristensson (1977) and various works by Lehnert (cf. 1990), gives a detailed account of the linguistic impact of English on German in the GDR. Press publications from 1983 to 1985 are used to discuss usage frequencies in relation to different newspapers and domains, including orthographic, morphological, and semantic questions, and motives for the adoption of anglicisms.

72. —— (1989), 'Aspekte der Wertung und Erforschung von Anglizismen in der deutschen Sprache der DDR. Tendenzen und Perspektiven', *ZAA* 37: 339–48.

The author provides an overview of the treatment of anglicisms in the GDR summarizing her dissertation and including an account of relevant research in the GDR and the FRG.

73. Herbst, Thomas (1994), *Linguistische Aspekte der Synchronisation von Fernsehserien. Phonetik, Textlinguistik, Übersetzungstheorie.* (LA 318; Tübingen: Niemeyer), 327 pp.

This comprehensive study of the linguistic problems involved in the dubbing of TV serials (considering synchronicity, paralinguistic equivalence, accent and dialect, and consequences for the theory of translation studies) also deals with Anglo-American influence (127–50). The corpus (4–6) consists of mostly Anglo-American serials shown on German TV, and a few dubbed German serials, such as *Derrick*, shown in anglophone countries. Herbst finds two major in-roads for anglicisms in the German audio-visual media: importations (foreign words or loanwords) abound in radio broadcasts and in the language of advertising. By contrast, television, due to the dominating position of English as a world language and the cultural hegemony of the US, shows a high degree of unintentional indirect interference. This includes various kinds of substitutions (loan translations, renditions, meanings, pragmatic errors, syntactic interference, etc.) which result mostly from thoughtlessness or oversight in translation. Some, like *realisieren* or *'Sinn machen'* (from *make sense*) have become fashionable and may be permanent additions to the German language.

74. —— (1995), 'Der Gebrauch des Englischen in den Medien und im *Showbusiness*', in Rüdiger Ahrens *et al.* (eds.), *Handbuch Englisch als Fremdsprache* (Berlin: E. Schmidt), 64–5.

The article (based on Herbst 1994) deals with the use and function of anglicisms in German TV and radio programmes; it covers the aspects of importation and substitution, especially interference due to translation dubbing.

75. Hilgendorf, Suzanne K. (1996), 'The impact of English in Germany' in *English Today*, 47 (12: 3), 3–14.

A quite well-informed survey of the state of play, written for a non-specialist readership and therefore lacking detail; the stress is somewhat on non-integrated specimens of English terms which might better be classified as quotation words, foreignisms or instances of code-switching. The short paper is important for the great number of readers it is likely to reach.

76. Issatschenko, Alexander V. (1979), 'Kein Kommentar zu

brandneuen Einwegübersetzungen aus dem Amerikanischen', in Walter Mair and Henry Vernay (eds.), *Sprachtheorie und Sprachenpraxis. Festschrift für Henri Vernay zu seinem 60. Geburtstag* (TBL 112; Tübingen: Narr), 81–4.

77. KIRKNESS, ALAN (1975), *Zur Sprachreinigung im Deutschen 1789–1871. Eine historische Dokumentation* (2 vols. Forschungsberichte des Instituts für deutsche Sprache 26.1., 26.2.; Tübingen: Narr).

A classic account of purist tendencies in German; the period treated does not have many anglicisms and in consequence purist reactions against them.

78. —— (1984), 'Aliens, Denizens, Hybrids and Natives: Foreign Influences on the Etymological Structure of German Vocabulary', in Charles V. J. Russ (ed.), *Foreign Influences on German: Proceedings of the Conference 'Foreign Influences on German: Past and Present', Held at the University of York, England, 28–30 March 1983* (Dundee: Lochee Publications), 1–26.

79. —— and HERBERT ERNST WIEGAND (1983), 'Wörterbuch der Anglizismen im heutigen Deutsch', *ZGL* 11: 321–8.

The authors give an account of the proceedings of the second colloquium organized at Paderborn on the occasion of the *Dictionary of Anglicisms* then in progress (cf. Carstensen and Busse 1993–1996).

80. KOZIOL, HERBERT (1974), *Zum englischen Einfluß auf den deutschen Wortschatz in den Jahrzehnten um 1800* (Sitzungsberichte der Österreichischen Akademie der Wissenschaften, philosophisch-historische Klasse, Bd. 298, 2. Abhandlung; Vienna: Österreichische Akademie der Wissenschaften), 56 pp.

This work centres on eighteenth-century loans in German. By taking into account sources other than Ganz, Palmer, and Stiven, for example older editions of dictionaries and encyclopaedias, Koziol is able to supply some antedatings to the earlier research. The later development of these loans is illustrated by reference to a nineteenth-century history book and the 1961 edition of the Duden orthographic dictionary.

81. KRAUSS, PAUL G. (1961), 'Anglo-American Influence on German Sport Terms', *American Speech*, 36: 41–7.

Krauss points out which sport terms current in the 1930s were still included in German dictionaries and which new items can be found in German newspapers and magazines published after 1955. The study is followed up in his 1962 article 'English Sport Terms in German', *American Speech*, 37: 123–9, and in his 1966 article 'The Continuing Anglo-American Influence on German', *American Speech*, 41: 28–38. Examples are taken from newspapers and magazines and it is checked whether they are included in German dictionaries. (Cf. the author's earlier papers employing the same method: 'The Increasing Use of English Words in German', *The German Quarterly*, 31 (1958), 272–86; 'The Anglo-American Influence on German', *American Speech*, 38: 257–69.)

82. KRISTENSSON, GÖRAN (1977), *Angloamerikanische Einflüsse in DDR-Zeitungstexten* (Stockholmer Germanistische Forschungen 23; Stockholm: Almqvist and Wiksell), 365 pp. (Summary in *Braun (ed.) (1979), 327–36). (Reviews: Carstensen, *Muttersprache*, 88 (1978), 132–6; Ising, *ZPSK* 35 (1982), 564–9; Koller, *Moderna Språk*, 72 (1978), 181–3; Koller, *Deutsche Sprache*, 6 (1978), 306–22; Korlén, *Moderna Språk*, 81 (1987), 112–18; Lehnert, *ZAA* 28 (1980), 67–70; Penzl, *Language*, 54 (1978), 1010–11.)

Kristensson finds that the lexical impact of English was not held up by the Iron Curtain. The major motivating factors appear to have been: actuality, partizan evaluation, expressiveness, precision, variation, local colouring, succinctness, and prestige; however, anglicisms were used with a higher degree of intentionality than in the West. In political contexts, they were often used with negative connotations (*manager*, *image*, *lobby*, etc.).

83. KÜFNER, RUTH *et al.* (1977), *Grosses Fremdwörterbuch* (Leipzig: VEB Bibliographisches Institut), 824 pp.

84. LANGNER, HEIDEMARIE C. (1995), *Die Schreibung englischer Entlehnungen im Deutschen* (Theorie und Vermittlung der Sprache 23; Frankfurt/M.: Lang), 305 pp.

This D.Phil. thesis is the most comprehensive monograph on the influence of the spelling and/or pronunciation of anglicisms on the German phono-graphemic system. The database used are the entries marked as 'from English' of twenty editions (1880–1991) of the Duden orthographic dictionary. The following aspects are analysed: factors governing the phonological and/or orthographical integration of an item in German, the differences between English and German inventories of sounds and letters, the relationships between these two levels, which anglicisms show 'transference', i.e. remain foreign, and which show various degrees of adaption and 'integration' in spelling and/or pronunciation. An alphabetical index (201–305) listing all the entries in the Duden editions is appended (cf. Busse 1993).

85. LANGNER, HELMUT (1986), 'Zum Einfluß des Angloamerikanischen auf die deutsche Sprache in der DDR', *Zeitschrift für Germanistik*, 7: 402–19.

The paper is mainly based on 1979–1985 daily and weekly German newspapers. The author treats categories and frequencies of usage in the corpus and suggests motives for borrowings, offering a balanced view of the English influence on the German language of the GDR.

86. LEHNERT, MARTIN (1986), 'Der angloamerikanische Einfluß auf die deutsche Sprache in der DDR', in Stiller, 8–88. (Review: Korlén, *Moderna Språk*, 81 (1987), 112–18).

The article is a precursor to his book of 1990; it also appeared in a shortened version in *Viereck and Bald, 129–57. Lehnert analyses with great insight the impact of English on a society officially opposed to such Western fashions. He discusses attitudes, the extent of the lexical imports, conditions and motives and forms of influence (loanwords, calques, blends, and semantic differentiation). Anglicisms imported via Russian and political considerations (including replacement of loanwords), technical vocabulary and individual words (*broiler*, *quark*) are dealt with at length.

87. —— (1990), *Anglo-Amerikanisches im Sprachgebrauch der DDR* (Berlin: Akademie-Verlag), 270 pp.

Lehnert provides the latest analysis of the specific influences of English on the German of the former East German state, analysing newspapers between 1984 and 1989 and concentrating on the domains of entertainment, sports, music, food, science, and technology. In spite of the anglophobe attitude of the regime, Lehnert found some 1,500 items in current use; there was no danger involved in this impact, it is claimed, since German will retain its character by selecting and adapting such loans.

This comprehensive study will prove to be of special documentary value as the last state-of-the-art account of anglicisms in the former socialist state.

88. LEOPOLD, WERNER F. (1967), *English Influence on Postwar German* (University of Nebraska Studies, new series No. 36; Lincoln: University of Nebraska Press). (Reviews: Butler, *GLL* 22 (1968/9), 279–80; Galinsky, *Anglia*, 89 (1971), 359–76.)

The German-educated author lived in the US and was thus well acquainted with problems of transference and interference. In his descriptive study he mainly presents the linguistic collections of a study trip to Germany in 1965–6 including observations in everyday contacts in speech and print and excluding the technical vocabulary of science and technology. He supplies comments on usage, frequency and attitude together with grammatical information on pronunciation, morphology, word-formation, and syntax. The data are presented in fifteen domains; a word-index is appended. (Cf. earlier observations by the same author: 'Recent Developments in the German Language', *JEGP* 57 (1958), 232–69 and 'Supplement: Comments about Recent German', *Die Sprache*, 6 (1960), 231–5.)

89. LIEBKNECHT, WILHELM (1874), *Volksstaat-Fremdwörterbuch* (Leipzig: Genossenschafts-Buchdruckerei); *Volksfremdwörterbuch*, [13]1912.

90. LÖWE, RUDOLF (1957), 'Der Einfluß des Englischen auf die Sprache von Karl Marx—Ein Beitrag zur Textkritik des "Kapital"', *ZAA* 5: 153–65.

91. MEYER, HANS-GÜNTHER (1974), 'Untersuchungen zum Einfluß des Englischen auf die deutsche Pressesprache—dargestellt an zwei deutschen Tageszeitungen', *Muttersprache*, 84: 97–134.

This article, based on a Mainz state examination thesis, analyses two 1972 issues of the German dailies *Allgemeine Zeitung* [Mainz] and the *Wiesbadener Kurier*, both regional newspapers from the Rhine-Main area. The author deals with semantic influences, largely neglecting morphological and syntactical problems. He concentrates on quantitative aspects, i.e. the percentage of anglicisms, the different categories of loans and the distribution of these in the different parts of the newspapers.

92. MOELLER-SCHINA, UTE (1969), 'Deutsche Lehnprägungen aus dem Englischen, von der althochdeutschen Zeit bis 1700', unpublished D.Phil. thesis (Tübingen). (Review: Gneuss, *Beiträge zur Namenforschung*, 9 (1974), 290–2.)

93. MUHVIĆ-DIMANOVSKI, VESNA (1982), 'The English Element in German—the Phonological and Morphological Adaptation', in *Filipović (ed.), 213–43.

94. —— (1991), 'The Semantic Adaptation of English Loan-words in German', in *Filipović (ed.), 109–21.

95. NESKE, FRITZ and INGEBORG (1970), *dtv-Wörterbuch englischer und amerikanischer Ausdrücke in der deutschen Sprache* (Munich: dtv), 313 pp.

The dictionary covers three thousand anglicisms of American and English origin in modern German, including a number of exotisms and internationalisms of neo-Latin or neo-Greek origin which supposedly entered German through mediation of English. In addition there is an introduction heavily relying on Carstensen (1965) and a bibliography. Until the publication of the *Dictionary of Anglicisms* (cf. Carstensen and Busse 1993–6) this was the only German dictionary entirely devoted to anglicisms. Its value is restricted since usage and frequency notations of the items listed are sometimes doubtful.

96. NITSCHKE, DIRK and PETER WIPPERMANN (eds.) (2000), *Duden. Wörterbuch der Szenensprachen.* (Mannheim: Dudenverlag), 224 pp.

Almost a thousand modern words current among young insiders in the fields of funsports, (pop) music, fashion, computer, sex and parties are almost entirely composed of anglicisms (and words fabricated from English elements), documenting the fashionable and largely transitory nature of this type of lexis. Only some 10% can be found in general newspaper diction, the remainder is clearly complementary to *DEA* lexis.

97. ORTNER, HANSPETER (1981), *Wortschatz der Mode. Das Vokabular der Modebeiträge in deutschen Modezeitschriften* (Sprache der Gegenwart 52; Düsseldorf: Schwann), 324 pp.

Ortner describes the lexical devices employed in the leading German fashion magazines (1960–74) for the presentation of garments and accessories. With due consideration of the linguistic peculiarities of this text genre and its communicative functions he catalogues, describes, and analyses the lexical influences. He covers a large number of anglicisms, gives reasons for lexical changes and shows which problems arise for a lexicographical description of these processes.

98. ORTNER, LORELIES (1982), *Wortschatz der Pop-/Rockmusik* (Sprache der Gegenwart 53; Düsseldorf: Schwann), 465 pp.

120 issues of German musical magazines (1972–5) are analysed to reveal the lexical devices employed in the wording of foreign phenomena in the English-dominated pop music business. The study is in three parts: the first is devoted to a lexicographical description, the second deals with the stratification, i.e. jargon, slang, fads, etc. and the third part explores the underlying stylistic and functional aspects. Although this study—like that of Hanspeter Ortner—is not explicitly devoted to anglicisms, they appear throughout the book, are concentrated in a chapter on transference and can be retrieved through a word-index.

99. OSCHLIES, WOLF (1988), 'Hat der Dispatcher die Broiler abgecheckt? Anglizismen im sprachlichen Alltag der DDR', *Muttersprache*, 98: 205–13.

Oschlies gives a personal review on the changing situation of English in the GDR from the 1950s until 1988, surveying the domains with the greatest influence, in particular, entertainment, sports, fashion, technology, and youth language. He concludes that English had a greater impact on (Eastern) German than Russian had.

100. PALMER, PHILIP MOTLEY (1933), *Der Einfluß der neuen Welt auf den deutschen Wortschatz 1492–1800* (Germanische Bibliothek 35; Heidelberg: Winter), 162 pp.

The thesis is based on an extensive study of primary sources from literature and history: the author provides word histories for 151 words from North and South America of non-Indo-European, esp. native Indian origin, describes their meaning, etymology, and gives quotations.

101. —— (1939), *Neuweltwörter im Deutschen* (Germanische Bibliothek 42; Heidelberg: Winter), 174 pp.

A continuation of his 1933 book; basing his statements on 450 primary sources, Palmer brings his research forward into the twentieth century.

102. —— (1950), *The Influence of English on the German Vocabulary to 1700* (Berkeley: University of California Press).

The author investigates the influence of English on the German vocabulary from the earliest contacts until 1700. The historical evidence for the language contact is compiled from German literary works and entries in German dictionaries. Palmer tries to answer which words German writers used to describe foreign ideas and objects and whether these words were taken over unchanged, in translation or with changes and adaptations. The paper is arranged in form of an alphabetical dictionary with fifty-six detailed word histories, grouped according to first occurrences. Their development is amply illustrated by references to attestations in contemporary dictionaries and citations from literary sources.

103. —— (1960), *The Influence of English on the German Vocabulary to 1800—A Supplement* (Berkeley: University of California Press).

This monograph covering the period from 1700 to 1800 is intended as a supplement to Palmer (1950) and to Ganz (1957); it includes 239 words. An alphabetical and chronological word-list arranged according to first occurrences and domains is given.

104. PFAFF, WILHELM (1933), *Zum Kampf um deutsche Ersatzwörter* (Gießener Beiträge zur deutschen Philologie 31; Gießen: v. Münchowsche Universitätsdruckerei, repr. 1968 Amsterdam), 62 pp.

105. PFITZNER, JÜRGEN (1978), *Der Anglizismus im Deutschen. Ein Beitrag zur Bestimmung seiner stilistischen Funktion in der heutigen Presse* (Schriftenreihe Amerikastudien 51; Stuttgart: Metzler), 254 pp. (Reviews: Carstensen, *Amerikastudien*, 25 (1980), 98–102; Stanforth, *Archiv*, 219 (1982), 163–6.)

The book is a revised version of a 1972 St Louis, Missouri, dissertation. It covers the stylistic function of anglicisms in four German newspapers in 1969, *viz*: *Die Welt*, *Süddeutsche Zeitung*, *Oberhessische Presse* and the popular mass-circulation daily *Die Bildzeitung*. Only direct loans are treated. After a theoretical discussion of the concept of foreign words and the terminology and the function of stylistics, the main part of the book is devoted to outlining the stylistic function of anglicisms and to suggesting reasons for their preference.

106. POLENZ, PETER VON (1967), 'Sprachpurismus und Nationalsozialismus: Die Fremdwortfrage gestern und heute', in B. von Wiese and R. Henß (eds.), *Nationalismus in Germanistik und Dichtung. Dokumentation des Germanistentages in München vom 17.–22.10.1966* (Berlin: Schmidt), 79–112.

107. —— (1991–4), *Deutsche Sprachgeschichte vom Spätmittelalter bis zur Gegenwart* (3 vols. Berlin: de Gruyter; new ed. 1999).

108. PROBST, ALFRED (1989), *Ami-Deutsch. Ein kritisch-polemisches Wörterbuch der anglo-deutschen Sprache* (Frankfurt/Main: Fischer), 176 pp.

This book comprises some six hundred entries of 'unnecessary' modern anglicisms; the headword is followed by its approximate pronunciation and the German word which would fully serve the purpose. Each entry has a quotation, most of which come from *Der Spiegel* (1986–9), and some flippant remarks on the passage quoted. It is interesting to note that a few of the objectionable terms have disappeared (by 1995), but others have lost their provocative novelty; a few quotes are plain nonsense and taken up as easy preys of an enthusiastic word-hunter.

109. REICHMANN, OSKAR and HERBERT E. WIEGAND (1980), 'Wörterbuch der Anglizismen im heutigen Deutsch', *ZGL* 8: 328–43.

The authors give an account of the proceedings of the first colloquium organized in Paderborn on the occasion of the planned *Dictionary of Anglicisms* (cf. Carstensen and Busse 1993–6).

110. SCHELPER, DUNJA (1995), *Anglizismen in der Pressesprache der BRD, der DDR, Österreichs und der Schweiz; eine vergleichende, typologische und chronologische Studie* (French text; Université Laval Québec).

The study examines the English influence on the German press language in four German-speaking states: the FRG, the GDR, Austria and Switzerland. One supraregional prestigious daily newspaper per state (*Die Welt, Neues Deutschland, Die Presse, Neue Zürcher Zeitung*) was searched diachronically (1949–89) and synchronically (four sections of politics, economics, culture, and sports). An average of fifty-seven to sixty-two tokens and thirty-nine to forty-five types was found. Based on the models of Betz and Haugen, a new classification system of loan types was established for the present study. The most numerous categories were, in this order: loanwords, hybrids, semantic loans, loan translations, and loan creations. Among the four newspaper sections the largest occurrence of anglicisms was found in the sports section.

111. SCHLICK, WERNER (1984), 'Die Kriterien für die deutsche Genuszuweisung bei substantivischen Anglizismen', *The German Quarterly*, 57: 402–31.

The author offers criteria and reasons for the noun gender assignment of English loans in German.

112. —— (1984/5), '"Diese verflixte englische Geschlechtslosigkeit" —zur deutschen Genuszuweisung bei neueren Lehnsubstantiven aus dem Englischen', *Muttersprache*, 95: 193–221.

This article tries to find answers for the mechanisms at work in the gender assignment of English noun loans in German. The author reviews previous research, presents a corpus with comments and gives reasons.

113. SCHÜTTE, DAGMAR (1996), *Das schöne Fremde. Anglo-amerikanische Einflüsse auf die Sprache der deutschen Zeitschriftenwerbung* (Studien zur Kommunikationswissenschaft 16; Opladen: Westdeutscher Verlag), 383 pp.

This dissertation is an empirical study of the Anglo-American influence on the language of advertising in German periodicals. The analysis is based on a 'systematic random sample' of three thousand advertisements of the 1951, 1961, 1971, 1981, and 1991 issues of *Stern, Spiegel*, and *Brigitte* from which a random sample is statistically analysed (163–8). In contrast to earlier studies (cf. Friman 1977) the author systematically interprets her empirical data as indicators of linguistic change and also as manifestations of a shift in social values. She divides the body of an advertisement into the sections of slogan, headline, and text. Frequencies are interpreted according to occurrence in these text types, according to parts of speech and type of product.

114. Siegl, Elke A. (1989), *Duden Ost—Duden West. Zur Sprache in Deutschland seit 1945. Ein Vergleich der Leipziger und der Mannheimer Dudenauflagen seit 1947* (Sprache der Gegenwart, 76; Düsseldorf: Schwann), 520 pp.

Siegl compares English-derived words on the basis of letter C (334–87); her general statistics for A–Z demonstrate that a) anglicisms are much less frequent than French-derived words; and b) that the Western Duden, unsurprisingly, has a wider coverage than its Eastern counterpart—rising from 868 to 1404 in (W) as against 824 to 952 in (E). This contrast reflects language policies rather than actual usage and thus serves to warn us not to take dictionary evidence *bona fide*. As far as domains are concerned, technology and the domains of leisure, sports, and music clearly predominate (cf. Busse 1993).

115. Söderberg, Barbro (1979), 'Pragmatik och angloamerikanskt långods i östtyskan' (Pragmatics and Anglo-American Borrowings in GDR German), *MINS* 4 (Stockholms Universitet: Institutionen för nordiska språk).

A discussion and evaluation of Kristensson (1977).

116. Sörensen, Ilse (1995), *Englisch im deutschen Wortschatz. Lehn- und Fremdwörter in der Umgangssprache* (Berlin: Volk & Wissen), 168 pp.

Some 2,500 anglicisms, including very recent colloquialisms and items from specialized jargons, exoticisms, names, and quotation words are here collected rather indiscriminately; no information about usage or frequency is provided. The popular character of the book excluded proper documentation in form of citations, dates, and stylistic analysis. Within these self-imposed limits the collection is informative and generally reliable; however, quite a few gaps might have been easily filled by consulting Carstensen and Busse (1993–6). (Review: Görlach *IJL*, 11 (1998), 164–6.)

117. Stanforth, Antony W. (1968), 'Deutsch-englischer Lehnwortaustausch', in Walther Mitzka (ed.), *Wortgeographie und Gesellschaft. Festgabe für Ludwig Erich Schmitt zum 60. Geburtstag am 10. Februar 1968* (Berlin: de Gruyter), 526–60.

The author first gives an overview of research on Anglo-German linguistic relations, then discusses the methodology and terminology of language contacts and provides a chronologically ordered survey of English-German and German-English borrowings from Old High German to the present times.

118. STEINBACH, HORST-RALF (1984), *Englisches im deutschen Werbefernsehen. Interlinguale Interferenzen in einer werbesprachlichen Textsorte* (Paderborn: Schöningh), 310 pp.

Steinbach analyses more than seven hundred commercials which were broadcast on German television in May 1978. The study begins with a semiotic definition of advertising and its special language, the pragma-linguistic function of commercials and a discussion of the English influence on German including theoretical and terminological matters. These foundations serve as a backdrop against which the encountered phenomena are interpreted. The corpus is presented in form of an alphabetical dictionary followed by detailed lexico-statistical analyses including pronunciation, orthography, morphology, and syntax (cf. Herbst 1994).

119. STICKEL, GERHARD (1984), 'Einstellungen zu Anglizismen', in Werner Besch *et al.* (eds.), *Festschrift für Siegfried Grosse zum 60. Geburtstag* (Göppinger Arbeiten zur Germanistik 423; Göppingen: Kümmerle), 279–310.

The author uses critical comments on foreign words and letters to the editor published in German newspapers to describe attitudes and motives for the preference, or more often rejection of anglicisms.

120. STILLER, HEINZ (ed.) (1986), *Der angloamerikanische Einfluß auf die deutsche Sprache der Gegenwart in der DDR* (Berlin: Akademieverlag), 128 pp.

Contributions dedicated to Martin Lehnert.

121. STIVEN, AGNES BAIN (1936), *Englands Einfluß auf den deutschen Wortschatz*, D.Phil. thesis (Marburg) (Zeulenroda: Sporn), 151 pp.

This Marburg D.Phil. thesis treats in chronological order the anglicisms that entered the German language from the thirteenth century up to the 1930s. The author relies mainly on secondary sources such as dictionaries and encyclopaedias. For this reason some of the datings have to be treated with caution: several words listed in dictionaries may have been quite peripheral. The work is the first comprehensive study of English loans in German; it has prepared the ground for the large number of publications after 1945.

122. TOWNSON, MICHAEL (1984), 'Nuclear Neologisms', in Charles V. J. Russ (ed.), *Foreign Influences on German* (Dundee: Lochee Publications), 88–108.

The article shows how the American terminology of military hardware and of (nuclear) military policy affected the German language.

123. —— (1986), 'Anglizismen in der Sprache der Verteidigungspolitik. Untersucht anhand der "Nachrüstungsdebatte"', *Muttersprache*, 96: 271–81.

A revised German version of the previous article investigating the communicative function of anglicisms in government publications and parliamentary debates.

124. URBANOVÁ, ANNA (1966), 'Zum Einfluß des amerikanischen Englisch auf die deutsche Gegenwartssprache. Ein Beitrag zur Frage sprachlicher Kontakte', *Muttersprache*, 76: 97–114.

The article is a summary of the author's 1963 Prague dissertation in which she scrutinizes the AmE influence on present-day German as reflected in the West German press, especially *Der Spiegel*. The Austrian and Swiss press, belles-lettres, and a systematic analysis of Max Frisch's *Homo Faber* are also included. Her article covers structural analyses including pronunciation, orthography, and morphology. In the field of lexis she pays special attention to loan shifts; the material is arranged according to domains.

125. VIERECK, KARIN (1980), *Englisches Wortgut, seine Häufigkeit und Integration in der österreichischen und bundesdeutschen Pressesprache* (Bamberger Beiträge zur Englischen Sprachwissenschaft 8; Frankfurt/M.: Lang), vi + 431 pp. (Review: Fink, *Amerikastudien*, 26 (1981), 361–7.)

This quantitative study comparing the two Austrian dailies *Kleine Zeitung* and *Die Presse* with the German *Süddeutsche Zeitung*, contrasts 1974 data with those of Fink (1970) of 1963, grouping the material into fourteen domains; unfortunately ten of these from her 1979 Innsbruck dissertation were omitted from the book version. A description of the items in form of a dictionary arranged according to subject areas constitutes the main part of the thesis. Brief summaries are followed by computer-based frequency counts and a word-index.

126. —— (1986), 'The Influence of English on Austrian German', in *Viereck and Bald (eds.), 159–77.

The author analyses anglicisms in two 1984 issues each of a regional and a national daily (*Kleine Zeitung*, *Die Presse*), to contrast with Viereck (1980), which is based on similar data. Her interpretation considers subject areas, educational, and social status of readers and investigates how far anglicisms are properly understood, also summarizing earlier studies on the impact of English on Austrian German.

127. —— WOLFGANG VIERECK, and INGRID WINTER (1975), 'Wie englisch ist unsere Pressesprache?', *Grazer Linguistische Studien*, 2: 205–26.

This article is a predecessor to Karin Viereck's 1980 dissertation. The authors analyse two 1974 issues of the *Kleine Zeitung*, *Die Presse*, and the *Süddeutsche Zeitung* in order to reveal the distribution of loans in respect to different domains, complementing their findings by a panel test which is intended to investigate the social and educational factors determining the understanding of anglicisms.

128. —— —— —— (1976), 'Englisches in der österreichischen Pressesprache. Ein Vergleich mit der "Süddeutschen Zeitung"', *Der Sprachdienst*, 20: 53–6; enlarged and revised repr. in Braun (ed.) (1979), 314–20.

The allegedly dominant influence of English in journalese is investigated in a comparison of two Austrian dailies with the *Süddeutsche Zeitung* (1974) and analysed according to subject areas.

129. VIERECK, WOLFGANG (ed.) (1980*a*), *Studien zum Einfluß der englischen Sprache auf das Deutsche. Studies on the Influence of the English Language on German* (TBL 132; Tübingen: Narr, repr. 1983), 323 pp. (Reviews: Clyne, *Leuvense Bijdragen*, 71 (1982), 358–61; Fink, *Amerikastudien*, 26 (1981), 454–9; Görlach, *EWW* 1 (1980), 287.)

Nine papers (some of them reprints; only one is in English) by leading specialists in the field on general problems, pronunciation, gender attribution and pseudo-loans, frequencies and reception lag, usage and domains (newspapers and advertising). The individual contributions are discussed under Carstensen 1980*a*, 1980*c*; Fink 1980; Galinsky 1980*a*; Viereck 1980*b*, 1980*c*.

130. VIERECK, WOLFGANG (1980*b*), 'Zur Thematik und Problematik von Anglizismen im Deutschen', in Viereck (ed.), 9–24.

Examples are presented of genuine loanwords, words in which only a part of their meaning was taken over into German and words which are used with a non-English meaning in German. Viereck points out the problem of determining the origin of genuine loans. After summarizing efforts to keep the German language pure by rejecting foreign words, he advises to which extent foreign words should be taken over.

131. —— (1980*c*), 'Empirische Untersuchungen insbesondere zum Verständnis und Gebrauch von Anglizismen im Deutschen', in Viereck (ed.), 237–321.

After discussing and commenting on various empirical investigations in this field, Viereck presents his own study based on a list of forty-two anglicisms handed out to test persons in order to determine the distinction between knowledge, understanding and active use of individual words. Viereck found that incorrect comprehension is largely independent of age, sex, and education.

132. —— (1982), 'The Influence of the English Language on German', *Amerikastudien / American Studies*, 27: 203–15.

The article offers a *tour d'horizon* of English–German interference problems, giving a brief historical survey and a state-of-the-art account of research.

133. —— (1984), 'Das Deutsche im Sprachkontakt. Britisches Englisch und Amerikanisches Englisch/Deutsch', in Werner Besch *et al.* (eds.), *Sprachgeschichte. Ein Handbuch zur Geschichte der deutschen Sprache und ihrer Erforschung* (HSK 2.1; Berlin: de Gruyter), 938–46.

A historical account of the impact of English on German and a survey of existing research, with sketches of the influence on individual linguistic levels and on spoken vs. written German.

134. —— (1986), 'The Influence of English on German in the Past and in the Federal Republic of Germany', in *Viereck and Bald (eds.), 107–28.

Viereck reviews the limited impact of English on German before 1800, sketches the increasing influence up to 1945 and analyses recent loans on the levels of spelling and pronunciation, morphology, and semantics and finally contrasts spoken and written German.

135. WÄCHTLER, KURT (1980), 'Was ist ein Amerikanismus—heute?', *AAA* 5: 145–58.

Wächtler argues for a narrowing of the gap between the linguistic definition of 'Americanisms' and 'Briticisms' and the labelling in English dictionaries where disregard of processes of assimilation, infiltration, and neutralization and mistaking origin for usage often result in misleading labels.

136. WENDELKEN, PETER (1967), 'Der Einfluß des Englischen auf das heutige Werbedeutsch', *Muttersprache*, 77: 289–308.

The article deals with English words in German advertising considering orthography, pronunciation, morphology, semantics, and also style and syntax and paying particular attention to brandnames.

137. WILSS, WOLFRAM (1958), 'Das Eindringen angloamerikanischer Fremdwörter in die deutsche Sprache seit Ende des zweiten Weltkrieges', *Muttersprache*, 68: 180–8.

Wilss claims that loans are mainly imported through the daily press. He outlines the German postwar situation by emphasizing the socio-political dominance of the USA and gives a balanced account of its linguistic impact on the German language. His arguments are expanded in his 1966 article 'Der Einfluß der englischen Sprache auf die deutsche seit 1945', *Beiträge zur Linguistik und Informationsverarbeitung* 8: 30–48.

138. WOJCIK, MANFRED (1982), *Der Einfluß des Englischen auf die Sprache Bertolt Brechts* (Brecht-Studien 11; Berlin: Brecht-Zentrum der DDR), 249 pp.

The study is a revised version of the author's 1967 D.Phil. thesis at the Humboldt University, Berlin.

139. Yang, Wenliang (1990), *Anglizismen im Deutschen. Am Beispiel des Nachrichtenmagazins Der Spiegel* (RGL 106; Tübingen: Niemeyer), ix + 237 pp. (Review: Görlach, *IJL* 5 (1992), 78–9.)

This revised Brunswick dissertation deals with anglicisms in the most 'English' German news magazine, modelled on *Time* in content and style. The analysis is based on six issues each of 1950, 1960, 1970, and 1980, which yielded 10,070 occurrences of 3,646 items (detailed in the word index, 181–237). Frequencies are analysed according to parts of speech, domains, text types, style and meaning, and the specific effectiveness is interpreted as a consequence of intended local colouring, linguistic economy, variation, euphemisms, and pedagogical aspects (118–35). The author does not attempt to place his data into a wider German context.

140. Zieglschmid, A. J. F. (1935), 'Englisch-amerikanischer Einfluß auf den Wortschatz der deutschen Sprache der Nachkriegszeit', *JEGPh* 34: 24–33.

The article covers the time between the two World Wars, and for the first time stresses the rising AmE influence on German, offering a cursory view of random findings in post-1918 literature, newspapers and periodicals without any aim (or claim) of completeness. The author notes that 1933 marks a decrease in the usage of foreign words.

141. Zimmer, Dieter E. (1997), 'Neuanglodeutsch: Über die Pidginisierung der Sprache', in Dieter E. Zimmer, *Deutsch und anders. Die Sprache im Modernisierungsfieber* (Reinbek: Rowohlt), 7–85.

142. Zindler, Horst (1959), 'Anglizismen in der deutschen Pressesprache nach 1945', unpublished D.Phil. thesis (Kiel).

This is the first extensive scholarly study of English (or mainly American) neologisms which entered German after 1945. As in many monographs that were to follow, Zindler analyses the language of the press: he claims that it is very open to foreign influences, has a great impact on its readers, and is moreover one of the important factors in the shaping of modern German. A shorter introductory part on theoretical and terminological problems concerning the assimilation of loans is followed by a dictionary with word histories and citations organized in subject groups. The author does not claim to be exhaustive; technical lexemes are excluded.

143. —— (1975), 'Anglizismen im heutigen Deutsch—beobachtet in der Sprache der Presse 1945–1960', *Beiträge zu den Fortbildungskursen des Goethe-Instituts für ausländische Deutschlehrer an Schulen und Hochschulen* (Munich: Goethe-Institut), 82–91.

Greek (Ekaterini Stathi)

1. ANASTASSIADIS-SYMÉONIDIS, ANNA (1990), 'To ghenos ton syghkhronon dhanion tis NE' (The Gender of Recent Loans in Modern Greek), *Studies in Greek Linguistics—Proceedings of the 10th Annual Meeting of the Department of Linguistics, Faculty of Philosophy, Aristotelian University of Thessaloniki, 9–11 May 1989* (Thessaloniki: Kyriakides), 155–77.

The author proposes a hierarchy of rules which apply in fixed order during gender assignment of French and English loans in Modern Greek. The analysis is based on the distinction between morphologically integrated and non-integrated loans. Three types of analogy play a central role: a) semantic analogy, which accounts for the agreement between natural and grammatical gender in the case of nouns referring to animates as well as the correspondence between the gender of the loan and a near-synonym or hyperonym; b) morphological analogy: this is used in the case of non-humans which are integrated into an inflectional paradigm, in which case they receive the gender of this class; c) interlingual analogy: the loan retains the gender of the source language.

2. —— (1994), *Neologhikos dhanismos tis Neoellinikis* (Neological Borrowing in Modern Greek. Direct Loans from French and Angloamerican. Morphophonological Analysis) (Thessaloniki).

This is an up-to-date linguistic analysis of loans in Modern Greek from a specialist in the field of neologisms. The book is divided into five major chapters. The first contains theoretical, methodological, and terminological preliminaries as well as a typology and the characteristics of loanwords. In the second chapter the author presents the direct loans of Modern Greek: lexical units, suffixes, and morphological/grammatical elements. The third chapter is on the mechanisms of borrowing and on Greek-French/English language contact. Chapter four contains the linguistic analysis of their integration on all levels (graphemic, phonological, morphological). Finally, the fifth chapter refers to purist reactions.

3. APOSTOLOU-PANARA, ATHENA-MARIA (1985), 'Ta dhania tis Neas Ellinikis apo tin Agliki. Fonologhiki edaksi ke afomiosi' (The

Phonological Integration of English Loanwords into Modern Greek), unpublished dissertation (Athens).

The first part of the dissertation is a contrastive analysis of the Greek and English phonemic systems. The second part describes the rules and systematic procedures by which borrowings from English are assimilated on the phonological level.

4. —— (1986), 'Gender Assignment of English Substantives in Modern Greek', *Parousia D*, 97–104.

In this article Apostolou-Panara distinguishes in a first step between nouns which refer to animates and those which refer to inanimates. Further analysis of her data leads to a model explaining gender assignment by two criteria: Morphophonologically adapted loans are both animate (and thus either masculine or feminine) and inanimate, in which case they may be assigned to all three genders. On the other hand, loans that are only phonologically integrated may be assigned to either feminine or neuter gender according to the underlying structural and lexical patterns.

5. —— (1988–9), 'The Significance of English Graphophonemic Relationships for English Loanword Integration into Modern Greek', *Glossologia*, 7–8: 193–205.

Since the written channel plays a major role in the process of borrowing, the graphemes of the source language are often interpreted in phonemic terms '(graphemic reinterpretation)'. The author distinguishes between a *systematic* and an *intuitive* graphemic interpretation. The former appears in the written medium and accounts for idiosyncrasies of the English phonological system due to its diachronic changes, while the latter is performed by a bilingual person who is more or less unaware of the graphophonemic correspondences of the English language.

6. Charalabakis, Chistophoros (1992), 'Metafrastika dhania tis Neas Ellinikis apo evropaikes ghlosses' (Loan Translations from European Languages in Modern Greek), *Neoellinikos Loghos* (Athens: Nefeli).

This article is a comment on the etymologies of the Dictionary of Modern Greek (LNE, Institute of M. Triantaphyllidis). Charalabakis observes that the etymologies provided neglect loan translations and the semantic extension of native words in Greek, processes which have become prolific during the last years. The author, after distinguishing between the different types of borrowing (borrowing proper vs. loan substitution) and its subtypes, lists and comments on some loan translations found in Modern Greek and their equivalents in other European languages. A short chapter on internationalisms follows. These chapters are particularly important because they contain many words coined from Ancient Greek elements, but which enter the Modern Greek vocabulary through English and/or French. Their easy translation and integration as well as their native-like shape make it difficult to think of them as non-Greek items. He also refers to the treatment of 'foreign words' by laymen, i.e. to purism in the past and today and concludes that the phenomenon of language contact should be given more importance in Greece and studied by linguists more thoroughly and systematically.

7. Cvjetković-Kurelec, Vesna (1993), 'Engleski element u novogrčkom jeziku—Adaptacija na fonološkoj razini' (The English Element in Modern Greek—Adaptation on the Phonological Level), *Suvremena lingvistika* 19 (1–2), no. 35–6, 49–57. (EEEL 4).

8. Kalioris, Jannis M. (1993), *O ghlossikos afellinismos* (The Linguistic Dehellenization) (Athens: Armos).

The aim of this book is to draw attention to the increasing influx of foreign—mostly English—words. The author is greatly concerned about the future of the Greek language which, he claims, is losing its identity through the import of foreign words, particularly because the loans have become very frequent and are not integrated graphemically, phonologically or morphologically into Modern Greek, as they used to be some decades ago. The author criticizes the unreflected adoption of the Latin alphabet in all domains (books, magazines, media, advertisements, signs, etc.) which he regards as harmful. His treatment of the subject is puristic, not linguistic, but it contains valuable data.

9. Stathi, Ekaterini (2000), 'Der lexikalische Einfluss des Englischen auf das Griechische: Integration und Produktivität', M.A. thesis (University of Cologne).

This thesis is the outcome of the data analysis of the *Dictionary of European Anglicisms*. It represents a preliminary attempt to describe in detail the phonological, graphemic, and morphological integration of English loanwords into Modern Greek. Furthermore, the productivity of certain morphological elements (affixes) is considered as well as trends in language change which may be triggered by language contact.

10. SWANSON, DONALD C. (1958), 'English Loanwords in Modern Greek', *Word*, 14: 26–46.

Swanson's article represents one of the earliest attempts to deal with English loanwords in Modern Greek in terms other than purist. In his introduction, the author refers to the setting of the contact establishing four different classes of loans: direct loans from British or American English, English words which have entered Modern Greek through French and Italian, words borrowed directly from French (but which also exist in English), and problematic words which are well-established in many European languages. He then offers his material in four lists with comments on each word, followed by a short morphological, phonological, semantic, and cultural analysis of the loans. In the final section he makes reference to loan translations and 'repatriated' words. This important article offers old material (many words quoted are now obsolete), and enables a comparison with older stages of language contact.

Hungarian (Judit Farkas and Veronika Kniezsa)

(see also *25)

1. BAKOS, F. (1994), *Idegen szavak és kifejezések kéziszótára* (A Dictionary of Foreign Words and Expressions) (Budapest: Akadémiai Kiadó).

No other language in Eastern Europe has had so many dictionaries of foreign words in its history. The aim of this one was to bring the foreign element in the Hungarian lexicon up-to-date including information about their phonemic, orthographic and morphological adaptation and their field-oriented usage. The primary aim is to serve the larger public; it does not replace a special dictionary of anglicisms which has in fact never been compiled for Hungarian.

2. BÁNHIDI, Z. (1971), *A magyar sportnyelv története, és jelene sportnyelvtörténeti szótárral* (The History and the Present of Hungarian Sports Language with a Historical Dictionary of Terms of Sports) (Budapest).

3. BÁRCZI, G. (1958), *A magyar szókészlet eredete* (Origins of the Hungarian Lexicon) (Egyetemi magyar nyelvészeti füzetek; Budapest: Tankönyvkiadó).

A university textbook giving a theoretical explanation of the borrowing process of foreign lexical elements. The author did not include English loanwords in his work, which is, however, important for the general background and theory.

4. —— (1963), *A magyar nyelv életrajza* (A Biography of the Hungarian Language) (Budapest: Akadémiai Kiadó).

One of the chapters gives a short summary of recent loanwords in Hungarian including a list of English borrowings.

5. CSAPÓ (1971*a*), 'A magyar sportnyelv angol eredetü elemei adaptációjának kérdéseihez' (On the Accommodation of English Elements in Hungarian Sports Vocabulary), *Magyar Nyelvjárások*, 17: 29–39.

6. —— (1971*b*), 'English Sporting Terminology in Hungarian, a Study of the Process of Assimilation and Rejection', *Angol Filológiai Tanulmányok*, 5: 5–50.

1895 marks the beginning of the wholesale infiltration of English sports terms into Hungarian (in boxing, football, wrestling, etc.). According to the author's account the sports terms in this period make up a total of six hundred to seven hundred words, but only a few dozen survived 'magyarization' in the 1930s. The rest of the article is on the problems of assimilation (spelling, phonetic-phonemic, morphological, and syntactic adaptation, calques, pseudo-English words, vernacular vs. alien terms in sports vocabulary). The recent tendency to use sports terms in their original English form is because sporting activities take place on a world-wide scale, and the official language of the really great and important sports events is English.

7. DEME, L. (1943), 'English Words in Hungarian', unpublished diploma thesis (Péter Pázmány University, Budapest).

This is one of the first monographs on anglicisms in Hungarian.

8. HUSZÁR, A. (1985), 'Idegenül hangzik' (It Sounds out of Place), in Ágnes Bíró and Gábor Tolcsvai Nagy (eds.), *Nyelvi divatok* (Bratislava: Madách Publishing House), 66–71.

Is the use of foreign words good or bad? The article describes research carried out in a large factory: a list of foreign words was given to persons with different levels of education asking for their meanings. The author found that the knowledge of these words differed a great deal between management and the apprentices. The result also confirmed the hypothesis that some anglicisms are useful, but others which can be exactly replaced by native terms, are superfluous. The recent wave of foreign terms, especially from English, is considered problematic.

9. JAKOBS-NÉMETH, ILONA (1982), 'Phonological Adaptation of English Loanwords in Hungarian', in *Filipović (ed.), 244–66.

10. KÁLMÁN, B. (1978), 'Szemle' (Review of Országh, László 1977), *Magyar Nyelv*, 74: 107–9.

Hungarian etymology classifies words according to their immediate source. Thus European cultural words count as German, or are described as 'international words' or 'wandering words'. Even before 1914, English words could be sporadically borrowed directly either through literature or from Hungarians returning from America. All through the twentieth century the possibility of direct borrowing has grown considerably, and in the last couple of decades there has hardly been any alternative.

11. Kiss, L. (1966), 'Müveltségszók, vándorszók, nemzetközi szók' (Cultural Words, Wandering Words, International Words), *Magyar Nyelv*, 62: 179–88.

Ernst Tappolet (1914) distinguished two types of loanwords: 'Luxuslehnwörter', which increase the number of synonyms, and 'Bedürfnislehnwörter', which are new words for new ideas. Among the borrowed elements of the cultural lexicon there are items which more or less accurately correspond in pronunciation and meaning in several, genetically not necessarily related and/or neighbouring languages. These can be travelling elements, usually adopted orally, as is the case with Hu *szekrény* = E. *shrine*, or international words reflecting close European inter-cultural relationships, which make it difficult to determine the original language, as with *telegráf*, *expressz* etc.

12. Kontra, Miklós (1975), 'Javaslatok orvosi nyelvünk angol szavainak fonetikai átírására' (Suggestions for the Phonetic Transcription of the English Words in our Medical Language), *Magyar Nyelvőr*, 99: 37–41.

The considerable differences between English and Hungarian spelling and pronunciation are a major obstacle for students. From printed texts it is difficult to conclude how the pronunciation of borrowed English terms has changed owing to the traditions of medical orthography. There are three features influencing the pronunciation of a given term: whether the student had learnt English or foreign languages, heard the term pronounced by his teacher, and whether there is a recognizably Greek or Latin element in the term. Pronunciation can be determined by spelling pronunciation, re-latinization, and French interference. Kontra's suggestion for general principles of transcription are: 1) As in early loanwords, the stress should be placed on the first syllable; 2) the unstressed *shwa* should be pronounced either with a full vowel, as in [dalla:r], [bairon], or uniformly with [e], [er], [or]; 3) certain diphthongs should be simplified (*grading* [gre:ding]), while others should not (*compound* [kompaund]).

13. —— (1977*a*), 'Néhány angol eredetű neoklassikus szavunkról' (About Some Neoclassical Words of English Origin), *Magyar Nyelvőr*, 101: 107–9.

14. —— (1977*b*), 'Egy új kölcsönhomonímánkról' (On a New Loan-synonym), *Magyar Nyelvőr*, 101: 109–10.

15. —— (1978), 'A művelt ujrakölcsönzésről, Shakespeare ürügyén' (On Educated Re-borrowing, on the Pretext of Shakespeare), *Magyar Nyelvőr*, 102: 109–10.

16. —— (1981), *A nyelvek közötti kölcsönzés néhány kérdéséröl, különös tekintettel 'elangolosodó' orvosi nyelvünkre* (On the Question of Borrowing from Different Languages, with Special Respect to our 'Anglicized' Medical Jargon) (Nyelvtudományi Ėrtekezések 109; Budapest: Akadémiai Kiadó).

The analysis is based on more than fifty medical text-books and periodicals, earlier papers on the topic of anglicisms in different fields, and various dictionaries. After a general treatment of language contacts, interference and borrowing in general, the author goes on to treat orthographical, phonetic-phonological, and morphological adaptation. He then discusses the influence of English words on Hungarian morphology and semantics. The article is a good summary of the adaptation of English words to Hungarian and a useful account illustrating changes in the language under the influence of English.

17. —— (1982*a*), *Amerikai magyar újságok nyelve a sztenderd magyarral összevetve* (The Usage of Hungarian Newspapers Edited in the USA Compared to Standard Hungarian) (Nyelvtudományi Értekezések 110; Budapest: Akadémiai Kiadó).

18. —— (1982*b*), 'Medical Language in Contact: English and Hungarian', *Hungarian Studies in English*, 15: 75–89.

A short survey of how English words are integrated, analysing the phenomenon on individual linguistic levels. The specimens used come from general vocabulary, but specialized medical terms were tested on students, which yielded, unsurprisingly, a great number of spelling pronunciations.

19. Magay, T. (1967), *Angol-Magyar és Magyar-Angol szótárak hazánkban 1945 előtt* (English-Hungarian and Hungarian-English

Dictionaries in Hungary before 1945) (Nyelvtudománi Értekezések, 57; Budapest: Akadémiai Kiadó).

This study offers a critical description and evaluation of the methods, resources, and techniques employed and the results achieved in the compilation and publication of English-Hungarian and Hungarian-English dictionaries in Hungary from 1860 to 1945. The works of the four major lexicographers—Dallos, Bizonfy, James-Endrei, and Yolland—are dealt with in detail.

20. MEDGYES, P. (1992), 'Angol a kommunikáció pótnyelve. Az angol nyelv jelenléte Magyarországon' (English as a Substitute-language of Communication. The Presence of English in Hungary), in *Magyar Pedagógia*, 4: 263–83.

The author demonstrates various aspects of the teaching and learning of English and the spread of English in present-day Hungary. In the light of statistical data, he shows the proportion of English taught, compared with that of Russian, German, and French, in various types of schools. Although Hungarians have long recognized the importance of English, the possibility for learning it remains limited, mainly because of the acute shortage of teachers. Nevertheless, the English language is ubiquitous, found in graffiti, posters, street signs, and job advertisements; it permeates the language of science, technology, business, pop-culture and mass media. Hunglish, the hybrid of Hungarian and English, is a constant source of amusement and irritation.

21. ORSZÁGH, L. (1968), 'The Life and Death of English Words in the Hungarian Language', *The New Hungarian Quarterly*, 31: 180–8.

22. —— (1975*a*), 'Ventillátor. Vécé', *Magyar Nyelvőr*, 99: 79–82.

Words such as: *bicikli, detektív, harmonika, kaleidoszkóp, koedukáció, lokomotív, propeller, revolver, traktor, utópia* consist of Latin or Ancient Greek elements, but were coined in English. *Ventillátor* appeared in English in 1743 and in Hungarian in 1834, *Vécé* (water closet) in 1865.

23. ORSZÁGH, L. (1975*b*), 'On a New Morpheme', *Studies in English and American* (Budapest: Eötvös University), 2: 371–8.

This essay treats the element *-tel* derived from *ho-tel* as a new formative element to indicate 'place of accommodation' as in *motel, rotel* and a Hungarian innovation *lotel* 'horse hotel'.

24. —— (1977), *Angol eredetü elemek a magyar szókészletben* (English Elements in the Hungarian Lexicon) (Nyelutudományi Értekezések, 93; Budapest: Akadémiai Kiadó) (Review: B. Kálmán, 'Szemle', *Magyar Nyelv*, 74 (1978), 107–9).

This monograph is the only major work dealing with anglicisms in Hungarian from many aspects; it also provides a consistent historical overview of English elements in the lexicon. The four major periods treated are: before the Reformation, 1610–1820; the Reformation era, 1820–1849; 1850–1920; between the two World Wars, 1920–1945; and 1945–1975. The material is arranged according to semantic fields, and the process of adaptation described (orthographic, phonetic-phonological, morphological, derivational, and semantic). Finally, the indirect impact of English is discussed. A special value of this monograph is that it summarizes the achievement of former (pre-1975) authors on this topic, and of the few dictionaries available. Because the author makes use of most of the relevant works, this present bibliography lists only those titles from before 1975 which made really important contributions to the question of anglicisms in Hungarian.

25. Révbíró, S. (1972), 'Angol kölcsönszavak a magyar időszaki sajtóban a Reformkor végén (1841)' (English Loanwords in the Hungarian Press at the End of the Age of Reform), unpublished M.A. thesis (Eötvös Loránd University, Budapest).

26. Rot, S. (1986), 'English in Contact with Hungarian', in *Viereck and Bald (eds.), 207–30.

Rot provides a short account of the history of language contact between English and Hungarian and of the relevant research and then analyses recent loans and calques in the light of multilingualism in Hungary and the possible transmission of anglicisms through German. His terminology and classifications are somewhat idiosyncratic.

27. Tolcsvai, G. (1985), 'Beat, rock, pop, diszkó' (Beat, rock, pop, disco), in Ágnes Bíró and Gábor Tolcsvai Nagy (eds.), *Nyelvi divatok Gondolat* (Bratislava: Madách), 72–7.

This essay deals with the history of the four words in Hungarian, their native derivatives and some changes in meaning. Because these words can be found in the language of the younger generation, it is important to standardize their spelling and pronunciation, in order to integrate them into the native lexicon.

28. VÖRÖS, F. (1966), *Angol jövevényszavak a magyar sportnyelvben a labdajátékok területén* (English Loanwords in Hungarian Sports Terminology in the Field of Ball Games), unpublished M.A. thesis (Budapest: Eötvös Loránd University).

Icelandic (Ásta Svavarsdóttir and Guðrún Kvaran)

(see also *25)

1. ÁRNASON, KRISTJÁN (1989), 'Engelsk-amerikansk indflydelse på islandsk sprog' (English-American Influence on the Icelandic Language), *Språk i Norden*, 57–66.

The paper is a part of a thematic discussion of English-American influence on the Scandinavian languages. The author treats the matter from a socio-cultural as well as from a linguistic point of view and gives a number of examples of potential English influence on various levels of the language: vocabulary, syntax, phonology, etc.; however, the discussion is mainly speculative.

2. ÁRNASON, MÖRÐUR, SVAVAR SIGMUNDSSON, and ÖRNÓLFUR THORSSON (1982), *Orðabók um slangur, slettur, bannorð og annað utangarðsmál* (A Dictionary of Slang) (Reykjavík: Svart á hvítu), 160 pp.

This first and only dictionary of Icelandic slang includes a considerable number of anglicisms, as well as more or less adopted words from other languages and slang words of native origin.

3. EIRÍKSSON, EYVINDUR (1975), 'Beyging nokkurra enskra tökuorða í nútíma-íslensku' (The Inflection of a Few English Loanwords in Modern Icelandic), *Mímir, blað félags stúdenta í íslenskum fræðum*, 23: 55–71.

The paper is based on the most extensive study of English loanwords in Modern Icelandic to date. The emphasis is on the inflectional adaptation of some 116 direct loans, over 80 per cent of them borrowed after 1940; these are mainly nouns, but also include a number of verbs, adjectives and interjections. There is also a brief mention of hybrids, i.e. nouns and adjectives based on an English stem and a native suffix/component, which decides the inflection. The main results of the study are that verbs are invariably fully adapted to the Icelandic conjugational system, that most nouns acquire grammatical gender and a declension, whereas adjectives tend to be uninflected in spite of a rich inflectional pattern for most, though not all, native adjectives. A revised version appeared as 'English Loanwords in Icelandic: Aspects of Morphology', in *Filipović (ed.) (1982), II: 266–300.

4. Eiríksson, Eyvindur (1979), 'Item uno trusso II C whyte lynnen cloth', *Íslenskt mál og almenn málfræði*, 1: 25–33.

The subject of this paper is early English influence on Icelandic, particularly in the fifteenth century. The author argues that the words *trúss* (noun) and *trússa* (verb) were borrowed from Middle English rather than Middle Low German as previously believed.

5. —— (1981), 'Burgeisar, ribbaldar, barúnar og allt það hafurtask', in *Afmæliskveðja til Halldórs Halldórssonar 13. júlí 1981* (Reykjavík, Íslenska málfræðifélagið), 85–96.

The paper discusses the inflectional adaptation of some Middle English loanwords borrowed into Icelandic in the fourteenth and fifteenth centuries when English had largely lost the old nominal and adjectival inflection. Most of the words discussed are nouns, but some verbs and adjectives are also included. Only a few of these words have survived in modern Icelandic. The author looks mainly at the grammatical gender acquired by the borrowed nouns in Icelandic, as well as at the inflectional classes adopted by both nouns and verbs.

6. Fjalldal, Magnús (1987), 'Leiðin frá *helvíti* til *hi* og *bye*' (The Way from *helvíti* 'hell' to *hi* and *bye*), *Íslenskt mál og almenn málfræði*, 9: 111–19.

The author gives a survey of the research on English loanwords in Icelandic and discusses the English influence in very general terms.

7. Groenke, Ulrich (1966), 'On Standard, Substandard, and Slang in Icelandic', *Scandinavian Studies*, 38: 217–30.

The author agrees with the claim that, at least as dialectal variation on the phonological level is concerned, there is no standard vs. substandard gradation in Icelandic. However, some variation on the morphological / syntactic level indicating such a gradation is pointed out. The subject of the remainder of the paper is standard/substandard gradation on the lexical level, especially with respect to the status of foreignisms, danicisms as well as anglicisms. The main emphasis is on the vocabulary of informal registers, colloquial language, and slang.

8. —— (1975), '*Sletta* and *götumál*: on Slangy Borrowings in Icelandic', in Karl-Hampus Dahlstedt (ed.), *The Nordic Languages and Modern Linguistics* (Stockholm: Almqvist and Wiksell), 2: 475–85.

The main emphasis is on danicisms in Icelandic slang and colloquial speech, but several examples of anglicisms are included as well. There is some discussion of the influence of the British/American contact during and after World War II on the development of slang in Iceland.

9. HALLDÓRSSON, HALLDÓR (1962), 'Kring språkliga nybildningar i nutida isländska' (On Linguistic Innovation in Modern Icelandic), *Scripta Islandica*, 13: 3–24.

The main topics of the article are neologisms and Icelandic language purism; borrowing is only a secondary subject. A historical overview of the official attitude towards innovation in the lexicon is of some interest, though, also with respect to foreignisms.

10. —— (1970), 'Determining the Lending Language', in Hreinn Benediktsson (ed.), *The Nordic Languages and Modern Linguistics*. Proceedings of the International Conference of Nordic and General Linguistics, University of Iceland, Reykjavík, 1969 (Reykjavík: Vísindafélag Íslendinga), 365–77.

The main topic of the paper is Old Icelandic borrowings from West Germanic languages, i.e. Old Saxon, Middle Low German, and Old and Middle English.

11. —— (1979), 'Icelandic Purism and its History', *Word*, 30 (1–2): 76–86.

This paper was published in a special issue of *Word*, which was devoted to national language planning and treatment. It contains a survey of the history of Icelandic purism, as well as an account of the official and general attitude towards the language at the time when the article was written.

12. JONES, OSCAR E. (1964), 'Some Icelandic *götumál* Expressions', *Scandinavian Studies*, 36: 59–64.

This is a small and rather loose collection of slang expressions with examples and explanations (some of them debatable). Some of the expressions are anglicisms, but others come from Danish or are of native origin.

13. Jónsson, Baldur (1987), 'Íslensk orðmyndun' (Icelandic Word-formation), *Andvari* (Nýr flokkur), 29: 88–102.

The last part of the article discusses loanwords and their integration from a language political point of view. It is mainly speculative, but a number of better integrated loanwords from various languages are mentioned as examples.

14. Jónsson, Jón Hilmar (1978), 'Zur Sprachpolitik und Sprachpflege in Island', *Muttersprache*, 88: 353–62.

The paper presents a historical summary of Icelandic purism and language policy. The author also discusses the various options available when a new word is needed, and the adaptability of the language system to integrate loanwords.

15. —— (1980), 'Om skrivemåte og bøyning av fremmedord i islandsk' (On the Orthography and Inflection of Foreign Words in Icelandic), *Språk i Norden*, 61–7.

In this paper the author discusses the orthography of loanwords in Icelandic. No research has been undertaken in the field, but the tendency seems to be to adapt foreign spelling to the Icelandic phonological system. The author also discusses the inflection of loanwords in a complicated system as in Icelandic, trying to determine what decides the gender of a loanword. The difference between foreign nouns and adjectives is also pointed out; in general nouns are inflected, whereas adjectives remain uninflected.

16. Jónsson, Sigurður (1984), 'Af hassistum og kontóristum', *Íslenskt mál og almenn málfræði*, 6: 155–65.

17. Kress, Bruno (1966*a*), 'Anglo-Amerikanisch und Isländisch', *Nordeuropa. Jahrbuch für Nordische Studien*, 1: 9–22.

The subject of the first part of this paper is the history of purism and language policy in Iceland and Danish influence on the language. In the second part, the author discusses the growing English influence during World War II, caused by the British and later American military occupation. Numerous examples are given of English loanwords and loan translations, and of pronunciation and inflectional adaptation.

18. —— (1966*b*), 'Anglo-Amerikanismen im Isländischen', in *Festschrift Walter Baetke* (Weimar), 210–14.

The subject of the paper is the inflectional adaption of English loanwords. (Partly the same as Kress 1966*a*.)

19. —— (1970), 'Zur Einpassung anglo-amerikanischer Wörter in das Isländische', in *Proceedings of the Sixth International Congress of Phonetic Sciences Prague 1967* (Prague), 507–9.

The subject of this paper is the adaptation of English loanwords to the Icelandic phonological system. (Partly the same as Kress 1966*a*.)

20. KRISTINSSON, ARI PÁLL (1990), 'Skvass eða squash. Nyorði eða slettur' (*Skvass* or *squash*. Neologisms or Foreignisms), *Málfregnir*, 8: 26–8.

The paper opens with the mention of a number of proposals that have been made to replace the English word *squash* with Icelandic neologisms or to adapt the foreign word phonologically and morphologically. This is followed by a more general discussion of neologisms, both the formation of new words from native sources, and the borrowing and adaptation of foreign words.

21. MAGNÚSSON, ÁSGEIR BLÖNDAL (1989), *Íslensk orðsifjabók* (Icelandic Etymological Dictionary) (Reykjavík: Orðabók Háskólans), 1231 pp.

This etymological dictionary of Icelandic includes a number of anglicisms introduced in the modern language.

22. OTTÓSSON, KJARTAN G. (1990), *Íslensk málhreinsun. Sögulegt yfirlit* (Icelandic Purism. A Historical Survey) (Rit Íslenskrar málnefndar 6; Reykjavík: Íslensk málnefnd), 168 pp.

An excellent and very extensive historical survey on Icelandic purism and language policy from the reformation until the present, which, among other things, touches upon foreign influences at various times and the reactions to this, 168 pp.

23. SIGMUNDSSON, SVAVAR (1984), 'Slang på Island' (Slang in Icelandic), in K. Ringgaard and Viggo Sørensen (eds.), *The Nordic Languages and Modern Linguistics*, 5: 369–73.

The paper discusses the main characteristics of Icelandic slang, especially as regards word-formation, with respect to the material collected for the then recently published dictionary of slang (cf. Árnason *et al.* 1982).

24. SVAVARSDÓTTIR, ÁSTA (1993), *Beygingakerfi nafnorða í nútímaíslensku* (The Inflectional System of Nouns in Modern Icelandic) Málfræðirannsóknir 5 (Reykjavík: Málvísindastofnun Háskóla Íslands), 156 pp.

The topic of this monograph is the inflectional system of Icelandic nouns in general, but a short chapter (5.2) is dedicated to the inflectional adaptation of loanwords.

25. —— and GUÐRÚN KVARAN (1996), 'Nye ord i islandsk' (New Words in Icelandic), *Språknytt*, 2: 6–8.

A short survey of neologisms in Icelandic, with special emphasis on loanwords.

26. VIKØR, LARS S. (1995), *The Nordic Languages. Their Status and Interrelations* (Nordic Language Secretariat, Publication no. 14; Oslo: Novus Press).

A general introduction to the Nordic languages and their internal and external sociolinguistic status. Among other things the author discusses foreign influence, which at present comes mainly from the English-speaking world.

27. VILHJÁLMSSON, BJARNI (1968), 'Sprogrensning og fremmedord' (Purism and Foreign words), *Nordiske sprogproblemer 1966 og 1967*, 25–8.

A contribution to a discussion at the Nordic language meeting in Norway 1967. The author gives an account of the Icelandic way of dealing with new concepts, most often by the formation of neologisms of native origin, which is the preferred method from the puristic point of view, but sometimes by the phonological and/or morphological adaptation of foreign words. Some of the examples given are anglicisms, but others are international terms.

Italian (Virginia Pulcini)

1. Amato, Antonio, Francesca Maria Andreoni, and Rita Salvi (eds.) (1990), *Prestiti linguistici dal mondo anglofono* (Rome: Bulzoni).

This compilation lists 2,300 English words collected from newspapers during 1987, grouped under seven subjects (politics, daily news, advertising, jobs, culture, economics, and science) and accompanied by quotations. No linguistic information about the English loanwords is provided.

2. Beccaria, Gian Luigi (1988), *Italiano antico e nuovo* (Milan: Garzanti).

The volume contains a very well-balanced and informative chapter ('La lingua dell'okey', 217–45) about the spread of English in Italy. Starting from a historical perspective on linguistic exchange, Beccaria praises the vitality of the English language, condemns purist policies directed against foreign words, as was the case in Italy during the Fascist regime, but also criticizes today's excessive use of English words in the press. Many examples of 'necessary' or 'redundant' anglicisms in the various areas of borrowing are discussed, with particular emphasis on features of English words which facilitate their adoption and use, *viz.* their brevity, onomatopoeic quality and syntactic flexibility.

3. Bencini, Andrea and Eugenia Citernesi (1992), *Parole degli anni novanta* (Florence: Le Monnier).

This dictionary gathers materials collected for the second edition of Devoto and Oli (1990).

4. Berruto, Gaetano (1987), *Sociolinguistica dell'Italiano contemporaneo* (Rome: La Nuova Italia Scientifica).

5. Bombi, Raffaella (1987–1988), 'Alcune tipologie di calchi sull'inglese in italiano', *Incontri Linguistici*, 12: 17–59.

The author examines some of the major typologies proposed for the analysis of calques, then illustrates a substantial number of these, grouping them into two types. Compositional calques faithfully reproduce the compositional pattern of the English model (*centre-forward* → *centravanti*). Bombi then considers the various types of compositional patterns, especially calques made up of verb + noun and Latin/Greek prefix + noun, the latter having considerably increased in Italian under the influence of English compounds. By contrast, derivational calques reproduce the pattern of the foreign model (*colonization* → *colonizzazione*), though in many cases they may be analysed as adapted borrowings, because of the common lexical heritage especially in the case of internationalisms.

6. Bombi, Raffaella (1989–90), 'Calchi sintagmatici, sintematici e semantici sull'inglese in italiano', *Incontri linguistici*, 13: 97–149.

The author discusses the formal characteristics of the major types of English-Italian calques. The English pattern 'determinans-determinatum' in N+N compounds may be rendered in Italian by the same syntagmatic sequence (*high fidelity* → *alta fedeltà*), a reverse order (*data bank* → *banca dati*) or a noun followed by a prepositional phrase (*summit conference* → *conferenza al vertice*). The influence of English has accelerated some processes in Italian word-formation such as juxtaposition. Meaning is taken into account with various examples of semantic calques.

7. —— (1991), 'Di alcuni falsi anglicismi nell'italiano contemporaneo', *Incontri Linguistici*, 14: 87–96.

The growing presence and the prestige of anglicisms in Italian have favoured the creation of pseudo-anglicisms. In this article two compositional models are considered. *Filipović (1985) distinguishes between: a) the combination of two pre-existing anglicisms (*tennisman* for *tennis player*); b) derivation (*speaker* for *newsreader*); c) morphological simplification (*happy end* for *happy ending*), and stresses the role of mediating languages. Spence's proposed typology (1989: 323–34 = French) includes: a) the combination of two pre-existing anglicisms and b) the attribution of new meaning to an anglicism (*slip* for *panties*), taking into account the diachronic evolution of loanwords. Several pseudo-anglicisms are analysed on the basis of these two models.

8. Brown, Virginia (1987), *Odd Pairs and False Friends* (Bologna: Zanichelli; new edition: V. Brown, E. Mendes, and G. Natali (1995), *More and More False Friends, Bugs & Bugbears. Dizionario di ambigue*

affinità e tranelli nella traduzione fra inglese e italiano (Bologna: Zanichelli)).

9. Bruni, Francesco (1984), *L'italiano: Elementi di storia della lingua e della cultura* (Torino: UTET).

This volume contains a synthetic overview of the influence of English on Italian (104–12), with typological and morphological observations on English loanwords and calques.

10. Caretti, Lanfranco (1951*a*), 'Noterelle calcistiche', *Lingua Nostra*, 13: 14–18.

When football was introduced into Italy at the end of the nineteenth century, its terminology was entirely English. In this article the author presents some of the main football terms and discusses the fortune of their Italian substitutions.

11. —— (1951*b*), 'Noterelle tennistiche', *Lingua Nostra*, 13: 77–80.

Tennis spread in Italy from the last decade of the nineteenth century. Much of its terminology was originally English, although during the 1930s and 1940s it was almost entirely replaced by Italian terms. The author discusses some of the most common English tennis terms and their Italian equivalents.

12. Carpitano, Samuele and Giorgio Casole (1989), *Dizionario delle parole straniere in uso nella lingua italiana* (Milan: Mondadori).

This dictionary of foreign and Latin words gathered from written and spoken media from the late 1970s to the 1980s is addressed to a non-specialist public; it contains some 2,300 anglicisms and provides information on their native and adapted pronunciations, grammar, meaning, adapted forms, Italian equivalents and calques.

13. Cartago, Gabriella (1994), 'L'apporto inglese', in Luca Serianni and Pietro Trifone (eds.), *Storia della lingua italiana, III, Le altre lingue* (Torino: Einaudi), 721–50.

This chapter offers a detailed historical treatment of the contacts between English and Italian from the fourteenth century to the present. It is extremely rich in examples, historical documentation and bibliographical references.

14. Castellani, Arrigo (1984), 'Terminologia linguistica', *Studi Linguistici Italiani*, 10: 153–61.

The author discusses the inadequacy of some linguistic terms of English origin and proposes substitutions.

15. Castellani, Arrigo (1987), 'Morbus Anglicus', *Studi Linguistici Italiani*, 10: 137–53.

As the title of this article suggests, the borrowing of English words is seen as a 'linguistic disease'. The author strongly advocates the application of purist rules to English loanwords, i.e. their adaptation to Italian morphology or replacement by native words or Italian neologisms. He points out some orthographic and phonetic incongruencies between Italian and English and, as a solution, proposes the addition of a vowel for words ending in consonants, the simplification of consonant clusters, and replacements even for well-established anglicisms.

16. Cerasuolo Pertusi and Maria Rosaria (1987–88), 'Sulla storia di alcuni anglicismi marinareschi italiani', *Incontri Linguistici*, 12: 61–4.

This article illustrates the origin and history of the anglicisms *skiff* and *schooner* in Italian.

17. Cortelazzo, Manlio and Ugo Cardinale (1986), *Dizionario di parole nuove, 1964–1984* (Torino: Loescher).

This dictionary contains frequent and accepted neologisms collected between 1964 and 1984, including about 960 English loanwords, which make up 18 per cent of the total of the new lexis. The source and first occurrence date of each headword are shown and the native pronunciation of anglicisms is indicated. This work aims at continuing a scholarly tradition begun by Panzini and Migliorini's work on new words. A new updated edition of the dictionary, with another three years covered, is available (*Dizionario di parole nuove, 1964–1987* (Torino: Loescher, 1989)). More recent collections of neologisms by the same author are: *Annali del lessico contemporaneo italiano. Neologismi 1993–94* (Padova: Esedra, 1995); *Annali del lessico contemporaneo italiano. Neologismi 1995* (Padova: Esedra, 1996).

18. Dardano, Maurizio (1978), *(s)Parliamo Italiano?* (Rome: Curcio).

A scholarly yet very readable book on linguistic innovations in Italian from the 1880s to the 1970s. References to the influence of

English on Italian are widespread in the text (see 75–94; 120–2; 234).

19. —— (1983, [2]1985), 'L'inglese quotidiano', in *Il linguaggio dei giornali italiani* (Bari: Laterza), 485–94.

20. —— (1986), 'The Influence of English on Italian', in *Viereck and Bald (eds.), 231–52.

Dardano sketches the historical change from dominant French to English influence and purist tendencies, and then analyses the phonetic and morphological adaptation of loanwords and the text genres most likely to contain them (including terminologies in technical language). The final chapter is devoted to semantics and calques.

21. *D.E.I.* = *Dizionario enciclopedico italiano* (1955–61), (12 vols., Rome: Istituto della Enciclopedia italiana; *Supplemento* 1974; *Secondo Supplemento* 1984).

22. *D.E.I.* = Battisti, Carlo and Giovanni Alessio (1950–57), *Dizionario Etimologico Italiano* (5 vols., Florence: Barbèra).

23. *D.E.L.I.* = Cortelazzo, Manlio and Paolo Zolli (1979–1988), *Dizionario Etimologico della Lingua Italiana* (5 vols., Bologna: Zanichelli), vol. 1: *A–C* (1979); 2: *D–H* (1980); 3: *I–N* (1983); 4: *O–R* (1985); 5: *S–Z* (1988).

24. De Mauro, Tullio (1963), ([2]1970), *Storia linguistica dell'Italia unita* (Bari: Laterza).

This classic account of the history of Italian from unity (1861) to the end of World War II deals with foreign borrowings in Italian, the incidence of anglicisms and purism (see 163–82, 214–15, 247–8, 365–72 in particular).

25. Devoto, Giacomo and Gian Carlo Oli (eds.) (1990), *Il dizionario della lingua italiana* (Florence: Le Monnier) (first ed. 1971; CD-Rom ed.: Le Monnier-Editoria Elettronica Editel, 1994).

26. Durante, Marcello (1981), *Dal latino all'italiano moderno* (Bologna: Zanichelli), 265–9.

27. Elliot, Giacomo (1977), *Parliamo itangliano* (Milan: Rizzoli).

The pseudonymous author labels as 'Itangliano' the excessive use and misuse of English words in Italian, especially when this is done simply for effect in some professional careers. In a humorous vein this book presents and comments on four hundred English words used in present-day Italian, discussing adapted pronunciations, new meanings, and calques. (Review: Dunlop, *English Today*, 18 (1989), 32–5.)

28. FANFANI, MASSIMO (1991–1995), 'Sugli anglicismi nell'italiano contemporaneo', *Lingua Nostra*, 52 (1991): 11–24, 73–89, 113–18; 53 (1992): 18–25, 79–86, 120–1; 54 (1993): 13–20, 63–71, 122–4; 55 (1994): 19–25, 76–7, 117–20; 56 (1995): 14–17.

This is a series of articles about anglicisms in contemporary Italian. The first contribution offers a clear introduction to anglicisms and a review of Rando's dictionary (1987). Rich bibliographical references on the contacts between English, Italian and other languages today and in the past are contained in explanatory footnotes. Fanfani points out several weaknesses of Rando's dictionary, such as the heterogeneous selection of anglicisms (with entries of an encyclopedic nature), unsatisfactory linguistic information included in the entries (archaic or dialect forms, inadequate mention of pronunciation variants) and unreliable dating. In the subsequent articles Fanfani presents additional anglicisms collected in recent years, with a view to future revision and updating of Rando's dictionary.

29. FANFANI, PIETRO and CESARE ARLÌA (1877), *Lessico della Corrotta Italianità* (Milano: Libreria d'Educazione e d'Istruzione di Paolo Carrara).

30. FURLAN, INGRID (1977), 'Termini della politica inglese e americana entrati italiano nel decennio 1951–60', *Lingua Nostra* 38: 64–8.

31. GUȚIA, IOAN, GRAZIA M. SENES, MARCELLA ZAPPIERI, and FRANCESCA CABASINO (1981), *Contatti interlinguistici e mass media* (Rome: La Goliardica Editrice).

This collection of essays on cross-linguistic contacts in the mass media focusses in particular on the use of English words in advertising, radio, television, and the press.

32. HASTINGS, ROBERT (1984), 'Juve is magic: the anglicisms of Italian football graffiti', *Italian Studies*, 39: 91–102.

This article considers the influence of English in the graffiti written by Italian football fans. This phenomenon, though ephemeral, is worthy of documentation from a sociolinguistic point of view. The author shows how the language of Italian football graffiti is modelled on English slogans but is influenced by Italian spelling, morphology, and syntax.

33. —— (1987), 'Lord Snoydon for Carnaby Street: anglicisms in the Italian footwear trade', *Italian Studies*, 42: 91–105.

This article examines the role of English in the naming and description of Italian shoes. The recourse to English is motivated by the prestige of the Anglo-Saxon society in the Italian public but peculiar deviations in English spelling, morphology, syntax and even cases of anglicized Italian are found. The author foresees negative effects on Italian vocabulary resulting from uncontrolled use of English in the language of footwear marketing.

34. HOPE, THOMAS (1971), *Lexical Borrowing in the Romance Languages: A Critical Study of Italianisms in French and Gallicisms in Italian from 1100 to 1900* (Oxford: Blackwell), 755 pp.

35. ITALIANO, GLORIA (1999), *Parole a buon rendere ovvero l'invasione dei termini anglo-italiani.* (Fiesole: Edizioni Cadmo).

This study analyses many English borrowings in Italian according to the criteria of semantics, phonetics, morphology, and gender, and emphasises how certain terms show a transparent linear continuity when crossing the linguistic barrier while others undergo adaptations of various kinds. Plausible explanations are given for the various processes of assimilation of English loanwords into Italian.

36. JEZEK, ELISABETTA (1983), 'L'inglese giovane', *Italiano e Oltre*, 8: 204–9.

The influence of English on the speech of young Italians is examined on the basis of a corpus of anglicisms collected from traditional lexicographic sources and magazines for young people. Various types of adaptation, derivation, and calquing are described, although the majority of anglicisms found are unadapted. The author shows that, in the speech of young people, anglicisms are used creatively and represent a marker of group identity.

37. KLAJN, IVAN (1972), *Influssi inglesi nella lingua italiana* (Florence: Leo Olschki Editore).

This is the only comprehensive scholarly treatment of linguistic borrowing from English into Italian to date. The book deals with some major aspects of the exchanges between English and Italian, such as the Latin substratum and the mediation of French. Borrowings are classified into unadapted and adapted loanwords and calques. Adaptation is examined in detail from an orthographic, phonological, morphological, and semantic perspective. This book provides an extremely rich body of examples (unfortunately not indexed), and thorough historical information on anglicisms, although its documentation does not go beyond the 1960s.

38. La Rana, Silvana (1989), 'La lingua inglese in Italia', in Thomas Frank (ed.), *Introduzione alla studio della lingua inglese* (Bologna: Il Mulino), 303–19.

This chapter sketches the linguistic and cultural influence of English in Italy after 1945, drawing especially on Klajn (1972) and Rando (1987), and gives some information about the teaching of English in Italy over the past few decades.

39. —— (1992), 'Anglicisms in Italian: Phonological Cross-Linguistic Influence' in Nicola Pantaleo (ed.), *Aspects of English Diachronic Linguistics* (Fasano: Schena), 161–74.

40. Luciani Creuly, Renée (1987), 'Tecnicismi e immagini di cultura: alcune riflessioni sui forestierismi dell'italiano colto e della lingua dei media', in Cesare Cecioni and Gabriella Del Lungo Camiciotti (eds.), *Lingua letteraria e lingua dei media nell'italiano contemporaneo* (Florence: Le Monnier), 293–302.

This article discusses the presence of French and English loanwords in the spoken and written language of the media.

41. *L.U.I.* = Bosco, Umberto (1968–81), *Lessico Universale Italiano* (14 vols., Rome: Istituto della Enciclopedia Italiana), supplement 1985–86.

42. Lurati, Ottavio (1995), *3000 parole nuove: la neologia negli anni 1980–1990* (Bologna: Zanichelli).

This dictionary of neologisms includes 360 anglicisms (11 per cent of all the entries), indicates their pronunciation and source and provides quotations.

43. Marri, Fabio (1994), 'La lingua dell'informatica', in Lucia Serianni and Pietro Trifone, *Storia della lingua italiana*, 3 vols. Torino: Einaudi, vol. II: 617–33.

The author illustrates the terminology of computer science in Italian which includes anglicisms and calques from American English.

44. McGraw-Hill = *Dizionario enciclopedico scientifico e tecnico. Inglese-italiano. Italiano-inglese* (1980) (Bologna: Zanichelli). (Italian adapted translation of the *Dictionary of Scientific and Technical Terms* (New York, 1978)).

45. Merlini, Madeleine (1987), 'Appunti sulla ricezione e l'uso di parole straniere in un quotidiano italiano', in Cesare Cecioni and Gabriella Del Lungo Camiciotti (eds.), *Lingua letteraria e lingua dei media nell'italiano contemporaneo* (Florence: Le Monnier), 313–21.

An analysis of foreign words in the Italian newspaper *La Stampa*, two-thirds of which are anglicisms (1057), grouped in semantic fields (music, sport, modern art, and fashion) and discussed in detail. There are some general considerations on their use and new meanings in Italian.

46. Messeri, Anna Laura (1954), 'Voci inglesi della moda accolte in italiano nel XIX secolo', *Lingua Nostra*, 15: 47–50.

In the nineteenth century the influence of English fashion in men's clothing was remarkable in Italy. This article provides linguistic documentation for anglicisms in the field of men's fashion.

47. —— (1955), 'Anglicismi ottocenteschi riferiti ai mezzi di comunicazione', *Lingua Nostra*, 16: 5–10.

The author considers the terms referring to means of transport which originated in England and began to be used in Italy during the nineteenth century. Whereas terms for carriages (*tilbury*, *brougham*) are now obsolete, Italian railway terminology still shows many traces of English influence, often through French mediation. A list of terms, accompanied by historical quotations and dates of adoption, is provided.

48. —— (1957), 'Anglicismi nel linguaggio politico italiano nel 700 e nell' 800', *Lingua Nostra*, 18: 100–8.

A large number of anglicisms relating to politics were adopted in

Italy in the eighteenth and nineteenth centuries. Formally, many terms were of Latin origin and therefore easily adapted or translated into Italian. The parallel influence of French in the borrowing process was also important. A glossary of political terminology, with dates of adoption and historical quotations, is given.

49. MIGLIORINI, BRUNO (1963*a*), *Parole nuove. Appendice di dodicimila voci al 'Dizionario Moderno' di Alfredo Panzini* (Milan: Hoepli).

50. —— (1939, [4]1963*b*), *Lingua contemporanea* (Florence: Sansoni).

51. —— (1990), *La lingua italiana del Novecento* (Florence: Le Lettere).

52. —— (1937, [2]1960, [3]1991), *Storia della lingua italiana* (Florence: Sansoni).

53. MINI, GUIDO (1994), *Parole senza frontiere. Dizionario delle parole straniere in uso nella lingua italiana* (Bologna: Zanichelli). (First ed.: *L'italiano integrato, l'apporto di voci straniere nel nostro linguaggio* (Padova: La Galiverna, 1990)).

This dictionary includes 6,500 frequent foreign words in Italian, about three thousand of which are anglicisms (45 per cent of all the entries). Each headword includes the original and adapted pronunciation, the meanings and derived forms.

54. MONELLI, PAOLO (1933, [3]1957), *Barbaro dominio* (Milan: Hoepli).

This is a classic account of purism in which the author expresses his opposition to the penetration of foreign words into Italian.

55. MOSS, HOWARD K. (1976), 'Borrowings from English in recent Italian', *Trivium*, 11: 49–63.

This article presents many examples of English loanwords and calques used in contemporary Italian and discusses the reasons why anglicisms may be preferred to indigenous words to name new concepts. Some linguistic problems deriving from the use of English borrowings in Italian are considered as well as favourable and unfavourable attitudes.

56. —— (1992), 'The Incidence of Anglicisms in Modern Italian: Considerations on its Overall Effect on the Language', *The Italianist:*

Journal of the Department of Italian Studies (University of Reading), 129–36.

Recent specialist and non-specialist literature on neologisms and anglicisms in Italian is reviewed on the basis of corpus studies carried out over the past few decades. The author concludes that the number of anglicisms used in contemporary Italian is very small (ranging from 0.44 to 1 per cent of the common lexis).

57. PALAZZI, FERNANDO and GIAN FRANCO FOLENA (1992), *Dizionario della lingua italiana* (Torino: Loescher).

58. PANZINI, ALFREDO (ed.) (1963), *Dizionario moderno* (Milan: Hoepli; 1st ed. 1923).

59. PASQUARELLI, GIANNI and GERMANO PALMIERI (1987), *Parole d'oggi: guida ai termini economici e d'uso corrente* (Rome: Buffetti).

This dictionary of terms used in business and commerce includes 1,250 anglicisms (30 per cent of the total entries).

60. PETRALLI, ALESSIO (1996), *Neologismi e nuovi media* (Bologna: CLUEB).

This book deals with linguistic innovation in Italian caused by the spread of the new electronic media from the 1980s onwards. Neology and the internationalization of the lexes of modern languages are explored, with special focus on the influence of American English.

61. PULCINI, VIRGINIA (1990), *Introduzione alla pronuncia inglese* (Alessandria: Edizioni dell'Orso).

62. —— (1994), 'The English Language in Italy', *English Today*, 10 (4): 49–52.

An overview of the educational, cultural, and linguistic impact of English on Italian, including a brief presentation of lexical borrowing.

63. —— (1995), 'Some New English Words in Italian', *Textus. English Studies in Italy*, 8: 267–80.

This study is based on a corpus of 567 anglicisms collected from Italian daily newspapers in 1995. The 110 anglicisms which appeared to be unrecorded by any Italian dictionary are analysed in terms of formal, stylistic, and semantic features.

64. Pulcini, Virginia (1997), 'Attitudes Toward the Spread of English in Italy', *World Englishes*, 16: 77–85.

Particular attention is given to the linguistic policy of the Fascist regime and the 'Americanization' of modern society after World War II. The penetration of the English language in Italy is examined, from the purist attitudes of the past to the unbiased standpoint of present-day Italian linguists.

65. —— (1999), 'Focus on Italian Anglicisms: A Comparative Study of Three Dictionaries', in *Transiti Linguistici e culturali.* Atti del XVIII Congresso nazionale dell'A.I.A. edited by G. Azzaro and M. Ulrych (Trieste: E.U.T.), 359–71.

Starting from different definitions of anglicisms, this article considers the different criteria for inclusion of anglicisms used in three dictionaries namely *Lo Zingarelli 1997. Vocabolario della Lingua Italiana* (1996), *Dizionario degli Anglicismi* by G. Rando (1987), and the *DEA* by M. Görlach (2001). Although the retention of the original English form is a condition for a word to qualify as an anglicism in Zingarelli and the *DEA*, some violations of this rule and problems with labelling can be found, whereas in Rando's dictionary looser and less rigorous selection criteria are used. A grid illustrates the differences in the entries for the letter 'J' in the three dictionaries as a result of their lexicographic choices.

66. Quarantotto, Claudio (1987), *Dizionario del nuovo italiano* (Rome: Newton Compton).

This dictionary of neologisms from the post-war period to the mid-1980s comprises 1450 unadapted anglicisms (14 per cent of the total).

67. Raffaelli, Sergio (1983), *Le parole proibite. Purismo di Stato e regolamentazione della pubblicità in Italia (1812–1945)* (Bologna: Il Mulino).

68. Ragazzini, Giuseppe ([1]1967, [3]1995), *Il Nuovo Ragazzini. Dizionario inglese-italiano, italiano-inglese* (Bologna: Zanichelli).

69. Rando, Gaetano (1969), 'Anglicismi nel *Dizionario moderno* dalla quarta alla decima edizione (1923–63)', *Lingua Nostra*, 30: 107–12.

Rando compares the number of anglicisms recorded in the *Dizionario Moderno* by Panzini, revised by Migliorini in 1942, throughout its ten editions from 1923 to 1963. The author also discusses several cases of uncertain classification, resulting from French mediation, which were initially recorded as French loan-words. A decrease in the number of anglicisms recorded is concurrent with political crises between Italy and English-speaking countries (after World War I and during the Fascist regime).

70. —— (1970*a*), 'The Assimilation of English Loan Words in Italian', *Italica*, 47 (2): 129–42.

This article presents the different types of adaptation which English words undergo during the borrowing process: orthographic, phonological (involving phonemes and accentual patterns), and morphological (including gender and number attribution). Because of the structural and phonetic differences between Italian and English, semantic borrowing (which, according to the author, coincides with calquing and translating) is preferred in contemporary Italian.

71. —— (1970*b*), 'Voci inglesi nelle relazioni cinquecentesche degli ambasciatori veneti in Inghilterra (1498–1557)', *Lingua Nostra*, 31: 104–9.

The commercial contacts between Italy and England in the sixteenth century are recorded in the writings of Italian ambassadors in England. This article presents some of the words used to refer to English institutions and customs, mainly in the form of calques (*chamber*/*camera*) and a few adaptations (*My Lord*/*Milord*).

72. —— (1971), 'The Semantic Influence of English on Italian', *Italica*, 48: 246–52.

The semantic influence of English on Italian is examined with reference to calques and loan translations. Transfer of meaning is noticeable in paronymous words of classical origin which have developed different meanings in Italian and English (*attitudine*, 'aptitude' is now understood as 'attitude'). Because of formal similarity, an Italian word may acquire a new meaning from its English counterpart, as evident in political, economic, scientific, and journalistic terms such as *parliament*/*parlamento*, *station*/

stazione, and *sophisticated/sofisticato*. In the case of English words of Germanic origin, the word or the component elements are translated separately, as in *loudspeaker/altoparlante*. The author suggests that semantic borrowing is easier in anglicisms which are formally compatible with Italian phonology and morphology rather than in adapted and derived loanwords.

73. RANDO, GAETANO (1973*a*), 'A Quantitative Analysis of the Use of Anglicisms in Written Standard Italian during the 1960s', *Italica*, 50: 73–9.

The article reports the results of a quantitative analysis of anglicisms found in fictional, nonfictional, and journalistic writings (magazines and newspapers). Data show that the incidence of anglicisms in written Italian is fairly low. It amounts to less than 1 per cent, with a slightly higher percentage in journalistic language, and is restricted to special fields of vocabulary (sports and politics). Rando also provides a frequency list of anglicisms in the four types of written materials.

74. —— (1973*b*), 'Influssi inglesi nel lessico italiano contemporaneo', *Lingua Nostra*, 34: 111–20.

The penetration of anglicisms in Italian in the twentieth century is examined in relation to some important historical and sociocultural events. For instance, the Fascist regime slowed down the phenomenon and encouraged the creation of native substitutes, and World War II caused a spread of American cultural products. Many anglicisms are presented and grouped into fields of major influence (sports, entertainment, politics, business, commerce, science, and technology).

75. —— (1987), *Dizionario degli anglicismi nell'italiano postunitario* (Florence: Leo S. Olschki Editore).

This is the only dictionary of anglicisms in Italian to date; it covers the period from the 1850s to the 1980s including more than 2,300 entries, unadapted and adapted loanwords, hybrids, pseudo-anglicisms, calques, and foreign words mediated through English and some internationalisms. The dictionary also contains encyclopedic information on institutions, geographical names, trademarks, and many technical acronyms. Some adapted forms and variants provided for anglicisms are archaic, popular, or dialectal. A second, updated edition is needed.

76. —— (1990), '*Capital Gain, Lunedì Nero, Money Manager* e altri anglicismi recentissimi nel linguaggio economico-borsistico-commerciale', *Lingua Nostra*, 51: 50–66.

This is a collection of 608 anglicisms (unadapted, adapted, and calques) relating to economics, commerce and the money market, taken from the Italian newspaper *La Repubblica* between 1985 and 1989. Each word has a frequency code and is illustrated with a quotation and the date of its first occurrence.

77. ROSSETTI, CARLO (1974), *I tranelli dell'inglese* (New enlarged edition; Milan: Mondadori).

78. ROTHENBERG, R. JULIUS (1969), 'Un hobby per i cocktails', *Italica*, 46: 149–65.

The author criticizes the use and misuse of English words in Italian, which he calls 'little monsters'. In his long presentation of examples, however, he fails to distinguish fully accepted adaptations, semantic shifts, and pseudo-anglicisms from instances of non-standard, dialectal or even erroneous uses of anglicisms.

79. SABATINI, FRANCESCO and VITTORIO COLETTI (1997), *DISC. Dizionario Italiano Sabatini-Coletti* (Florence: Giunti). (Paper and CD-Rom edition.)

80. SANGA, GLAUCO (1981), 'Les dynamiques linguistiques de la société italienne (1861–1980)', *Languages*, 61: 93–115.

81. SCHMID, BONA (1989), *Words. Guida ai termini inglesi d'uso corrente e al loro giusto impiego* (Florence: Sansoni).

This dictionary includes about one thousand anglicisms used in present-day Italian. Each word is accompanied by the phonetic transcription of its pronunciation, etymology, meaning, and historical profile.

82. SCOTTI MORGANA, SILVIA (1981), *Le parole nuove* (Bologna: Zanichelli).

83. SENES, GRAZIA M. (1981), 'L'inglese nella pubblicità alla radiotelevisione e sulla stampa', in Guţia *et al.*, 67–110.

84. SIMONE, RAFFAELE (1988), 'Che lingua parleremo nel Duemila?', in *Maistock: il linguaggio spiegato da una bambina* (Florence: La Nuova Italia), 187–205.

85. Sočanac, Lelija (1990), 'Engleski element u talijanskom jeziku' (The English Element in Italian), *Filologija*, 18: 49–59. (EEEL 4).

The author gives a brief historical survey of anglicisms in Italian and analyses the orthographical, morphological, and semantic levels. Most English loans retain their original spelling. The phonological form of an English loan is determined either on the basis of spelling or pronunciation. Morphological accommodation is rather rare, except in the case of verbal loans. Some Italian words have acquired new meanings under the influence of English. A short survey of anglicisms in Italian dialects is also given.

86. —— (1993*a*), 'Morfološka adaptacija anglicizama u talijanskom jeziku' (The Morphological Adaptation of Anglicisms in Italian), *Filologija*, 20–21: 413–24. (EEEL 4).

The author concludes that the process of importation of anglicisms on the morphological level is stronger than the process of substitution. English loan verbs always receive the characteristic infinitive ending, while most of the borrowed nouns and adjectives remain unadapted.

87. —— (1993*b*), 'Sekundarna adaptacija anglicizama u talijanskom jeziku: tvorba riječi' (Secondary Adaptation of English Loanwords in Italian: Word-formation), *Suvremena lingvistika*, 35–36: 171–6. (EEEL 4).

The author analyses the process of word-formation with respect to English loanwords in Italian. A few Italian suffixes which are commonly joined to English loanwords, such as *-ista*, *-ggio*, *-ata*, *-iano*, *-ese*, and *-esco*, are listed along with examples, as well as frequent prefixes such as *anti-*, *post-*, and *super-*. A few examples of hybrid compounds are also discussed. In present-day Italian, word-formation is more productive than adaptation of anglicisms on the morphological level.

88. —— (1995), 'Sekundarna adaptacija anglicizama u talijanskom jeziku na semantickoj razini' (The Secondary Adaptation of Anglicisms in Italian on the Semantic Level), *Filologija*, 24–5: 325–30.

The author discusses changes in meaning, such as expansion in number, expansion in field, ellipsis, metaphor, metonymy, and pejoration. These changes occur in words which have become completely integrated into the system of the receiving language.

89. UPWARD, CHRISTOPHER and VIRGINIA PULCINI (1996), 'Italian Spelling and How It Treats English Loanwords', *Journal of the Simplified Spelling Society*, 20: 19–24.

90. VERARDI, GIUSEPPE M. (1995), *Le parole veloci. Neologia e mass media negli anni 90* (Locarno: Dadò Editore).

This book is about neologisms in the Italian mass-media in the 1990s. It includes a section on the influence of English (225–37) and many examples throughout the text.

91. *V.O.L.I.T.* = DURO, ALDO (1986–94), *Vocabolario della lingua Italiana* (5 vols., Rome: Istituto della Enciclopedia Italiana). CD-Rom ed. 1997.

92. ZINGARELLI, NICOLA (1922, [10]1970), ([11]1983), ([12]1993), *Vocabolario della lingua italiana* (ed. by Miro Dogliotti and Luigi Rosiello; Bologna: Zanichelli), ([12]1993 reprinted with additions every year, latest repr. *Lo Zingarelli 2001*; CD-Rom ed.: 1996, with *Le parole straniere dello Zingarelli*).

93. ZOLLI, PAOLO (1976, [2]1991), *Le parole straniere* (Bologna: Zanichelli).

This is a scholarly treatment of the penetration of foreign words into Italian from the Middle Ages to the present time. The long chapter devoted to anglicisms traces the history of linguistic contacts between Italian and English and illustrates English borrowings in chronological order, with dates of first occurrence, explanation, indication of the Italian equivalent, and historical references. This book is written in an expository style and includes a wealth of cultural information. It is a major work for the study of foreign language contact in Italian.

Norwegian (Anne-Line Graedler)

(see also *25)

1. AWEDYK, WITOSŁAW (1993), 'Engelsk påvirkning på norske ungdommers tale' (English Influence on the Speech of Norwegian Teenagers), unpublished thesis (Poznań: Adam Mickiewicz University), 51 pp. (summary in Polish).

A sociolinguistic study of the influence of English on the speech of forty-six upper secondary school students from two schools in the same socio-geographic area of Oslo. The survey takes up the informants' contact with and attitudes toward English, and the question of whether their use of English in Norwegian is systematic and conscious.

2. BLAAUW, KNUD, TROND VERNEGG, and LARS ROAR LANGSLET (eds.) (1996), *Engelske ord med norsk rettskrivning? Seks seminarforedrag 1996* (English Words with Norwegian Orthography? Six Seminar Lectures 1996) (Bergen: Bergens Riksmålsforening, Riksmålsforbundet and Det Norske Akademi for Sprog og Litteratur), 120 pp.

Six lectures about the standardization of foreign words and the attitude towards them, with topics ranging from standardization in a historical perspective and German orthographic principles, to ardent contributions to the current debate. The seminar was held after a controversial suggestion by the Norwegian Language Concil to Norwegianize the spelling of approximately sixty English loanwords; the book includes some of the official documents.

3. BRATLIEN, OLAF (1967), 'English Loan Words in a Norwegian Newspaper,' unpublished *hovedfag* thesis (University of Oslo).

This study of all the English loanwords found in the July–September 1960 issues of the national newspaper *Dagbladet* contains a number of diagrams and several lists of interest, but the conclusions drawn on the basis of the lists are often superficial or seem ill-founded, because the author is trying to do too many things at the same time.

4. BRUNSTAD, ENDRE (2001), 'Det reine språket. Om purisme i dansk, svensk, færøysk og norsk' (The Pure Language. Purism in Danish, Swedish, Faroese, and Norwegian). Dr.Art. thesis (University of Bergen).

5. CHRISTENSEN, NILS B. (1994), 'The Use of English in Three Major Norwegian Companies', unpublished *hovedfag* thesis (University of Oslo).

An investigation of the use of English in three Norwegian companies: Elkem, a metal and material company (6,000+ employees), Statoil, a government controlled oil drilling, producing and distributing company (some 12,000 employees), and Kværner, an industrial company (22,000+ employees). Total number of respondents: 291. Among other results, the thesis reveals that more than 90 per cent of the respondents in all groups considered English skills to be necessary to perform their job.

6. DEVENISH, INGRID ANN (1990), 'English Influence on Norwegian Pop Music Language', unpublished *hovedfag* thesis (University of Oslo), 119 pp. + appendices.

A study of relatively recent English loans in a text corpus composed of articles and advertisements about pop music in three national newspapers and one magazine. The material is analysed in terms of content categories, formal aspects, and aspects of semantics and function. The thesis also includes interviews with some musicians and journalists.

7. ERIKSEN, ANNE KRISTIN (1992), 'English Loan Words in some Recent Norwegian Novels and Short Stories', unpublished *hovedfag* thesis (University of Oslo), 262 pp.

A study of direct English loanwords in ten recent Norwegian works of fiction, mostly crime (totalling approximately 678,000 words), in terms of morphological, orthographic, and semantic features. The overall frequency of relatively recent borrowed English items was found to be rather low, on average 1.91 tokens per one thousand words.

8. FAUSA, KRISTIN (1994), 'English Loan Words in Norwegian: Some Aspects of the Adoption, Adaptation and Establishment of Loan Words', unpublished *hovedfag* thesis (University of Oslo), 102 pp. + appendices.

A thorough study of 1,256 loanwords, classified according to word class, gender, semantic domain, and age, and statistically analysed with respect to the processes of adoption, adaptation, and establishment in Norwegian. The thesis examines factors which might promote or hinder the different stages in the borrowing process.

9. Flydal, Einar (1983), *Oljespråk: Språklige lovbrudd og lovlige språkbrudd på sokkelen (Sluttrapport fra Sikkerhet på Sokkelen-prosjektet nr. 351 'Språk og sikkerhet')* (Oil Language: Linguistic Violations of Law and Legal Violations of Language on the Continental Shelf) (Stavanger, Oslo, Bergen, and Tromsø: Universitetsforlaget), 165 pp.

Final report on a research project on security on oil platforms in the North Sea, dealing with 'Language and security'. The use and spread of English are analysed from a cultural, political, organizational and work environments perspective. The extensive use of English on board oil platforms with Norwegian workers is seen as a safety hazard, and translation and Norwegianization of English terminology are considered necessary measures to improve safety.

10. Graedler, Anne-Line (1992), 'Orientiering om prosjektet "Norsk anglisismeordbok"' (Orientation about the Project 'Norwegian Anglicism Dictionary'), in Ruth Vatvedt Fjeld (ed.), *Nordiske studier i leksikografi. Rapport fra Konferanse om leksikografi i Norden 28.–31. Mai 1991* (Skrifter utgitt av Nordisk forening for leksikografi, nr. 1), 307–14.

Brief orientation about the function, source material, and the criteria for selection of words in connection with the planned dictionary, with examples of finished entries.

11. —— (1994), 'Betydningsendring hos engelske lånond i norsk' (Semantic Change in English Loanwords in Norwegian), in Ulla-Britt Kotsinas and John Helgander (eds.), *Dialektkontakt, språkkontakt och språkförändring i Norden. Föredrag från ett forskarsymposium* (Meddelanden från institutionen för nordiska språk vid Stockholms universitet MINS), 210–19.

Survey of different types of semantic change found in English loanwords in Norwegian, and a discussion of various factors that seem to play a role in this process, both language-system related, language-user related, and more strictly formal (e.g. morphological) factors.

12. —— (1996), 'Forholdet mellom stavemåte og bøyning i engelske lånord' (The Relationship between Spelling and Inflection in English Loanwords), in Blaauw *et al.* (eds.), 67–80.

The article takes up for special consideration the spelling and inflection of borrowed verbs and nouns with plural *-s*, and concludes that there is indeed a correlation between certain types of morphological integration and altered spelling of some loanwords.

13. —— (1998), *Morphological, Semantic, and Functional Aspects of English Lexical Borrowings in Norwegian.* (Oslo: Scandinavian University Press), xxi + 368 pp.

This is the first major analysis of anglicisms in Norwegian for some time. Graedler first describes the contact situation past and present and defines types of borrowing. She then discusses in four chapters the morphological integration of anglicisms (gender allocation, pluralization, adaptations of verb morphology and aspects of word-formation) before treating the semantic and communicational/stylistic function of anglicisms in Norwegian. The book is an excellent companion volume to the dictionary edited jointly with Stig Johansson in 1997. Very valuable comments by three 'opponents' of the (1995) thesis and a response to these were published in the *Norsk Lingvistik Tidssrift*, 15 (1997), 83–114 (incorporated in the book version).

14. —— and Stig Johansson (1995), '*Rocka, hipt* and *snacksy*: Some Aspects of English Influence on Present-Day Norwegian', in Gunnel Melchers and Beatrice Warren (eds.), *Studies in Anglistics* (Stockholm Studies in English 85; Stockholm: Almqvist & Wiksell), 269–87.

Overview and summary of the research project 'English in Norway', with a presentation of theses and results so far. Brief comparison with the situation in Sweden.

15. —— —— (eds.) (1997), *Anglisismeordboka. Engelske lånord i norsk* (A Dictionary of Anglicisms. English Loanwords in Norwegian) (Oslo: Universitetsforlaget), 466 pp.

The first Norwegian dictionary that deals specifically with English loanwords. Contains approximately four thousand entries, mostly direct loans, ranging from old and established words, through typically oral expressions and more specialized terms, to quite recent words. The dictionary is descriptive in outlook, and each entry contains information about alternative forms of spelling, about pronunciation, some grammatical and often etymological information, a definition/explanation and/or a Norwegian synonym of the loanword, data about inclusion in other Norwegian dictionaries, (a number of) illustrative authentic examples of the word as used in Norwegian texts, information about any substantial differences in usage or meaning between English and Norwegian, and lists of derivations and compounds. The dictionary is based on a large computerized corpus of examples, which has been complemented with specimens from other sources.

16. GRØNLI, GRETE (1990), 'The Influence of English on Norwegian Advertising', unpublished *hovedfag* thesis (University of Oslo), 220 pp.

A study of English loanwords and text in the commercial advertisements of one week's morning issues and weekly supplement of the national newspaper *Aftenposten* from 1989, and a comparison with corresponding issues from 1969. The advertisements are classified in terms of subject area, and the words studied with respect to social and linguistic integration and textual function. The thesis also contains an investigation of attitudes towards the use of English among people in the advertising business.

17. GULDBRANSEN, TONE (1985), *Med fireflaiten åffsjår: norske oljearbeideres bruk av anglisismer* (With Flight Four Off-shore: Norwegian Oil Workers' Use of Anglicisms) (Stavanger: Universitetsforlaget), 117 pp.

A sociolinguistic study of the use of English among Norwegian oil workers, based on field observation. Two kinds of oil language are distinguished: that of the (American) management, and the offshore jargon of the workers. One of the conclusions is that the Norwegian offshore language mainly serves to strengthen the group-identity of the workers, and is not of major importance in the exchange of factual information on the platform, contrary to the conviction of the language users themselves.

18. GULLIKSEN, ØYVIND (1980*a*), 'Ned i self-servicen å shoppe. Om engelsk-amerikanske lånord og kulturpåverknad, Del 1' (Down to the Self-service to Shop. About English-American Loanwords and Cultural Influence, Part 1), *Språklig samling*, 21 (1): 4–8.

19. —— (1980*b*), 'Med panoramavindu og air-condition. Om engelsk-amerikanske lånord og kulturpåverknad, Del 2' (With Panorama Window and Air Conditioning. About English-American Loanwords and Cultural Influence, Part 2), *Språklig samling*, 21 (2): 10–14.

The two articles describe borrowing in terms of the notion of 'language pressure', i.e. as a cultural, not a linguistic problem. The author fears that increased knowledge of English may become a power factor that will separate the experts from the common man, but also notes that Norwegian counter- or sub-culture has made innovative use of English.

20. HALVORSEN, PER-KRISTIAN (1978), 'An Acquisitional Approach to Norwegian Noun Morphology', in John Weinstock (ed.), *The Nordic Languages and Modern Linguistics 3. Proceedings of the Third International Conference of Nordic and General Linguistics [1976]* (Austin: The University of Texas at Austin), 366–73.

Can acquisitional theory explain certain data from Norwegian noun morphology? The assignment of gender to English nouns that were borrowed into American Norwegian, with data from Haugen (1969), is used as a test case.

21. HAUGEN, EINAR (1969), *The Norwegian Language in America: A Study in Bilingual Behavior* (Bloomington, Ind.: Indiana University Press).

22. —— (1976), *The Scandinavian Languages: An Introduction to Their History* (London: Faber & Faber), esp. 63–71.

23. —— (1978), 'The English Language as an Instrument of Modernization in Scandinavia', in R. Zeitler (ed.), *Det moderna Skandinaviens framväxt. Bidrag till de nordiska ländernas moderna historia* (Uppsala).

24. —— (1988), 'The Influence of English: A Transatlantic Perspective', *Folia Linguistica* 22, 2–9.

The article discusses differences between cultural and intimate borrowing, with examples from English in Norwegian in

Norway (Stene 1945) and in America (Haugen's own studies). A number of examples illustrate differences in form (spelling, pronunciation), which are used as evidence of different ways and routes of borrowing.

25. Hellevik, Alf (1963), 'Den engelsk-amerikanske påverknaden på norsk' (The English-American Influence on Norwegian), in *Lånordproblemet. To foredrag i norsk språknemnd, Norsk språknemnd småskrifter* (Oslo: J. W. Cappelens), 2: 15–25.

26. —— (1970), 'Engelsk-amerikanske lånord og språklig sjølvhjelp' (English-American Loanwords and Linguistic Self-Help), in *Det rette ordet. Ord og ordlegging i skrift og tale* (Oslo: Det norske samlaget), 48–54.

27. —— (1979), 'Språklig påverknad frå engelsk og amerikansk' (Linguistic Influence from English and American), in *Språkrøkt og målstyring. Eit utval av artiklar* (Oslo: Det norske samlaget), 71–80.

The three articles deal with influences from English as a problem and describe the borrowing in terms of a linguistic 'invasion'. The author warns that the influence of English will continue to increase.

28. Jespersen, Otto (1902), 'Engelsk og nordisk. En afhandling om låneord' (English and the Nordic Languages. A Treatise on Loanwords), *Nordisk tidskrift för vetenskap, konst och industri*, 500–14.

The author's chief concern is the contribution that a study of loanwords can give towards a fuller understanding of historical processes; Jespersen compares the role of the early Scandinavian influence on the English language with the present role played by English and American. The article contains a list of about seventy English loanwords then in use in the Scandinavian countries, characteristically technical terms.

29. Johannessen, Steinar (1963), 'English Loan-words in a Norwegian Newspaper', unpublished *hovedfag* thesis (University of Oslo), 78 pp.

A study of all the English loanwords found in the January–March 1960 issues of the national newspaper *Dagbladet*, with a vocabulary of approximately 320 words. The loanwords are divided first into semantic groups, and then into three groups according to their hypothesized future in Norwegian.

30. Johansson, Stig (1992), 'Engelsk—et *must* i norsk? On the Role of English in Norwegian Language and Society', in Anne-Marie Langvall Olsen and Aud Marit Simensen (eds.), *Om språk og utdanning. Essays in Honour of Eva Sivertsen* (Oslo: Universitetsforlaget), 65–84.

A clear account of the situation with respect to English in Norwegian, with a summary of the research project 'English in Norway', where data and results form theses by Devenish, Grønli, and Valberg are presented and discussed.

31. Kilarski, Marcin (1994), 'Morphological Adaptation of English Loans in the Scandinavian Languages', unpublished thesis (Adam Mickiewicz University, Poznań).

32. Kristensen, Anne-Bente (1995), 'An Analysis of English Influence in two Lillehammer Newspapers from 1988 and 1993, with Special Reference to the XVII Olympic Winter Games', unpublished *hovedfag* thesis (University of Oslo).

33. Lyngstadaas, Kari (1965), 'A Study of English Loan-words', unpublished *hovedfag* thesis (University of Oslo), 95 pp.

A study of all the English loanwords found in the April–June 1960 issues of the national newspaper *Dagbladet*, with a vocabulary of 407 items. The final section is a survey of the thirty-nine words in the vocabulary that have been adapted in spelling.

34. Lystad, Mari (1994), 'The Americanization of Norwegian Culture and Language through American Films', unpublished *hovedfag* thesis (University of Oslo), 114 pp.

The author discusses the cultural effect of American films on the Norwegian film industry, investigates a collection of loanwords found in film reports and reviews, and also discusses current attitudes towards the alleged influence of American films on Norwegian culture.

35. Masvie, Inger Lise (1992), 'English in Norway—a Sociolinguistic Study', unpublished *hovedfag* thesis (University of Oslo), 128 pp. + appendices.

The study is based on a survey of attitudes towards English, use of English, comprehension, etc. Some fifty students from two different Norwegian upper secondary schools and some fifty adults enrolled in adult education classes participated by answering a comprehensive questionnaire. The results reveal differences related to age, sex, and region.

36. Mey, Jakob (1978), 'Sexism and Loans', in Moira Linnarud and Jan Svartvik (eds.), *Kommunikativ kompetens och fackspråk* (Föredrag hållna vid ett symposium om Språket i bruk i Södertälje 6–8. Oktober 1978 och utgivna av Svenska föreningen för tillämpad språkvetenskap (ASLA)), 241–52.

A discussion of the English elements in a Norwegian crime novel. The conclusion is that 'the loans . . . primarily characterize men and their exploits, and . . . they do this in a decidedly and unilaterally favourable manner, thus reflecting and maintaining the sexist and male-dominated orientation of society-at-large'.

37. Norsk språkråd (ed.) (1973–), *Språknytt. Meldingsblad for Norsk språkråd* (Bulletin from the Norwegian Language Council).

Contains shorter articles, debate, book reviews, lists and examples of new words, etc. Distributed free of charge and written for a wider audience.

38. —— (1982), *Nyord i norsk 1945–1975* (New Words in Norwegian 1945–1975) (Oslo: Universitetsforlaget).

39. Rafnung, Bjørn Thrane (1965), 'English Loan-words in a Norwegian Newspaper with Special Reference to Hybrid Compounds', unpublished *hovedfag* thesis (University of Oslo), 343 pp.

A study of all the English loanwords found in the October–December, 1963 issues of the national newspaper *Morgenbladet*, with a vocabulary of approximately 1,200 words. A final section deals with 'hybrid compounds', which are said to make up 53 per cent of the words (types) in the vocabulary list. The most common variety is English noun + Norwegian noun combinations.

40. Sandøy, H. (2000), *Lånte fjører eller bunad? Om importord i norsk*. (Foreign Chic or National Costume? On Imported Words in Norwegian) (Oslo: LNU/Cappelen).

41. Schmidt, Kari Anne Rand (1982), 'The Adaptation of English Loanwords in Norwegian', in *Filipović (ed.), 338–78.

An overview of the research in the field, with a good presentation and summary of the results. Treats the adaptation of English loanwords at the levels of phonology, morphology, tonemes, and semantics, and suggests a 'scale of adaptation' for nouns. The author's conclusion is that Norwegian accommodates English loanwords easily.

42. SIMONSEN, DAG FINN and HELENE URI (1992), 'Skoleelevers holdninger til anglonorsk' (School Children's Attitudes to Anglo-Norwegian), *Norsklæreren*, 1: 27–34.

An investigation of young people's attitudes to the use of English in Norway. Ninety-one respondents from three upper secondary schools in Oslo answered a questionnaire with sixteen questions about their attitudes to, e.g. English names of shops and particular word pairs. Respondents were also tested for English language skills and comprehension.

43. SJÅHEIM, ANNE ELISABETH (1994), 'The Use of English on Norwegian Television', unpublished *hovedfag* thesis (University of Oslo), 130 pp.

The study is based on 64.5 hours of watching four different Norwegian TV channels over a period of seven months. The average amount of programming in English varies from 9.5 per cent on the NRK (the Norwegian Broadcasting Corporation), to 54.4 per cent on TV Norge, a commercial channel. English loanwords in Norwegian programmes are also examined, with respect to frequency and formal, semantic and functional aspects. The use of English on TV commercials is also discussed.

44. SØRLAND, S. A. (1993), '"Trick", "trikk", or "triks"? Some Aspects of Orthographic Adaptation of English Loanwords in Standard Norwegian', unpublished *hovedfag* thesis (University of Oslo), 148 pp. and appendices.

A study of direct English loans in Norwegian and their adaptation to Norwegian spelling conventions, based on 380 adapted and 640 unadapted English forms listed in a major dictionary (*Bokmålsordboka* 1986). Changes and patterns of orthographic adaptation are analysed with respect to factors furthering or counteracting adaptation.

45. SPANGEN, AMUND (1965), 'English Loan-words in a Norwegian Newspaper', unpublished *hovedfag* thesis (University of Oslo), 269 pp.

A study of all the English loanwords found in the October–December 1960 issues of the national newspaper *Dagbladet*, with a vocabulary of approximately seven hundred words. The final chapter deals with the phonological adaptation of the loanwords and discusses the various solutions adopted by Norwegians when there is no exact equivalent to a given English sound.

46. STANDWELL, GRAHAM (1962), 'Contemporary Linguistic Borrowings by Norwegian from American and English', unpublished MA thesis (University of Durham), 142 pp. + appendices.

A study of English loanwords in use in Norway around 1960, partly based on daily newspapers. The study is modelled on that of Stene (1945), and besides a vocabulary of five hundred words, the thesis contains sections on the reasons for borrowing, pronunciation and spelling, morphology, meaning, translation of loans, and a semantic classification.

47. STENE, AASTA (1945), *English Loanwords in Modern Norwegian: A Study of Linguistic Borrowing in the Process* (London/Oslo: Oxford University Press, Johan Grundt Tanum Forlag), 222 pp. (Review: Haugen, *Language*, 27 (1949), 63–8.)

This has been for many years the most comprehensive study of English loanwords in Norwegian, based on a vocabulary compiled (mainly by introspection) before the war of 531 words/440 entries. The main object of the study is to establish a method for the synchronic identification of words as foreign (i.e. as loanwords), by the aid of a set of formal criteria—a thorough analysis of the orthography, pronunciation, accent, morphology, and semantics of loanwords.

48. VALBERG, INGER (1990), '"The perfect look"—A Study of the Influence of English on Norwegian in the Area of Fashion and Beauty', unpublished *hovedfag* thesis (University of Oslo), 150 pp.

A study of relatively recent English loans in a corpus of approximately 67,000 words composed of articles about fashion and beauty in the daily and weekly press. The study is partly modelled on that of Crystal (1988), and the material is analysed in terms of content categories, formal features, and aspects of semantics and function.

APPENDIX

The following titles were published after the collections for this bibliography were complete. The information impressively shows the great interest that the topic continues to have in Norway (and elsewhere).

GRAEDLER, ANNE-LINE (1999), 'Where English and Norwegian Meet: Codeswitching in Written Texts', in Hilde Hasselgård and Signe Oksefjell (eds.), *Out of Corpora. Studies in Honour of Stig Johansson* (Amsterdam: Rodopi), 327–43.

—— and STIG JOHANSSON (forthcoming 2002), *Rocka, hipt og snacksy. Engelsk i norsk språk og samfunn* (*Rocka, Hipt* and *Snacksy*. English in the Norwegian Language and Society) Kristiansand: Høyskoleforlaget).

JOHANNESSEN, HANNE K. (1999), 'On the Role of English in Norwegian Civil Aviation Administration', unpublished *hovedfag* thesis (University of Oslo), 101 pp. + appendices.

KOBBERSTAD, NILS (1999), 'The Influence of English on Norwegian in the Football Columns of Two Norwegian Newspapers: A Synchronic and Diachronic Study', unpublished *hovedfag* thesis (University of Oslo).

MØLLER, GUDVEIG (1996), 'The Acquisition of English Among Norwegian Children Before Formal English Teaching', unpublished *hovedfag* thesis (University of Oslo).

NORDLI, LISE TRANUM (1998), 'Internet Chatting: English Influence on Norwegian Chat Room Language', unpublished *hovedfag* thesis (University of Oslo), 87 pp. + appendices.

PETTERSEN, KARIN DAHLBERG (1999), 'English in Norway: Attitudes among Military Recruits and Teacher Trainees', unpublished *hovedfag* thesis (University of Oslo).

Polish (Elżbieta Mańczak-Wohlfeld)

(see also *45, *60)

BPTJ	*Biuletyn Polskiego Towarzystwa Językoznawczego* (Bulletin of the Polish Linguistic Society)
JP	*Język Polski* (The Polish Language)
KN	*Kwartalnik Neofilologiczny* (Neophilological Quarterly)
ŁTN	*Łódzkie Towarzystwo Naukowe* (Łódź Scientific Society)
PF	*Prace Filologiczne* (Philological Works)
PH	*Przegląd Humanistyczny* (Humanistic Review)
PorJ	*Poradnik Językowy* (Language Adviser)
SAP	*Studia Anglica Posnaniensia*
ZNUJ	*Zeszyty Naukowe Uniwersytetu Jagiellońskiego* (Scientific Issues of the Jagiellonian University)

1. ALTBAUER, M. (1955), 'O kilku przykładach depluralizacji zapożyczeń w języku polskim' (On Some Examples of Double Plural in the Polish Language), *JP* 35: 42–6.

The author discusses the so-called double plural of loanwords in Polish, illustrating the phenomenon with some borrowings taken from different languages, including English, Hebrew, etc.

2. BAJEROWA, I. (1976), 'Nowe wyrazy w języku współczesnym a zagrożenie komunikacji językowej' (New Words in Contemporary Polish and the Danger in Language Communication), *Zaranie Śląskie*, 39: 279–92.

3. BARTMIŃSKA, I. and J. BARTMIŃSKI (1978), *Nazwiska obce w języku polskim* (Foreign Proper Names in the Polish Language) (Warsaw: PWN).

4. BASAJ, M. (1982), 'Wpływy obce na polszczyznę w sześćdziesięcioleciu' (The Influence of Foreign Languages on Polish in the 60s), in J. Rieger and M. Szymczak (eds.), *Język i językoznawstwo polskie w sześćdziesięcioleciu* (The Polish Language and Linguistics in the 60s) (Wrocław: Ossolineum), 41–6.

5. BIŁYK, A. (1968), 'Zapożyczenia i neologizmy w świetle sporów o słownictwo powojennej polszczyzny' (Loanwords and Neologisms in

the Light of Controversy with Post-war Polish Lexis), *Językoznawca*, 18–19: 36–7.

6. BRÜCKNER, A. (1907), 'Wyrazy obce w języku polskim' (Foreign Words in the Polish Language), *PF* 6: 1–55.

The scholar deals with various loanwords in Polish and claims that there are very few anglicisms and therefore they are not worth discussing.

7. BUTTLER, D. (1978), 'Powojenne innowacje w polskim zasobie słownym' (Post-war Innovation in Polish Vocabulary), *PH* 5: 55–67.

The article includes the influence of English. According to the author anglicisms are mainly introduced by scientists and young people. English scientific terms infrequently enter everyday Polish but English borrowings introduced by the youth, concerning fashion, sports, and entertainmant, are generally accepted.

8. —— (1982), 'Rozwój słownictwa polskiego w sześćdziesięcioleciu' (The Development of Polish Lexis in the 60s), in J. Rieger and M. Szymczak (eds.), *Język i językoznawstwo w sześćdziesięcioleciu niepodległości* (The Polish Language and Linguistics in Sixty Years of Independence) (Wrocław: Ossolineum), 57–63.

The scholar discusses developments since 1918, including the introduction of English loans.

9. CUDAK, R. and J. TAMBOR (1995), 'O języku "komputerowców"' (On the Language of 'Computer Experts'), *JP* 75: 197–204.

10. CYRAN, W. (1959), 'Dżez czy dżaz' (Dżez or Dżaz), *JP* 39: 388.

The note is devoted to the pronunciation of the English loanword *jazz*. The problem lies in the choice of [∊] and [a] since English [æ] does not exist in Polish.

11. —— (1975), 'Krakersy' (Crackers), *JP* 55: 239–40.

The note deals with the so-called double plural illustrated by the analysis of *krakersy* < *crackers*.

12. DAMBORSKÝ, J. (1974), 'Wyrazy obce w języku polskim' (Loanwords in the Polish Language), *PorJ* 7: 341–55.

13. DOROSZEWSKI, W. (1938–9), 'Siła nurtu swojskiego w języku polskim' (The Power of Native Trends in Polish), *PorJ* 8: 137–9.

The author argues that despite the impact of borrowings from different languages (including English), Polish will remain a Slavic language.

14. Doroszewski, W. (1952), 'O rodzaju gramatycznym wyrazów obcych w języku polskim' (On the Grammatical Gender of Foreign Words in the Polish Language), *Sprawozdania z posiedzeń Komisji Językoznawczej WTN* (Reports from Meetings of Warsaw Linguistic Board), 4: 58–61.

Doroszewski enumerates morphological as well as semantic reasons for assigning different genders to loanwords, including anglicisms, in Polish.

15. —— (1971), 'Parę uwag o wyrazie *handicap*' (Some Remarks on the Word *handicap*), *PorJ* 4: 259–60.

The note is on the meaning of *handicap*, whose sense is opposite to the one found in English.

16. Du Feu, V. M. (1962), 'English Sports Terms in Polish', *Canadian Slavonic Papers*, 4: 155–9.

The author characterizes English sports terms in Polish on graphic, phonetic, morphological, and semantic levels. She also points to the use of originally English proper names, such as common *rower* 'bicycle' < *Rover*.

17. Dunaj, B. (1993), 'Żeńskie odpowiedniki wyrazu *biznesmen: bizneswomen, kobieta interesu, biznesmenka*' (Feminine Equivalents of the Word *biznesmen: bizneswomen, kobieta interesu, biznesmenka*), *JP* 73: 167–72.

Dunaj provides and discusses a number of words used to indicate 'a female businessman', some of them being of English origin.

18. Fisiak, J. (1961*a*), 'Zapożyczenia angielskie w języku polskim: analiza interpretacji leksykalnej' (English Loanwords in Polish), unpublished D.Phil. thesis (University of Łódź).

Fisiak's thesis provides a thorough formal and semantic analysis of about seven hundred English loanwords attested in Polish before 1960.

19. —— (1961*b*), 'Zjawisko depluralizacji niektórych rzeczowników angielskich zapożyczonych przez język polski' (The Phenomenon

of Double Plural of some English Nouns Borrowed in Polish), *JP* 41: 138–9.

20. —— (1962), 'Złożony kontakt językowy w procesie zapożyczania z języka angielskiego do polskiego' (Problems in the Language Contact in Borrowing from English into Polish), *JP* 42: 286–94.

Fisiak makes a distinction between anglicisms borrowed into Polish directly or indirectly (mainly through German, French, or Russian). He also points to the fact that in some cases English only serves as a mediating language.

21. —— (1964), 'English Sports Terms in Modern Polish', *English Studies*, 45: 230–6.

22. —— (1968), 'Phonemics of English Loanwords in Polish', *Biuletyn Fonograficzny*, 9: 69–79.

23. —— (1970), 'The Semantics of English Loanwords in Polish', *SAP* 2: 41–9.

Fisiak classifies over seven hundred English loanwords into different semantic categories like 'sport', 'music', 'literature', etc.

24. —— (1975), 'Some Remarks Concerning the Noun Gender Assignment of Loanwords', *BPTJ* 35: 59–63. (Polish original 1963.)

The majority of anglicisms are assigned the masculine gender; fewer nouns take the feminine, neuter (or no) gender.

25. —— (1985), 'A Note on the Adaption of English Loanwords in Polish: Verbs', *ITL Review of Applied Linguistics*, 67–8: 69–75.

Fisiak discusses the adaptation of English verbs in Polish, distinguishing defective loans (only one category is formed), partly adapted borrowings (some morphological categories are missing), and fully adapted anglicisms (all morphological categories are present).

26. —— (1986), 'The Word-Formation of English Loanwords in Polish', in *Viereck and Bald (eds.), 253–63.

The problems which occur within the process of derivation and compounding of loanwords are illustrated with many examples.

27. Górny, W. (1959), 'Jeszcze o budżecie . . . strzycie' (On *budżet . . . strzyc* Once Again), *JP* 39: 295–8.

The pronunciation of the English loan *budżet* < *budget* is contrasted with the phonetics of the Polish word *strzyc*.

28. Grabowska, L. and M. Grabowska (1971), 'Uwagi o "żargonie" marynarzy' (Remarks on the 'Jargon' Used by Sailors), *Językoznawca*, 23–24: 88–95.

The article is devoted to sailors' jargon which is full of anglicisms referring to the names of people and equipment.

29. Grabowski, Y. (1971), 'Recent English Loanwords Denoting Sciences, Technology, Music, Fashion, and Politics in the Polish Language', *Canadian Slavonic Papers*, 13: 65–71.

30. Grzebieniowski, T. (1962), *Słownictwo i słowotwórstwo angielskie* (English Words and Word-formation) (Warsaw: PWN).

The author includes a number of anglicisms formed from proper names and provides their historical account, e.g. *szrapnel* < *shrappnel* < *Shrapnel* (the name of a British general).

31. Hofman, L. (1967), *Procesy przyswajania wyrazów angielskich w języku polskim* (The Process of Adaption of Anglicisms in Polish) (London: Polski Universytet na Obczyźnie).

32. Kajetanowicz, H. (1993), 'Adaptacja zapożyczeń w terminologii fizyki ciała stałego' (The Adaptation of Borrowings in Physics), *PorJ* 8: 446–55.

The author analyses the assimilation of English terminology used in Polish physics. He analyses its adaptation on the graphic, phonetic, morphological, and semantic levels.

33. Kania, S. (1974), 'Z najnowszych zapożyczeń—*streaking, streakers*' (The Most Recent Borrowings—*streaking, streakers*), *PorJ* 7: 440.

34. —— (1975), 'Zapożyczenia angielskie w polskiej gwarze żołnierskiej' (Anglicisms in the Slang of Polish Soldiers), *JP* 55: 212–16.

35. —— (1978*a*), 'Jeszcze raz o pochodzeniu cinkciarza' (The Origin of *cinkciarz* Revisited), *PorJ* 2: 79–80.

It is claimed that the word *cinkciarz*, 'someone who changes money on the black market', is derived from English *chunk*.

36. —— (1978*b*), 'O UFO czyli o latających talerzach' (On UFO or on Flying Objects), *JP* 58: 306–7.

37. Kasprzycka, A. (1971), 'Materiały do polskiej leksykografii nautycznej XVIII w.' (Materials to Polish Nautical Lexicography from the 18th Century), *Nautologia*, 2–4: 57–70.

Some eighteenth-century nautical terms, including anglicisms *bord* < *board, jacht* < *yacht, ketch, kutter* < *cutter, sloop* are discussed.

38. Klemensiewicz, Z. (1953), 'Jeszcze o wymowie ang. *joule*' (On the Pronunciation of English *joule*), *JP* 33: 119–20.

39. —— (1972), *Historia języka polskiego* (History of Polish), vol. III (Warsaw: PWN).

A history of the Polish language; in volume III the author erroneously claims that the influence of English on Polish began only at the beginning of the twentieth century and that it has never been strong.

40. Kołodziejek, E. (1990), 'Zapożyczenia w gwarze marynarzy (typy i funkcje)' (The Jargon of Sailors—Types and Functions), *PorJ* 2: 112–18.

41. Koneczna, H. (1936–7), 'Wyrazy angielskie w języku polskim' (English Words in Polish), *PorJ* 9: 161–70.

Koneczna enumerates and analyses about 500 English loans found in Polish in the 1930s, some of which have disappeared.

42. Konopczyński, W. (1947), 'Anglia a Polska w XVIII w.' (England and Poland in the Eighteenth Century), *Pamiętnik Biblioteki Kórnickiej*, 4: 93–129.

43. Kreja, B. (1963), 'O tzw. depluralizacji w języku polskim' (On the So-called Double Plural in Polish), *JP* 43: 27–36.

44. —— (1993), 'O formancie *-gate* "afera, skandal"' (On the Morpheme *-gate* 'affair, scandal'), *JP* 73: 63–8.

The linguist comments and discusses a number of words formed by the addition of the English morpheme *-gate* to Polish lexical items, like *Sanepidgate*.

45. Lipoński, W. (1974), *Sport. Literatura. Sztuka* (Sport. Literature. Art) (Warsaw).

Some anglicisms concerned with sports, literature, and art are marginally discussed in the book.

46. Lipoński, W. (1978), *Polska a Brytania 1801–1830* (Poland and Britain 1801–1830) (Poznań).

47. Malinowski, L. (1888), 'Studia nad etymologią ludową' (Studies on Folk Etymologies), *PF* 2: 240–62.

The scholar provides some examples of English loans like *tramba, trąba < tramway.*

48. Mańczak-Wohlfeld, E. (1987*a*), 'Najstarsze zapożyczenia angielskie w polszczyźnie' (The Oldest English Borrowings in Polish), *JP* 67: 25–31.

The article deals with fourteen borrowings attested in Polish at the end of the eighteenth century (e.g. *galon < gallon, klub < club, kwakier < quaker, rum*).

49. —— (1987*b*), 'Efemerydy pochodzenia angielskiego w Słowniku wileńskim' (Ephemeral Anglicisms in the Vilnius Dictionary), *PorJ* 2: 100–3.

180 English borrowings found in the so-called *Vilnius Dictionary* (1861) are discussed; about thirty are ephemeral.

50. —— (1988*a*), 'Anglicyzmy w *Słowniku warszawskim*' (Anglicisms in the *Warsaw Dictionary*), *JP* 68: 24–9.

An analysis of about 250 anglicisms found in the *Warsaw Dictionary* (1900–23).

51. —— (1988*b*), 'Semantic Fields of English Loanwords in Modern Polish', *KN* 35: 275–88.

About 1500 English borrowings are classified into different semantic fields like 'sport', 'man', 'clothing', etc.

52. —— (1988*c*), 'Liczba mnoga zapożyczeń angielskich' (The Plural of English Loanwords), *PorJ* 7: 512–14.

The author discusses different ways of forming the plural of English loans in Polish, e.g. by the addition of Polish endings, by the introduction of the so-called double plural and by the omission of *-s* in *pluralia tantum.*

53. —— (1988*d*), 'The Semantic Integration of English Loanwords in Polish', *KN* 38: 45–54.

This article suggests that decomposition analysis and field theory is the most adequate framework for a semantic description of English loans in Polish.

54. —— (1991*a*), '*Tamersi*—nowa tendencja w języku polskim' (*Tamersi*—a New Tendency in Polish), *PorJ* 9–10: 429–31.

The article discusses the formation of the plural by means of both English and Polish endings.

55. —— (1991*b*), 'Dopełniacz niektórych zapożyczeń angielskich w języku polskim' (The Genitive of Some Anglicisms in Polish), *PorJ* 9–10: 431–2.

The note is on the formation of the so-called double genitive of some English proper names in Polish: apart from the marker of the English genitive the Polish ending is added, as in *Longmansa, McDonald'sa.*

56. —— (1992), *Analiza dekompozycyjna zapożyczeń angielskich w języku polskim* (Decomposition Analysis of English Borrowings in Polish) (Cracow: Wydawnictwo Uniwersytetu Jagiellońskiego).

About 1600 English borrowings have been attested in Polish; since a thorough discussion of all is impossible, the analysis is here limited to the field of 'clothing'. The characterization of these loans concerns their formal and semantic adaptation in Polish. By formal adaptation we mean their change on graphic, phonological, and morphological levels. The semantic analysis is conducted within the framework of decomposition analysis, and field theory.

57. —— (1993), 'Uwagi o wpływie języka angielskiego na polszczyznę końca XX w' (Some Remarks on the Influence of English and Polish at the End of the 20th Century), *JP* 73: 279–81.

Non-lexical influence of English on Polish, like the usage of the -'*s* genitive, the English plural, or the English word order (modifier + noun) is summarized.

58. —— (1994*a*), *Angielskie elementy leksykalne w języku polskim* (English Lexical Elements in the Polish Language) (Cracow: Universitas).

This dictionary describes about 1600 English loanwords. Each lexical entry consists of the headword and the following constituents: graphic variant(s) if present, phonetic transcription if pronunciation differs from spelling, morphological information, etymology in the case of words that do not belong to the stock of lexical items found in Middle English, the approximate time of its first occurrence, its meaning in Polish and in English if different, derivational affixes, and set phrases if they occur in Polish.

59. Mańczak-Wohlfeld, E. (1994*b*), 'English Loanwords in Amszejewicz's Dictionary', *KN* 41: 251–4.

About one hundred English loanwords attested in the first comprehensive dictionary of foreign words in Polish (1859) are discussed at length.

60. —— (1994*c*), 'Leksykon zapożyczeń angielskich w języku polskim' (The Lexicon of Anglicisms in the Polish Language), *BPTJ* 50: 101–8.

61. —— (1995), *Tendencje rozwojowe współczesnych zapożyczeń angielskich w języku polskim* (Tendencies in the Assimilation of Contemporary English Loanwords in Polish) (Cracow: Universitas).

An analysis of about 1700 English borrowings used in Polish. Most English loans entered Polish after 1945 and particularly after the change in the political system in Poland. However, a thorough analysis of a number of Polish dictionaries shows that the process of borrowing had begun in the eighteenth century. Older borrowings are very well-adapted and are not even felt as loans by Poles not knowing English. By contrast, the spelling of recent loans varies, we observe a certain degree of hesitation in their pronunciation and they easily follow the rules of Polish grammar. Since a majority of anglicisms are nouns (94 per cent) they are assigned an appropriate gender (in most cases the masculine) and are declined accordingly. There are about 3 per cent verbs, about 1 per cent adjectives and less than 1 per cent adverbs. Semantic fields such as 'sport', 'man', 'clothing', 'music' are the most numerous. Usually anglicisms in Polish retain the meanings of their English etymons.

62. —— (1996*a*), 'The Frequency of English Loanwords in Written Polish', *Suvremena Lingvistica* 22. 1–2: 643–8.

63. —— (1996*b*), 'The Influence of English on the Language of Polish Teenagers', *Studia Etymologica Cracoviensia*, 1: 45–8.

Although the influence of English on the language of teenagers is not very strong, it has a certain significance.

64. —— (1996*c*), 'Parę uwag o pierwszej gramatyce języka angielskiego wydanej w Polsce' (Some Remarks on the First English Grammar Published in Poland), *Języki Obce w Szkole*, 5: 395–8.

65. MARKOWSKI, A. (1991), 'Językowe kłopoty z AIDS' (Language Problems with AIDS), *PorJ* 7–8: 338–9.

66. —— (1992*a*), 'Nowsze anglicyzmy semantyczne w polszczyźnie' (Most Recent English Semantic Loanwords in Polish), *PorJ* 2: 165–9.

67. —— (1992*b*), 'Nowsze zapożyczenia w polszczyźnie: anglicyzmy gramatyczne i leksykalne' (Most Recent Borrowings in Polish: Grammatical and Lexical Anglicisms), *PorJ* 3: 237–41.

68. —— (1995), *Praktyczny słownik wyrazów obcych używanych w prasie, radiu i telewizji* (A Practical Dictionary of Foreign Words Used in the Press, Radio, and Television) (Warsaw: Twòj Styl).

This is a dictionary consisting of over one thousand loanwords most frequently used in the press, radio, and television in the 1990s; over one hundred lexical and semantic borrowings are of English origin.

69. MIODEK, J. (1971), 'Spór o *handicap*' (Dispute on *Handicap*), *PorJ* 4: 257–9.

70. —— (1983), *Rzecz o języku* (On Language) (Wrocław: Ossolineum).

Miodek discusses different changes in the Polish language, including the occurrence of a few anglicisms, like *handicap*, *o.k.* and *sparring partner*.

71. MOSZYŃSKI, L. (1975), 'Sposób przejmowania obcych dyftongów przez język polski' (The Method of Assimilation of Foreign Diphthongs in Polish), *PF* 25: 93–102.

Since Polish does not have diphthongs, those occurring in foreign words may be interpreted in different ways; for instance, English *cowboy* is pronounced [-ou-] whereas *clown* is rendered by [-au-].

72. MYSONA, M. and E. MARCINKOWSKA (1977), 'O zapożyczonych w języku polskim nazwach wyrobów skórzanych' (On Loanwords

Denoting Leather Products in Polish), *Przegląd Skórzany*, 32 (3): 77–81.

The authors are concerned with different loans (including anglicisms) denoting leather terms, like *obuwie Desty*, *obuwie Golfy*, both denoting different types of shoes.

73. OŻDŻYŃSKI, J. (1970), *Polskie słownictwo sportowe* (Polish Sports Terminology) (Wrocław: Ossolineum).

The book deals with Polish sports terms, including a number of English borrowings.

74. PARAFINOWICZ, Z. (1972/5), 'Niektóre obcojęzyczne nazwy rodzajów odzieży występujące w słownictwie odzieżowym' (On Some Borrowings Denoting Clothes Products), *Odzież*, 23: 373–6; 26 (1975): 353–7.

In a series of articles, Parafinowicz only enumerates and describes the meanings of several loanwords (including anglicisms) denoting 'clothing'.

75. PARYSKI, W. H. (1957), 'O wyrazach angielskich w gwarach spiskich i podkarpackich' (On English Words in the Dialects of Spisz and Podkarpaty), *JP* 37: 204–6.

76. PEPŁOWSKI, F. (1957), 'W sprawie *budżetu*' (On the Word *budżet*), *JP* 37: 202–4.

77. PISARKOWA, K. (1972), 'Nazwy nowoczesnych zespołów muzycznych (zespoły obce)' (The Names of Modern Music Groups—Foreign Groups), *Onomastica*, 17: 167–86.

Pisarkowa comments on the names of different music groups, most of them coined from English words.

78. PISARSKI, A. (1990), 'Some Problems of the Acceptance of Recent Borrowings of Hi-tech Terminology into Polish', unpublished paper delivered at the *SLE Annual Meeting*, Switzerland.

Despite the strong impact of English on Polish hi-tech terminology, it is hoped that in future Polish speakers will oppose this tendency as is already being seen in the field of computer terminology where more and more Polish words are being introduced.

79. PLUTA, F. (1971–2), 'Z badań nad słownictwem polskim w okresie II wojny światowej' (Research on Polish Lexis from the Period of

World War II), parts I and II, *Sprawozdania Opolskiego TPN*, 9: 55–74, 10: 29–62.

80. Przybylska, R. (1992), 'O współczesnych nazwach firm' (On Contemporary Names of Firms), *JP* 72: 138–50.

    Przybylska comments on different names of Polish firms focusing on names of English origin, like *The Best, All*, etc.

81. Ropa, A. (1974), 'O najnowszych zapożyczeniach' (On the Most Recent Borrowings), *PorJ* 7: 518–26.

    Ropa analyses some of the most recent English loanwords in Polish dealing with their formal and semantic assimilation.

82. Rybicka-Nowacka, H. (1967), 'W sprawie wyrazów obcych w języku polskim' (On Foreign Words in the Polish Language), *PorJ* 2: 93–8.

    The author discusses the adaptation of some borrowings, including anglicisms, on four levels of linguistic analysis.

83. —— (1976), *Losy wyrazów obcych w języku polskim* (The Future of Borrowings in the Polish Language) (Warsaw: PWN).

    The book is devoted to a detailed analysis of loanwords of various origins (including English).

84. Sawicka, G. (1995), 'Norma a problem tak zwanych "zapożyczeń"' (The Norm and the Problem of the So-called 'Borrowings'), *PorJ* 9–10: 78–84.

    It is argued that not only lexical items have been borrowed from English, but also some letters (e.g. *x* instead of Polish *ks*) and the morpheme -*'s*.

85. Schabowska, M. (1972), 'Apelatywizacja rzeczowników własnych na przykładzie wyrazów zapożyczonych do języka polskiego' (Appelativization of Proper Nouns Illustrated by Loanwords in Polish), in J. Zaleski (ed.), *Symbolae Polonicae in honorem Stanislai Jodłowski* (Wrocław), 155–64.

    Borrowings (mainly from English) formed from proper names, like *czester* 'a kind of cheese', are discussed.

86. Sieczkowski, A. (1948), 'Trolleybus', *PorJ* 1: 26–8.

87. Sieczkowski, E. (1956), 'O wymowie budżet i Kambod-ża' (On the pronunciation of *budżet* and *Kambod-ża*), *JP* 36: 388–90.

88. Steffen, A. (1972), 'Rozważania etymologiczne: *korman*, *noktajza*, "*krawat*"' (Etymological Considerations: *korman*, *noktajza* '*necktie*'), *JP* 52: 51–3.

Steffen discusses a couple of loanwords occurring in Polish dialects, including the anglicism *noktajza* < *necktie*, which was introduced by Polish emigrants.

89. Tekiel, D. (ed.) (1988–9), *Nowe słownictwo polskie. Materiały z prasy z lat 1972–82* (Recent Polish Vocabulary. Data from the Press 1972–82), parts I and II (Wrocław).

This is a list of neologisms and borrowings, each defined and accompanied by quotations from the press.

90. Tokarski, J. (1968), 'Język polski w pięćdziesięcioleciu' (The Polish Language in the 50s), *PorJ* 9: 428–41.

The article deals with the characteristics of the Polish language since 1918, including the influence of English. It is illustrated by a lengthy discussion of the borrowing *nylon* and the calque *drapacz chmur* < *skyscraper*.

91. Truszkowski, W. (1958), 'Hierarchizacja funkcji przyrostków wielofunkcyjnych na przykładzie przyrostka *-k* w wyrazach zapożyczonych' (The Hierarchy of the Functions of the Multifunctional Suffix *-k* in Borrowings), *JP* 38: 93–7.

The author discusses the word *uska* 'a bag from the USA' formed by adding the Polish suffix *-ka* to the abbreviation *U.S.*

92. Ułaszyn, H. (1957), 'Wojna i język. Słownictwo polskie z II wojny światowej' (War and Language. The Polish Lexis from World War II), *Rozprawy Komisji Językowej ŁTN*, 5: 7–41.

Ułaszyn presents the vocabulary used during World War II, also paying attention to anglicisms. The discussion is limited to a list of English borrowings and their semantic interpretation.

93. Walczak, B. (1983), 'The Earliest Borrowings from English into Polish', *SAP* 16: 121–33.

Walczak provides a list of about 180 English loans found in one of the oldest dictionaries of the Polish language, the *Vilnius Dictionary* from 1861. The linguist is particularly interested in their semantics.

94. Walczak-Asp, A. (1978), 'O neologizmach typu *dżinsówa, młodzieżówa* w języku polskim' (On Neologisms of the Type *dżinsówa, młodzieżówa* in Polish), *JP* 58: 346–52.

The article deals with word-formation in Polish including an analysis of the anglicism *dżins* < *jeans* and the Polish suffix *-owa*.

95. Wilczewska, K. (1970), 'O słownictwie współczesnej mody' (On the Vocabulary of Contemporary Fashion), *JP* 50: 97–109.

Wilczewska describes different terms denoting 'fashion', pointing to some anglicisms in this field. She claims that they are recent borrowings except *smoking*.

96. Wojciechowska, A. (1992), '*Kolegium* czy *college*' (*Kolegium* or *college*), *PorJ* 1: 83–8.

An argument whether one should use the assimilated Latin loan *kolegium* or the English borrowing *college* to denote recently introduced three years' teachers' training schools.

97. Wróblewski, K. (1991), '*Fan*—moda czy językowa konieczność' (*Fan*—Fashion or Linguistic Necessity), *PorJ* 3–4: 142–5.

It is claimed that the English loan *fan* should be used instead of the Polish word *wielbiciel*.

98. Zagrodnikowa, A. (1978), 'Nowe słownictwo w prasie: rodzaje, źródła, funkcje' (New Lexis in the Press: Types, Sources, Functions), *Zeszyty Prasoznawcze*, 19 (2): 9–28.

The author pays close attention to the analysis of loanwords, including anglicisms.

99. Zaręba, A. (1949), 'Nieco uwag o polskim słownictwie powojennym' (Some Remarks on Post-war Polish Vocabulary), *PJ* 29: 116–22.

A description of Polish during the first three years after World War II, mentioning the (very modest) influence of English.

100. Zarębina, M. (1974), 'Dystrybucja wyrazów zapożyczonych Panu Tadeuszu / na przyktadzie księgi VII' (The Distribution of Borrowings in *Pan Tadeusz*'s VIIth Book), *JP* 54: 388–94.

An analysis of a fifteenth century epic poem, which includes a single borrowing from English (*dżokej* < *jockey*).

Romanian (Ilinca Constantinescu and Ariadna Ştefănescu)

(see also *25, *63, *64)

ACIL-X — *Actes du Xe Congrès International des Linguistes, Bucarest (28 août–2 sept. 1967)* (Bucharest: Editions de l'Académie de la République Socialiste de Roumanie, 1969, 1970).

AUBFIL — *Analele Universităţii din Bucureşti, Seria Ştiinţe Sociale: Filologie* (Annals of the University of Bucharest, Social Science Series. Philology), Bucharest, 1964– .

AUT — *Analele Universităţii din Timişoara, Seria Ştiinţe Filologice* (Annals of the University of Timişoara, Philological Series), Timişoara, 1963– .

LL — *Limbă şi Literatură* (Language and Literature), Bucharest: SSF, 1955– .

LLR — *Limba şi Literatura Română* (Romanian Language and Literature), Bucharest: SSF, 1975– .

LR — *Limba Română* (The Romanian Language), Bucharest: Editura Academiei, 1952– .

RECAP — *The Romanian-English Contrastive Analysis Project*, Bucharest, 1971–84.

RRL — *Revue Roumaine de Linguistique*, Bucharest: Editura Academiei, 1956– .

SCL — *Studii şi Cercetări Lingvistice* (Linguistic Studies and Research), Bucharest: Editura Academiei, 1950– .

1. AVRAM, MIOARA (1975), 'Desinenţe pentru cuvinte străine în limba română contemporană' (Endings of Foreign Words in Contemporary Romanian), *SCL* 26: 319–24.

2. —— (1997), 'Anglicismele în limba română actuală' (Anglicisms in Contemporary Romanian), conference speech delivered at the Romanian Academy, February 13 (Bucharest: Editura Academiei), 31 pp.

The conference was devoted to the massive influx of anglicisms after 1989 (not looked upon as an 'attack' on the vernacular, but rather as compensating for the purist attitude favoured under the totalitarian regime). A vast range of problems was mentioned: from etymology (straight or multiple) to phonetic, graphic, and morphological adaptation; the semantics of anglicisms (e.g. loan translations; 'false friends', homonymic and paronymic collisions, semantic loans, phrasal borrowings, etc.), as well as lexical productivity and stylistics. Pertinent remarks on rich inventory of recent anglicisms and matters of usage.

3. BĂNCIULESCU, VICTOR (1984), *Limbajul sportiv. O investigație sentimentală* (Sports Language. A Sentimental Approach) (Bucharest: Editura Sport-Turism), 180 pp.

4. BANTAȘ, ANDREI (1977), 'A Bird's Eye-View of English Influences upon the Romanian Lexis', *Studia Anglica Posnaniensia*, 9: 119–33.

The author outlines the complexity of the phenomenon: from the different ways in which the influence was exerted—through the written language or orally, straight from the donor or mediated through another language (mostly French)—to problems of degrees of adaptation and of usage and misuse (embracing a wide range of aspects). This attempt to cover a great range of problems in a limited space is a starting point for further research regarding the English element in the Romanian lexis.

5. —— (1979), 'For Dictionaries of Foreign Influences', *Buletinul Științific al Institutului de Învățământ Superior Pitești*, 195–9.

6. —— (1981), 'The English Element Revisited', *Buletinul Științific al Institutului de Învățământ Superior Sibiu*, 85–105.

7. —— (1982), 'Aspects of Applied Semantics: For Modernizing Bilingual Dictionaries', *RRL* 27: 219–26.

This study briefly presents the specifics of different types of bilingual dictionaries. Besides the traditional types enumerated, it proposes a series of lexicons recording the influence of English, French, Spanish, Russian, German, etc. upon other languages. They should describe the history and particularly the contemporary status of foreignisms (e.g. of anglicisms). As regards the English element in Romanian, the nearly four thousand words, derivatives, compounds, and phrases involved point to a situation similar to that of *franglais* as Bantaș claims.

8. —— (1992), 'Mass media', *LR* 41: 131–3.

9. BANTAŞ, ANDREI, ILINCA CONSTANTINESCU, and PAULA ŞENDREA (1983), 'Observaţii pe marginea înregistrării cuvintelor de origine engleză în lucrări lexicografice româneşti' (Remarks on how Words of English Origin are Registered in Romanian Lexicographic Works), *SCL* 34: 543–8.

The continuous penetration of a great number of English words into Romanian vocabulary in the second half of this century is only to a small extent reflected in the general lexicographic works. Since usage varies and is often unstable, it raises many questions as to correctness. Studies devoted to the subject are partial (both in respect of topics and inventories considered). The study points out a number of directions that need further investigation (from etymology to translation accuracy). Mention is made of what specialists call the 're-Latinizing' of the Romanian lexis through the international scientific vocabulary of English conception.

10. —— and MIHAI RĂDULESCU (1967), *'Capcanele' vocabularului englez* ('Pitfalls' of the English Vocabulary) (Bucharest: Editura Ştiinţifică), 310 pp.

Formal resemblance of some words in English and Romanian often induces in the Romanian speaker the assumption that the respective lexical items are identical in meaning, too. Thus, tricky resemblances—especially in the case of words of Latin and Romance origin—lead to misuse. The authors try to make the learner aware of the 'pitfalls' of semantic differences in such cases. The work is structured in three parts: an English-Romanian dictionary (of approximately 1500 entries), a Romanian-English dictionary (of approximately 1100 entries), and an exercise section.

11. BĂNCILĂ, FLORICA and DUMITRU CHIŢORAN (1976), 'Remarks on the Morphological Adaptation of English Loanwords in Romanian', *AUBFIL* 25: 35–44.

Observations made on some four hundred anglicisms, mostly nouns, most of which are listed in the *Dicţionar de neologisme* (1966). Compared to the donor language, Romanian has a richer system of morphological marking. The adaptation of loanwords entails alterations and accommodation affecting mainly word-final segments. The role of semantic fields and of associative processes in gender assignment are pointed out. The semantic features of sex and animateness are of primary importance in the adaptation of English nouns to Romanian morphophonemic patterns.

12. ——— (1982), 'The English Element in Contemporary Romanian', in *Filipović (ed.), 378–420.

The analysis made by Băncilă and Chiţoran in 1976 is brought to the attention of anglicists from abroad, in an enriched and updated version. The factors influencing the distribution of nominal borrowings of English extraction into Romanian subclasses marked for gender are thoroughly described and commented.

13. BELCHIŢĂ, ANCA (1971), 'Some Aspects of the Contrastive Analysis of English and Romanian Morphophonemics', *RECAP* 2: 109–12.

14. —— (1972), 'The Contrastive Morphophonology of Romanian and English', *RECAP* (Monograph Series), 7–66.

15. BELCHIŢĂ-HARTULAR, ANCA (1982), 'Metalinguistic Remarks in a Linguistic Interview', *RRL* 27: 235–41.

The article contains data on the American-Romanian patois of immigrants to the USA.

16. BERINDEI, MIHAI (1976), *Dicţionar de jazz* (A Dictionary of Jazz) (Bucharest: Editura Ştiinţifică şi Enciclopedică), 292 pp.

The work gives in alphabetical order both short biographies of the most outstanding jazz musicians and jazz terminology up to the 1960s. The English pronunciation of the terms is given in IPA. If a term has been adapted, its Romanian pronunciation is added in parentheses.

17. BOGDAN, MIHAIL (1970), 'English Loanwords in Romanian', *ACIL-X* 4: 741–5.

The number of anglicisms borrowed directly from English (British or American) is greater than lexicographers were inclined to admit. Trofin's study on the adaptation of English sports terminology is compared with Romanian anglicisms from other spheres of activity (politics, banking, communications, architecture, clothing, recreation, etc.). The main morphological characteristics are briefly enumerated.

18. Bota, Maria (1978), 'Observaţii asupra morfologiei neologismelor de origine engleză în limba română literară' (Observations on the Morphology of English Neologisms in Romanian), *LL* 23: 34–8.

Bota describes the various morphological devices at work when English words are integrated into Romanian. Most of the borrowed nouns behave as neuters. The agglutination of the enclitic definite article is a sign of integration. Adjectives tend to get inflectional endings. Some anglicisms have an incomplete paradigm. In the case of verbs, there seems to be a tendency to use them mostly as past participles.

19. Bujeniţă, M. (1966), 'Din terminologia nautică românească. II. Termeni marinăreşti de origine engleză' (Romanian Maritime Language. II. Maritime Terms of English Origin), *LR* 15: 83–91.

Sixty-seven English nautical terms have entered the Romanian language owing to merchant navigation—some at the end of the nineteenth century. In this field there was direct English-Romanian contact, prior to the intermediary function of French in other domains.

20. Buzdugan, Gheorghe (1994), 'Un neologism mai dificil: design' (A Rather Difficult Neologism: Design), *Academica*, 4: 24–5.

21. Candrea, I.-Aurel and Gh. Adamescu (1926–31), *Dicţionarul enciclopedic ilustrat* (Illustrated Encyclopedic Dictionary) (Bucharest: Editura Cartea românească).

22. Chiţoran, Dumitru (1980), 'Studiile de anglistică la Universitatea din Bucureşti' (English Studies at Bucharest University), in *Momente din istoria învăţământului limbilor străine la Universitatea din Bucureşti* (Bucharest: Universitatea din Bucureşti), 89–99.

23. —— (1986), 'The English Element in Romanian: A Case Study in Linguistic Borrowing', in *Viereck and Bald (eds.), 287–307.

The author sketches the complex language history of Romanian and the high degree of assimilation of loanwords which explains the great number of foreign words with multiple etymologies; before 1945 English words used to be transmitted through French, but their form does not permit a clear account of the paths of borrowing. Since 1945, subject areas and often the form of loanwords make a classification as anglicisms much easier, as Chiţoran's detailed phonemic and morphological analysis shows in a chapter which is the most comprehensive and insightful account devoted to the topic to date. The article thus covers a variety of aspects: from a general characterization of the structure of the Romanian vocabulary to the expanding place occupied since World War II by the English element. Previous studies dealing with anglicisms are reviewed. After placing in a proper perspective the specific features of English borrowings into Romanian, the author proceeds to a linguistic analysis of the process of penetration. Most of the space is allotted to phonetic and phonological considerations. The part devoted to morphology is mainly on gender assignment with nouns, outlining noticeable tendencies. A few semantic aspects are briefly enumerated in the final section.

24. —— James E. Augerot, and Hortensia Pârlog (eds.) (1984), *The Sounds of English and Romanian, RECAP* (Bucharest: Bucharest University Press), 158 pp.

25. Ciobanu, Georgeta (1983), 'Adaptarea fonetică a cuvintelor româneşti de origine engleză' (The Phonetic Adaptation of Romanian Words of English Origin), unpublished D.Phil. thesis (Bucharest University).

A first systematic approach to the intricacies of phonetic (and graphic) adaptation of anglicisms to Romanian patterns, based on the careful analysis of a great number of words borrowed from English in various domains.

26. —— (1990), 'The English Element in Romanian—the Phonetic Level', in *Filipović (ed.), 358–63. (EEEL 4).

27. —— (1991), 'Phonological Adaptation of Anglicisms in Romanian', in *Filipović (ed.), 30–58.

Since the essential factor determining the structure of an English loanword is the phonological system of the receiving language, the author focussed her attention on transphonemization. Tape-recorded material was analysed in order to account for peculiarities of the transfer in the vowel system, the consonant system, accentual patterns, and syllable division. The pronunciation given in some of the Romanian dictionaries is compared with the data in the corpus. This contains many English borrowings introduced by the mass media not yet included in dictionaries.

28. CIOBANU, GEORGETA (1996), *Anglicisme în limba română* (Anglicisms in the Romanian language) (Timişoara: Editura Amphora), 135 pp.

The first Romanian book listing alphabetically a representative inventory of anglicisms, with comments on meaning, pronunciation, gender assignment, and etymology. The anglicisms were extracted from the main dictionaries published during the last four decades, newspapers, magazines, almanacs, and articles published in linguistic journals, as well as from oral sources (including mass media). Set phrases and phraseological units are also registered, as their number keeps increasing in present-day Romanian. Words pertaining to highly specialized terminologies are not included. Although descriptive in its presentation, the work is prescriptive in intent and effect. It relies on a thorough linguistic analysis of the data and will contribute to the correct usage of hundreds of recent anglicisms. Its reader-friendly form hides the great amount of work incorporated.

29. —— (1997*a*), *Adaptation of the English Element in Romanian* (Timişoara: Editura Mirton), 212 pp.

30. —— (1997*b*), *Romanian Words of English Origin* (Timişoara: Editura Amphora), 144 pp.

31. CONSTANTINESCU, ILINCA (1972), 'Influenţa limbii engleze în vocabularul sportiv românesc, I.' (The English Influence on Romanian Sports Vocabulary), *LR* 21: 527–37.

A summary of previous opinions on anglicisms in Romanian sports terminology. Though French often served as an intermediary, this is not the case with the entire sports lexis. The author discusses about one hundred words (and derivatives) of wide circulation, adapted phonetically and morphologically. Most of them have been included in dictionaries of contemporary Romanian or, at least, have attracted the attention of modern linguists.

32. —— (1973), 'Influenţa limbii engleze în vocabularul sportiv românesc, II. & III.', *LR* 22, 1: 25–35; 22, 2: 109–17.

A continuation of her 1972 article adding words with a technical character. A hundred lexical items taken from dictionaries, scientific articles, and the newspaper *Sportul* of the 1960s have their etymology, meaning, usage peculiarities, and derivative force pointed out. A last category discussed is that of 'journalistic anglicisms' encompassing less integrated borrowings. Some of these are terms used in games not practised in Romania, others are merely equivalents for existing words, picked up by sportswriters in order to give more colour to their comments. The study ends with generalized remarks on the process and phases of integration and a few prescriptive recommendations (some invalidated by further usage developments).

33. —— (1989), 'Asimilarea numelor proprii englezeşti în limba română' (On the Adaptation of English Names in Romanian), *SCL* 40: 219–23.

34. Coteanu, Ion and Marius Sala (1987), *Etimologia şi limba română* (Etymology and the Romanian Language) (Bucharest: Editura Academiei Republicii Socialiste România), 160 pp.

35. Diaconovici, C. (1889–94), *Enciclopedia română* (Romanian Encyclopedia) (3 vols. Sibiu: Editura şi tiparul lui W. Krafft).

36. *Dicţionarul explicativ al limbii române* (An Explanatory Dictionary of the Romanian Language) (1975) (Bucharest: Institutul de Lingvistică din Bucureşti, Editura Academiei Republicii Socialiste România), 1049 pp. [DEX1].

37. —— (²1996), (Bucharest: Institutul de Lingvistică 'Jorgu Jordan', Univers Enciclopedic), 1192 pp. [DEX2].

38. *Dicţionarul limbii române* (Dictionary of the Romanian Language) (1913–2000), (14 vols. Bucharest: Academia Română). Librăriile Socec & Comp. şi C. Sfetea / Monitorul Oficial şi Imprimeriile Statului / Editura Academiei. [DA/DLR].

39. *Dicţionarul limbii române moderne* (The Dictionary of Modern Romanian) (1958) (Bucharest: Editura Academiei Republicii Populare Române). [DLRM].

40. *Dicţionarul ortografic, ortoepic şi morfologic al limbii române* (An Orthographical, Orthoepical and Morphological Dictionary of the Romanian Language) (1982), (Bucharest: Institutul de Lingvistică al Universităţii Bucureşti, Editura Academiei Republicii Socialiste România), 696 pp. [DOOM].

41. DIMITRESCU, FLORICA (1975), 'Un "verbum vicarium": a realiza "réaliser"', *RRL* 20: 333–6.

In Romanian the verb *a realiza* 'to achieve, to accomplish, to finish successfully' has developed many new meanings, tending to be used instead of a large number of existent verbs. The senses 'to grasp or understand clearly; to become aware of' come from English. For other meanings French was the source or at least the intermediary.

42. —— (1980), 'Impact', *LR* 29: 201–4.

Usage and misuse of borrowed meanings of the word *impact* are brought to the attention of the Romanian speaker.

43. —— (1982), *Dicţionar de cuvinte recente* (Dictionary of Recent Words) (Bucharest: Editura Albatros), 536 pp. [DCR].

44. —— (1993), 'Etimologia sensurilor noi' (The Etymology of New Meanings), *SCL* 44: 211–16.

Recent semantic loans from French and English are discussed.

45. —— (1995), *Dinamica lexicului românesc* (The Dynamics of Romanian Lexis) (Cluj-Napoca: Editura Clusium-Logos), 336 pp.

46. DRAGOŞ, CLARA LILIANA (1996), *Anglia—model în cultura română modernă (1800–1850)* (England—a Model for Modern Romanian Culture (1800–1850)) (Bucharest: Editura Tehnică), 184 pp.

47. DUMITRIU, GETA (1987), 'English Studies at the University of Bucharest', *Analele Universităţii Bucureşti. Limbi şi literaturi străine*, 36: 61–75.

The author reviews a variety of papers (on language, literature, culture, and civilization) and recollections of the beginnings of teaching English presented on the occasion of the 1986 jubilee celebrating the introduction of English studies at the University of Bucharest.

48. GHEŢIE, ION (1957), 'Observaţii asupra limbii folosite în "Sportul popular"' (Remarks on the Language Used in 'Sportul Popular'), *LR* 4: 19–25.

The author has a prescriptive attitude, advocating Romanian phonetic spelling of neologisms, including anglicisms (e.g. *iaht-*

ing, *iolă*, *rugbi*, *snaip*). Anglicisms easily rendered through equivalent words or expressions in Romanian should be avoided. Words like *corner*, *penalti*, *draw*, *fair*, *out-sider*, *sparing-partener*, *daviscupman* often used in the newspaper *Sportul popular* are considered unnecessary.

49. GRAUR, A. (1963), *Etimologii românești* (Romanian Etymologies) (Bucharest: Editura Academiei Republicii Populare Române).

50. —— (1967), *The Romance Character of Romanian* (Bucharest: Publishing House of the Academy of the Socialist Republic of Romania), 75 pp.

51. —— (1968), *Tendințele actuale ale limbii române* (Present-day Tendencies of the Romanian Language) (Bucharest: Editura Științifică), 439 pp.

52. —— (1969), 'Alternanțe sp/șp, st/șt' (The Alternation sp/șp, st/șt), *SCL* 20: 335–7.

53. GRUIȚĂ, MARIANA (1974), 'Adaptarea cuvintelor de origine engleză la sistemul fonetic și ortografic al limbii române actuale' (The Adaptation of Words of English Origin to the Phonetic and Orthographic System of Present-Day Romanian), *LL* 19: 51–7.

The study of the phonetic adaptation of loanwords according to the spelling or pronunciation of the English word analyses the 'accidental phonetic adaptation' and indirectly proves that the 'accidental' character is motivated by some specific occurrences of consonantic clusters or diphthongs in Romanian, by the pressure of other Romanian words, by morphological constraints, by indirect borrowing or by hypercorrectness. The rebirth of anglophilia in the seventies diminished the number of indirect borrowings so that nowadays the adaptation follows more and more the phonetic form of the English word.

54. HANEA, VICTOR (1963), 'Referiri la limba engleză în opera lui Timotei Cipariu' (References to the English Language in Timotei Cipariu's Work), *AUBFIL* 12: 25–30.

55. HRISTEA, THEODOR (1968*a*), *Probleme de etimologie* (Problems of Etymology) (Bucharest: Editura Științifică), 384 pp.

56. Hristea, Theodor (1968*b*), 'Conceptul de "hipercorectitudine". Hipercorectitudinea latentă' (The Concept of 'Hypercorrection': Latent Hypercorrection), in Hristea (1968*a*), 277–86.

The concept of hypercorrection is illustrated through anglicisms beginning with the sounds [sp] often pronounced [ʃp], as in words of German origin, by Romanians who do not know English. As knowledge of English spreads, the correct [sp] forms tend to replace the hypercorrect ones. A number of English names are misspelt by using the letter *w* for the sound [v]. Hypercorrection accounts for these forms, too.

57. —— (1972*a*), 'Împrumuturi şi creaţii lexicale neologice în limba română contemporană' (Borrowings and Neologistic Lexical Coinages in Contemporary Romanian), *LR* 21: 185–98.

Lexical borrowings in contemporary Romanian are discussed in general. Foreign words (including anglicisms) have entered Romanian mainly via French.

58. —— (1972*b*), 'Observaţii asupra folosirii neologismelor în limba română contemporană' (On the Use of Neologisms in Contemporary Romanian), *LL* 17: 591–605.

The article contains prescriptive recommendations as to how some neologisms should be used in Romanian (among them anglicisms such as *smash*, *safe*, *game*).

59. —— (1974), 'Pseudoanglicisme de provenienţă franceză în limba română' (Pseudo-Anglicisms of French Origin), *LR* 23: 61–71.

Hristea discusses the words *tenisman/-ă*, *cupman*, *Daviscupman*, *recordman/-ă*, *vatman* and *handbal* (with their written and oral variants) refuting the current opinion put forward in dictionaries and articles that they are anglicisms. *Handbal* comes from German, because the game originated in Germany, while the others, non-existent as such in English, were coined in French with English morphemes.

60. —— (1975*a*), 'Un nou element de compunere: *-averaj*' (A New Element of Composition: *-averaj*), *SCL* 26: 375–9.

61. —— (1975*b*), 'Calcul internaţional' (The International Calque), *SCL* 26: 499–504.

62. —— (1977), 'Contribuţii la studiul etimologic al frazeologiei

românești moderne' (Contributions to the Etymologic Study of Modern Romanian Phraseology), *LR* 25: 588–92.

Most of the phrases of English origin were probably taken through the mediation of other languages (French, German, Italian, Russian). Hristea illustrates in this article the concept of 'multiple etymology' and discusses semantic loans from this viewpoint.

63. —— (1978*a*), 'Neologisme de proveniență engleză' (Neologisms of English Extraction), *România literară*, 18: 19: 588–92.

64. —— (1978*b*), 'Romanian Vocabulary and Etymology', in A. Rosetti and Sanda Golopenția-Eretescu (eds.), *Current Trends in Romanian Linguistics* (Revue roumaine de linguistique 23; Cahiers de linguistique téorique et appliquée 15; Bucharest: Editura Academiei Republicii Socialiste România), 203–54.

65. —— (1978*c*), 'Anglicisme reale și aparente' (Real and Seeming Anglicisms), *România literară*, 50: 8.

66. —— ([3]1984), *Sinteze de limba română* (Syntheses of the Romanian Language) (Bucharest: Editura Albatros), 384 pp.

67. Iarovici, Edith (1967), 'Unele aspecte ale influenței limbii engleze asupra limbii românilor din SUA' (Some Aspects of the Influence Exerted by English on the Language of the Romanians Residing in USA), *AUBFIL* 16: 223–38.

68. —— and Rodica Mihăilă (1970), 'Introduction to a Contrastive Analysis of the English and Romanian Vocabularies', *Analele Universității București. Limbi germanice*, 19: 23–37.

69. —— and Rodica Mihăilă-Cova (1979), *Lexicul de bază al limbii engleze. Dicționar contrastiv* (Lexicon of Basic English. A Contrastive Dictionary) (Bucharest: Editura științifică și enciclopedică), 680 pp.

This bilingual dictionary lists about 2700 English words selected mainly from *A General Service List of English Words* by Michael West (London, 1959). On the basis of a rigorous contrastive analysis of both form and meaning the following classes and subclasses of equivalences are established: cognates, diversified cognates, diversified partial cognates, deceptive cognates, partly deceptive cognates, different forms and identical meanings, different forms and partly identical meanings, different forms and diversified meanings. The words are then classified according to the predicted degree of difficulty.

70. IORDAN, IORGU ([2]1947), *Limba română actuală. O gramatică a 'greşelilor'* (Present-day Romanian. A Grammar of 'Errors') (Bucharest: Editura Socec), 540 pp.

71. —— (1956), *Limba română contemporană* (Contemporary Romanian) (Bucharest: Editura Ministerului Învăţământului), 831 pp.

72. LIUTAKOVA, RUMIANA (1993*a*), 'Trăsături specifice ale împrumuturilor englezeşti în limbile română şi bulgară' (Specific Features of English Loanwords in Romanian and in Bulgarian), *SCL* 44: 151–62.

The article contains more than one hundred anglicisms found both in Romanian and in Bulgarian. Formal differences are due to phonetic differences between the two receiving languages. By transcribing them in the Cyrillic alphabet anglicisms sooner acquire a standardized form in Bulgarian, as compared to Romanian. Semantic differences are accounted for by different intermediary languages.

73. —— (1993*b*), 'English Loan-Words in Romanian and Bulgarian', *Zeitschrift der Germanisten Rumäniens*, 2: 62–3.

74. MACREA, D. (1942), 'Circulaţia cuvintelor în limba română' (Currency of Romanian Words), *Transilvania*, 73: 268 *et seq*.

75. —— (1961), *Probleme de lingvistică română* (Problems of Romanian Linguistics) (Bucharest: Editura Ştiinţifică), 30–5.

76. MANOLESCU, ZOIA (1990), 'Proportions of the English Element in Contemporary Romanian', in *Filipović (ed.), 120–5. (EEEL 4).

Recent English borrowings are analysed on the basis of counts made on six letters of *DEX* (1975) and its *Supplement* (1988). A comparison is drawn with the data found under the same letters (i.e. C, S, Ş, Q, W, Y) in two general dictionaries of the Romanian language published half a century earlier, namely L. Şăineanu, *Dicţionar universal al limbii române* (1929), I. A. Candrea and G. Adamescu, *Dicţionar enciclopedic ilustrat al limbii române* (1931). The figures show that the English element is on the increase.

77. —— (1999), *The English Element in Contemporary Romanian* (Bucharest: Conspress), 291 pp.

The work is the result of research carried out for the doctoral degree. In order to draw up the inventory of the English words borrowed into Romanian the main dictionaries were analysed starting with the first modern dictionary published in 1898 and continuing up to the mid-1990s. The vocabulary of some newspapers from the last decade was also examined. Statistics and counts (in domains) substantiate the conclusions. The author lists 3,820 anglicisms (including acronyms, pseudo-anglicisms and semantic loans—all of them representing 'the English element in contemporary Romanian').

78. MARCU, FLORIN (1997), *Noul dicționar de neologisme* (The New Dictionary of Neologisms). Bucharest: Editura Academiei Române, 1556 pp.

A considerable number of anglicisms are recorded. The work does not mention the dates of their introduction.

79. —— and CONSTANT MANECA (1961, ^{2}1966, ^{3}1978), *Dicționar de neologisme* (Dictionary of Neologisms) (Bucharest: Editura Academiei Republicii Socialiste România). [DN].

80. MOCIORNIȚĂ, MARIA (1980), 'Momente premergătoare semnificative pentru instituirea învățământului universitar de limbă engleză' (Important Moments in the History of Teaching English at the University), in *Momente din istoria învățământului limbilor străine la Universitatea din București* (Bucharest: Universitatea din București), 83–8.

The article surveys the most important Anglo-Romanian cultural contacts preceding the introduction of English studies in the university curricula of Jassy (1917), Cluj (1921), and Bucharest (1936). Credit is given to N. Iorga for his historiographic studies: *Les premières relations entre l'Angleterre et les Pays Roumains (1427–1611)* and *Histoire des relations anglo-roumaines* published in 1913 and, respectively, 1917. Other research done in Romania and Great Britain reveals interesting data regarding literature, religion, travelogues, history, and politics.

81. MOCIORNIŢĂ, MARIA (1983), 'Romanian-English Cultural Relations in the 16th and 17th Centuries', in Ioan Aurel Preda (ed.), *English Literature and Civilization. The Renaissance and the Restoration Period* (Bucharest: Editura Didactică şi Pedagogică), 188–92, 211–13.

82. —— (1992), 'Contacte anglo-române: un incitant domeniu de cercetare' (Anglo-Romanian Contacts: A Challenging Research Subject), *Comunicările 'Hyperion'*, 124–32.

83. MUNTEANU, ŞTEFAN and ŢÂRA, VASILE D. (1983), *Istoria limbii române literare* (History of the Romanian Literary Language) (Bucharest: Editura Didactică şi Pedagogică), 372 pp.

84. OLOS, ANA (1974), 'Numele proprii englezeşti în limba română' (English Names in the Romanian Language), *LR* 23: 201–3.

According to the recommendations regarding the written form of foreign names dating from the beginning of the nineteenth century (and reinforced thereafter), the original spelling of a name should be retained. English personal names are very difficult to read by native speakers of Romanian who are used to a phonetic writing system. English nouns are more amenable to orthographic and/or phonetic adjustments than names. There are brief suggestions for a guidebook to the pronunciation of English names.

85. PĂDUREANU, OCTAV (1946), *Anglo-Romanian and Romanian-English Bibliography* (Bucharest: Monitorul Oficial şi Imprimeriile Statului, Imprimeria Naţională).

86. PÂRLOG, HORTENSIA (1971), 'Termeni de origine engleză în publicistica română contemporană' (Terms of English Origin in Present-Day Romanian Periodicals), *AUT* 9: 55–68.

The author's attention is focused on the increasing influence of the English language on Romanian, documented in newspaper articles in the 1970s. Examples are taken from the weekly *Contemporanul* and the daily *Scânteia*. About 213 words and phrases (in 550 occurrences) were found in materials dealing with film, theatre, TV, music, the arts, science and technology, social and political life, fashion, sports, and varia. Of the 213 words and phrases only thirty-five are recorded in *Dicţionarul limbii române moderne* (1958) and *Dicţionar de neologisme* (1961). The author points out the tendency to use English spelling even for borrowings that have already been considered by lexicographers to have been adapted to Romanian orthography (i.e. *jazz/jaz*, *sketch/scheci*, *interview/interviu*, *leader/lider*, etc.). Some English loanwords are considered unnecessary because they have perfect equivalents in Romanian (e.g. *show/spectacol*, *step by step/pas cu pas*). A few remarks are made on Romanian derivatives from anglicisms (such as the adjectives *clown+esc*, *jazz+istic*, or the nouns *hobby+iști*, *kidnap+ist*). An alphabetic list of 160 anglicisms makes clear what each word means in English and then gives a short syntagmatic illustration of the way it was used in the excerpted Romanian newspapers.

87. —— (1972), 'The Auditory Discrimination of the English Element in Contemporary Romanian', *RECAP* 3: 89–101.

88. —— (1973*a*), 'The Interpretation of the English Velar Nasal by Romanian Speakers', *RECAP* 4: 86–92.

89. —— (1973*b*), 'Some Remarks on the Disyllabic Structures in English and Romanian', *RECAP* 4: 105–23.

90. —— (1976), 'Romanian and English Stops. A Contrastive Analysis', *RECAP* 7: 341–53.

91. —— (1977), 'The Interpretation of the English Interdental Fricatives by Romanian Speakers of English', *AUT* 15: 1663–8.

92. —— (1978), 'Monosyllabic Structures in English and Romanian', *AUT* 16: 129–41.

93. —— (1983), 'English Loanwords in Romanian', in *Sajavaara (ed.), 241–53.

The paper contains remarks on the various degrees of linguistic integration into Romanian of neologisms of English origin collected mainly from newspapers in the 1970s and early 1980s. Only those (ca. 140) borrowings have been considered which are not found in such reference works as *Dicționarul explicativ al limbii române* (1975) or in *Dicționar de neologisme* (1978), most of them nouns. A first step towards the morphological integration of nouns is their use with determinatives. The author analyses, on the basis of examples, the way in which a) a demonstrative adjective, b) the adjectival phrase *așa-numitul*, or c) some qualitative adjectives indicate in their inflected forms the gender, the number or the case of substantial anglicisms in a given Romanian context. Further morphological adaptation is shown by their use with the articles (indefinite and definite) and finally, their use with inflexional endings specific to Romanian. Most of the borrowed nouns are characterized as inanimate and accordingly neuter. Many pertinent remarks are made on a variety of aspects related to the behaviour of anglicisms in an inflected language such as Romanian.

94. PÂRLOG, HORTENSIA (1993), 'On Politeness in English and Romanian', *Studii de limbi şi literaturi moderne*, 140–51.

95. POPOVICI, DAN (1992), *Good Friends, False Friends Dictionary. Dicţionar de cuvinte asemănătoare în limbile engleză şi română* (Bucharest: Editura Sigma), 126 pp.

96. RAEVSKI, N. and M. GABINSKI (eds.) (1987), *Scurt dicţionar etimologic al limbii moldoveneşti* (A Short Etymological Dictionary of the Moldavian Language) (Kishinev: Redacţia principală a enciclopediei sovietice moldoveneşti), 678 pp. [SDEM].

97. ŞANDRU-OLTEANU, TUDORA (1993), '"Americanismele" din Diccionario de la lengua española (ediţia a 21-a)', *SCL* 44: 87–92.

98. SCHWEICKHARD, WOLFGANG (1986), '*Etimologie distinctivă*. Methodische Überlegungen zur Herkunftsbestimmung neuerer Entlehnungen des Rumänischen am Beispiel des sportsprachlichen Vokabulars', in Gunter Holtus and Edgar Radtke (eds.), *Rumänistik in der Diskussion. Sprache, Literatur und Geschichte* (Tübinger Beiträge zur Linguistik: 259; Tübingen: Narr), 129–63.

Phonetic, morphological, semantic, and extralinguistic criteria are proposed for distinguishing between anglicisms borrowed straight from English and those taken via French. The study is based on a rich bibliography devoted to etymology in general and to Romanian sports terminology in particular.

99. SECHE, LUIZA (1974), 'Englezisme terminate în *-ing* folosite în presă' (Anglicisms Ending in *-ing* in Newspapers), *Presa noastră*, 20: 43–5.

100. —— and MIRCEA SECHE (1965), 'Despre adaptarea neologismelor în limba română literară' (On the Adaptation of Neologisms in Literary Romanian), *LR* 13: 678–87.

The authors analyse six thousand neologisms attested in Romanian in the eighteenth and nineteenth centuries. Parallel forms are explained as borrowings from more than one donor language, or adaptations to the native phonetic system. Sometimes also folk etymology and hypercorrection are at work. Neological variants are usually monosemic. In the nineteenth and twentieth centuries most foreign words came via French.

101. Seche, Mircea (1959), 'Despre stilul sportiv' (On Sports Language), *LR* 2: 80–98.

The language of sports publications starting with the first Romanian periodical in the field, *Sportul*, dating back to 1880 has its peculiarities. The vocabulary was soon enriched with foreign words—anglicisms among them. The adaptation of lexical loans to the phonetic spelling of Romanian contributed to the integration of the borrowings. Other aspects, such as derivation, semantic loans, synonymy, polysemy, and metonymic usage are also considered.

102. Stoichițoiu, Adriana (1986), 'A Functional Approach to the Study of Recent English Borrowings in Romanian', *Analele Universității București. LLR* 35: 84–92.

103. —— (1992), 'Împrumuturi "necesare" şi împrumuturi "de lux" în limbajul publicistic actual' ('Necessary' Loanwords and 'Luxury' Loanwords in Present-Day Journalese), *Comunicările 'Hyperion'*, 169–76.

Recent English and French borrowings are interpreted from a functional perspective, taking into account the complex interplay of the socio-cultural, psychological, and linguistic factors involved in the acceptance and diffusion of such words in contemporary journalism. There are distinguished technical (denotative) vs. stylistic (connotative) borrowings. The assimilation of a borrowed word can be speeded up if it is a common word or may be slowed down if it is a technical term, or a borrowing meant to suggest a foreign cultural context.

104. Stoichițoiu-Ichim, Adriana (1993), 'Anglomania—o formă de snobism lingvistic' (Anglomania—A Form of Linguistic Snobbism), *Comunicările 'Hyperion'*, 2: 270–80.

105. Stoichiţoiu-Ichim, Adriana (1996), 'Observaţii privind influenţa engleză în limbajul publicistic actual (I; II)' (Notes Regarding the English Influence on Contemporary Journalese), *LLR* 2: 37–46; 3/4: 25–34.

106. —— (1997), 'Influenţa engleză în limbajul presei actuale: o perspectivă normativă' (The Influence of English on the Language of Present-Day Newspapers: A Prescriptive View), *Comunicările 'Hyperion'*, 6: 167–81.

107. Ştefănescu-Drăgăneşti, Virgil (1966), 'Comparaţie între sistemul fonologic al limbii engleze şi cel al limbii române' (A Comparison Between the English Phonological System and the Romanian One), *AUBFIL* 15: 285–96.

108. Tătaru, Ana (1961), 'Despre unele vocale ale limbii engleze privite comparativ cu vocalele limbii române' (On Comparing Some English Vowels to the Romanian Ones), *Cercetări de lingvistică*, 2: 339–49.

109. —— (1967), 'Consoanele oclusive în limba engleză şi în limba română' (Occlusive Consonants in English and Romanian), *Cercetări de lingvistică*, 2: 215–23.

110. —— (1978), *The Pronunciation of Romanian and English: Two Basic Contrastive Analyses* (Frankfurt am Main: Haag Kerchen), xxviii + 211 pp.

111. Teleagă, Maria (1986), 'Influenţa limbii engleze asupra limbajului românesc de management şi marketing' (The Influence of English on the Romanian Language of Management and Marketing), *Studii de limbi şi literaturi străine*, 106–8.

112. Trofin, Aurel (1967), 'Observaţii cu privire la adaptarea terminologiei de origine engleză în limba română' (Notes Regarding the Adaptation of Terminology of English Origin in Romanian), *Studia Universitatis Babeş-Bolyai. Series Philologia*, 2: 125–30.

Analysing the lexis of sports, the author disagrees with those linguists who maintained that all English borrowings came via French. Therefore one should study the history of each discipline in order to ascertain whether an anglicism was taken over directly or not. In a number of cases the presence of an English term in French (and in the international vocabulary) contributed to the survival of the borrowing in Romanian. One may notice the tendency to re-anglicize the spelling of some early neologisms.

113. —— (1975), 'Istoria anglisticii româneşti—privire specială asupra predării limbii engleze în România' (History of English Studies—Research on the Teaching of English in Romania), unpublished D.Phil. thesis (Cluj-Napoca), 198 pp.

114. ULIVI, ANCA (1973), 'Notes on the Consonant [ŋ] in Romanian and English', *RECAP* 4: 74–85.

115. VASILE, ECATERINA (1994), 'Influenţe româno-americane în lexicul românesc' (Romanian-American Influences on the Romanian Vocabulary), *LLR* 23: 9–10.

116. VASILIU, EMANUEL (1965), *Fonologia limbii române* (The Phonology of the Romanian Language) (Bucharest: Editura Ştiinţifică), 150 pp.

Russian (Tamara Maximova and Helen Pelikh)

(see also *45)

Étimologicheskie issledovaniya po russkomu yazyku (Etymological studies of the Russian language) Moscow.

1. ARISTOVA, V. M. (1980), 'Anglo-russkie yazykovye kontakty i zaimstvovaniya' (Anglo-Russian Linguistic Contacts and Borrowing), unpublished Ph.D. thesis (Leningrad), 400 pp.

The author investigates English loanwords which first appeared in the sixteenth to twentieth centuries, taking into account the history and culture of the two nations. She gives a detailed semantic classification and then considers different semantic changes that cause the adoption of anglicisms in Russian: 1) they enlarge synonymic groups; 2) they often replace long word combinations or compound words; 3) they are sometimes more specific than Russian synonyms; and 4) they either make Russian synonyms archaic or become archaic themselves.

2. —— (1985), *Angliĭskie slova v russkom yazyke* (English Words in the Russian Language) (Kaliningrad: Kaliningradskiĭ gosudarstvennyĭ universitet), 105 pp.

The author considers 1) problems of language contacts; 2) forms of borrowing (words, word-combinations, calques); and 3) the evolution of English loanwords in Russian. She distinguishes between grammatical and semantic types of evolution, stating that all English words undergo grammatical adaptation regardless of whether analogous categories exist in English or not. After a while loanwords tend to acquire certain meanings and connotations due to Russian usage.

3. ARKAD'EVA, É. V. (1974), 'Iz istorii nekotorykh zaimstvovannykh slov v russkom yazyke' (On the History of some Loanwords in the Russian Language), *Russkiĭ yazyk v shkole*, 2: 106–10.

The author provides detailed word histories of some borrowed words including anglicisms and states that in the course of time loanwords undergo both semantic and stylistic changes.

4. AVAKOVA, A. S. (1976), 'Naimenovanie sportsmenov—igrokov v

sovremennom russkom yazyke' (Terms for Sportsmen—Players in Contemporary Russian), *Étimologicheskie issledovaniya po russkomu yazyku, vypusk*, 8: 15–29.

Avakova gives a detailed account of the impact of a group of anglicisms on the Russian language. She divides all sports terms into two groups—proper terms and those which are accepted into general use.

5. AVILOVA, N. S. (1967), *Slova internatsional'nogo proiskhozhdeniya v russkom literaturnom yazyke novogo vremeni* (Words of International Origin in the Contemporary Russian Literary Language) (Moscow), 244 pp.

6. BABKIN, A. M. and V. V. SHENDETSOV (1992), *Slovar' inoyazychnykh slov i vyrazheniĭ, upotreblyayushchikhsya v russkom yazyke bez perevoda* (Dictionary of Foreign Words and Expressions Employed in the Russian Language without Translation), (3 vols., St. Petersburg), 1344 pp.

The dictionary is compiled on the basis of more than a hundred thousand citations, selected from scientific, periodical, high, and trivial literature from the nineteenth century onwards. It includes foreign words and phrases (including English) used without translations. The source of borrowings, their domains, stylistic, and grammatical features are indicated.

7. BASH, L. M. (1989), 'Differentsiatsiya termina "zaimstvovanie": khronologicheskie i étimologicheskie aspekty' (Differentiation of the Term 'Loanword': Chronological and Etymological Aspects), *Vestnik Moskovskogo universiteta*, seriya 9, Filologiya, 4: 22–34.

Bash divides all loanwords into borrowings and quasi-borrowings, and gives a detailed description of each group. The author's method seems to be reliable and applicable to loanwords in all languages.

8. BELYAEVA, S. A. (1984*a*), *Angliĭskie slova v russkom yazyke XVI–XX vv* (English Words in the Russian Language of the 16th–20th Centuries) (Vladivostok), 108 pp.

The author investigates some peculiarities of lexico-semantic adaptation of anglicisms analysing about two thousand words selected from dictionaries and newspapers. There are 'ups and downs' in the spread of anglicisms. According to the degree of assimilation three main types of loanwords can be distinguished: unassimilated, partially assimilated, and fully assimilated. Each type is characterized in detail.

9. Belyaeva, S. A. (1984*b*), 'Izmenenie stilisticheskikh kharakteristik kak pokazatel' stepeni semanticheskoĭ assimilyatsii zaimstvovannogo slova' (Stylistic Changes Indicating the Steps of Semantic Assimilation of the Loanword), *Filologicheskie Nauki*, 2: 78–80.

In their assimilation loanwords undergo many changes, including stylistic ones. These are closely connected with semantic changes in the receptor language. Their use in different contexts leads to various stylistic characteristics: from neutral to negative, from positive to ironical, etc. All the claims are well illustrated.

10. Benson, Morton (1958), 'English Loanwords in Russian Sports Terminology', *American Speech*, 33: 252–9.

English loanwords in Russian sports terminology are either generally used in present-day Russian sports literature or also (rarely) used in present-day standard Russian. The more widely used Russian equivalents are added.

11. Birzhakova, E. E., L. A. Voĭnova, and L. L. Kutina (1972), 'Ocherki po istoricheskoĭ leksikologii russkogo yazyka XVIII v' (Studies in the Historical Lexicology of Eighteenth-century Russian), in *Yazykovye kontakty i zaimstvovaniya* (Language Contacts and Borrowings) (Leningrad), 350 pp.

The etymology and chronology of foreign words used in the eighteenth century are analysed, which includes their phonetic, morphological, and semantic adaptation. The authors state that the period is characterized by a small number of anglicisms, naval terminology being an exception.

12. Bobrova, A. V. (1982), 'Imena sushchestvitel'nye na -ing v russkom yazyke' (Nouns Ending in *-ing* in Russian), unpublished avtoreferat kandidatskoĭ dissertatsii (Moscow), 21 pp.

A thorough investigation of the nouns ending in *-ing* first registered in the epoch of Peter I is provided. The author's main objectives are to analyse and describe phonetic, morphological, and semantic processes of adaptation of anglicisms and to classify them according to subject matter. Furthermore, the author shows how anglicisms (many of which are technical terms) change their semantic structure acquiring new meanings and losing their stylistic reference.

13. *Bol'shoĭ tolkovyĭ slovar' inostrannykh slov* (New Explanatory Dictionary of Foreign Words) (1995) (Rostov/Don), 1546 pp.

The authors M. A. Nadel'-Chervinskaya and P. P. Chervinskiĭ have compiled an explanatory dictionary of foreign words characterizing them in terms of meanings and usage. This dictionary differs from previous ones for many reasons: the authors note that many loanwords are stylistically marked as terms of different branches of science, and they paid great attention to the meanings of loanwords and various peculiarities. Moreover, the dictionary includes many new words.

14. Bondarenko, I. V. (1992), 'Angliĭskaya terminologiya kak predmet filologicheskogo issledovaniya' (English Terminology as a Subject of Philological Studies), unpublished avtoreferat kandidatskoĭ dissertatsii (Moscow), 24 pp.

The author analyses 3,500 naval terms classifying them according to different criteria. Etymologically they may be native or borrowed (Dutch, Latin); semantically they are either monosemic or polysemic, concrete or abstract; structurally the terms are subdivided into words and attributive word groups. Bondarenko also describes methods of creating new sea terms and underlines their instability, descriptive character, and variability.

15. Bragina, A. A. (1973), *Neologizmy v russkom yazyke* (Neologisms in the Russian Language) (Moscow), 224 pp.

One chapter of the book, 'Ustoĭchivye i vremennye zaimstvovaniya' (Stable and Temporary Borrowings) (pp. 84–161), is devoted to the integration of loanwords into Russian in the 1960–70s. The author distinguishes three groups: fully assimilated, assimilated but stylistically restricted, and temporary, unstable borrowings. Consequently, the function of each group is different.

16. Elizova, T. K. (1978), 'Zaimstvovanie angliĭskoĭ leksiki v russkiĭ yazyk v 60–70 gg. XX v' (The Borrowing of English Words in the Russian Language in the 60–70s), unpublished avtoreferat kandidatskoĭ dissertatsii (Rostov/Don), 19 pp.

The author investigates six hundred English words and set

phrases documented in periodicals of the 1960–70s. The process of their incorporation (lexicosemantic, grammatical, and derivational development) exhibits the opposite tendencies of assimilation or retention of the original form.

17. Filipović, Rudolf and Antica Menac (1993), 'Transfonemizacija u *Rječniku anglicizama u ruskom jeziku*: teorija i primjena' (Transphonemization in the *Dictionary of Anglicisms in Russian*: Theory and Application), *Suvremena lingvistika*, 35–6: 59–75.

Three types of transphonemization (zero, compromise, and free) are used in the analysis of anglicisms in Russian. The first type appears quite often in the transphonemization of seven English vowels and fourteen English consonants, equivalents being available in Russian. The second type occurs in four vowels that differ in their degree of opening and in four consonants with a different place of articulation. The third type comprises several phonemes which have no equivalents in the other language.

18. Frone, G. (1968), 'Ob angliĭskikh zaimstvovaniyakh v russkom yazyke' (On English Loanwords in the Russian Language), *Russkiĭ yazyk v shkole*, 3: 76–8.

A brief account of the English lexical impact on the Russian language is given in accordance with the major historical stages.

19. Gorbachevich, K. S. (1984), *Russkiĭ yazyk—proshloe, nastoyashchee, budushchee* (The Russian Language—the Past, Present, Future) (Moscow: Prosveshchenie), 190 pp.

The study based on different periods of Russian gives convincing statistics on loanwords from English. The process of borrowing is inevitable in some periods of language development, and attempts of some purists to translate borrowings are not always justified (cf. *lift* vs. *samopodymal'shchik*).

20. Gorlenko, V. (1989), 'Ékologiya yazyka' (The Ecology of Language), *Pravda*, 17 March.

The penetration of anglicisms into Russian through the mass media sometimes results in a distortion of sense.

21. Goryaev, N. V. (1896), *Sravnitel'nyĭ étimologicheskiĭ slovar' russkogo yazyka* (Comparative Etymological Dictionary of the Russian Language) (Tbilisi).

22. HOLDEN, K. T. (1980), 'Russian Borrowing of English [æ]', *Slavic and East European Journal*, 24: 387–99.

23. HÜTTL-WORTH, G. (1963), *Foreign Words in Russian—A Historical Sketch: 1550–1800* (University of California Publications in Linguistics: 28; Berkeley and Los Angeles).

This study contains lists of foreign words in Russian, including their various sources, the date of their first appearance, and the route of adaptation. A dictionary of foreign words is presented at the end of the study.

24. KAL'NOVA, O. I. (1986), 'Funktsionirovanie ékzotizmov v russkikh tekstakh' (The Function of Exoticisms in Russian Texts), unpublished avtoreferat kandidatskoĭ dissertatsii (Voronezh), 19 pp.

The author investigates the graphic, orthographic, and grammatical forms of 1900 exotic words (including a limited number of English and American ones). She defines the subject area and the markers of their lexical semantic assimilation. The work is based on citations from magazines and scientific literature and intended for a wide range of readers.

25. KARAPETYAN, V. V. (1987), *Semantiko-stilisticheskie sdvigi v anglitsizmakh v sovremennom russkom yazyke* (Semantic and Stylistic Changes of Anglicisms in Contemporary Russian) (Erevan), 177 pp.

All anglicisms undergo adaptation in Russian, and in the course of time change both semantic and stylistic characteristics. The main factors in this process are the time of their borrowing and the ideological content which anglicisms acquire in Russian as well as their context. The latter is of greater importance; anglicisms may become specialized or enlarge their semantic structure and lose or acquire stylistic reference.

26. KESIĆ-ŠAFAR, B. (1972), 'Engleske posuđenice u ruskom sportskom vokabularu', *Kineziologija*, 2: 137–49.

27. —— (1979), 'Historical Background of Anglo-Russian Borrowing', *Studia Romanica et Anglica Zagrabiensia*, 24: 265–277. (EEEL 4).

28. —— (1982), 'Semantička adaptacija engleskih, njemačkih i francuskih posuđenica u Tolstojevo doba' (The Semantic Adaptation of English, German, and French Loanwords in Tolstoi's Time), *Filologija*, 10: 223–42. (EEEL 4).

29. KESIĆ-ŠAFAR, B. (1991), 'The Analysis of Anglicisms in Russian', in *Filipović (ed.), 3: 91–103.

30. KOMLEV, N. G. (1992), *Inostrannoe slovo v delovoĭ rechi* (Foreign Words in the Business Language) (Moscow), 127 pp.

The dictionary contains five hundred current anglicisms in present-day Russian chosen from Russian newspapers, periodicals, advertisements, magazines, etc. The focus is on recent adoptions (after 1975), which are not found in dictionaries of foreign words or encyclopaedias. The author gives translations and information about dates, stress, and stylistic aspects.

31. —— (1995), *Slovar' novykh inostrannykh slov (S perevodom, étimologieĭ i tolkovaniem)* (Dictionary of New Foreign Words. With Translation, Etymology and Explanation) (Moscow), 144 pp.

The dictionary includes 1,500 neologisms recently borrowed into Russian; they are predominantly from English, but also from French, German, and other languages. The author gives Russian spelling and stress, and the English etymon with its translation and a definition.

32. KOTELOVA, N. Z. (ed.) (1995), *Slovar' novykh slov russkogo yazyka (seredina 50-kh—seredina 80-kh godov)* (Dictionary of New Words in the Russian Language (1950s–1980s)) (Moscow), 876 pp.

The dictionary consists of ten thousand words (including anglicisms) which have come into use since the middle of the twentieth century, with data on the time of entry, usage and illustrative examples.

33. —— and Y. S. SOROKIN (eds.) (1973), *Novye slova i znacheniya—Slovar'-spravochnik po materialam pressy i literatury 60-kh godov* (New Words and Meanings—Dictionary Material from Periodical and Non-periodical Literature of the 60s) (Moscow: Sovetskaya Éntsiklopediya), 543 pp.

The dictionary includes 3,500 new words which have not yet been registered in dictionaries. Each entry contains information on spelling, stress, grammatical marking, definition, and citations which show how to use the new words correctly.

34. KRYSIN, L. P. (1965), 'Inoyazychnye slova v sovremennom russkom yazyke' (Foreign Words in Contemporary Russian), in

Izmeneniya v leksike sovremennogo russkogo yazyka (Changes in the Lexis of Contemporary Russian) (Moscow), 22–37.

To become part of the lexical system of the receptor language a foreign word must meet the following requirements: it must be phonetically and grammatically adapted, have a definite meaning, be regularly used in speech, and be able to form derivatives. The author does not differentiate between foreignisms and loanwords.

35. —— (1968), *Inoyazychnye zaimstvovaniya v sovremennom russkom yazyke* (Foreign Borrowings in Contemporary Russian) (Moscow), 208 pp.

The author provides a thorough description of foreign influence on the Russian vocabulary within the Soviet period. The first part of the book is devoted to the theoretical problems of borrowing. The second part gives a historical account of the process at different stages of language development. The book includes a list of writings on problems of borrowing, vocabularies, and a word index. The post-war period (1940–50s) is characterized by the elimination of loanwords in the spheres of terminology and everyday speech. The process corresponds to the general ideological tendency of the government. The author expresses his negative attitude towards the elimination of fully integrated loanwords especially as far as sports terminology is concerned.

36. —— (1986), *Inoyazychnye slova v russkom yazyke* (Foreign Words in the Russian Language) (Moscow: Nauka).

37. —— (1995*a*), 'Tipy leksikograficheskoĭ informatsii ob inoyazychnom slove' (The Types of Lexicographical Information about a Loanword), *Rusistika segodnya* (Institut russkogo yazyka: Russian Academy of Sciences), 3: 66–81.

All dictionaries of loanwords are mainly encyclopaedic, informing readers about the realia and notions. By contrast, linguistic data concerning grammatical categories, stylistic properties, derivatives, peculiarities of pronunciation tend to be absent. Krysin works out a structure of an ideal entry which is both linguistic and encyclopaedic.

38. —— (1995*b*), 'Yazykovoe zaimstvovanie: vzaimodeĭstvie vnutrennikh i vneshnikh faktorov' (Linguistic Borrowing: Interrelation

Between Inner and Outer Factors), *Rusistika segodnya* (Institut russkogo yazyka: Russian Academy of Sciences), 1: 117–34.

Social, psychological, political, and other reasons have played a different role in the process of borrowing. Purist attitudes towards loanwords, typical of most languages, prevailed in the 1940s–50s; later on, the Russian society started tolerating them. We are experiencing a boom of anglicisms, but there are good reasons, the author claims, to save Russian from the domination of foreign words.

39. Kul'chitskiĭ, G. (1990), 'Bez 'yazykovaya glasnost" (Extralinguistic glasnost'), *Vek XX i mir*, 9 (Moscow).

The adoption of foreignisms contributes to the enrichment of the vocabulary. However, the author criticizes cases like the extension of the semantic group of 'director, administrator, etc.' by 'manager'.

40. Larionova, E. V. (1993), 'Noveĭshie anglitsizmy v sovremennom russkom yazyke' (The Latest Anglicisms in Contemporary Russian), unpublished D.Phil. thesis (Moscow), 179 pp.

The main tendencies in borrowing English words into present-day Russian are discussed. The author traces the development of loanwords from their first appearance in Russian, taking into account extralinguistic (social) and linguistic factors. She stresses the importance of distinguishing between occasional anglicisms and anglicisms proper. Occasional anglicisms are found in the speech of bilinguals, whereas anglicisms proper may denote new phenomena and/or new concepts (*dealer, holding, broker, leasing, marketing, price list*). According to the functional frequency value they may be of three types: rare, active, and superactive.

41. *Leksika russkogo literaturnogo yazyka XIX—n. XX v* (The Vocabulary of the Russian Literary Language of the 19th–20th Centuries) (1981) (Moscow), 360 pp.

This collective work, edited by Prof. Filin, treats the two most important periods from the 1870s up to 1917. The chapters devoted to loanwords and word history were written by I. A. Vasilevskaya, and V. K. Yunosheva, who discuss the sources of borrowings and the place of anglicisms in the system of lexical borrowings; they also give social reasons for the increasing influence of English.

42. LOGINOVA, Z. S. (1978), 'Anglitsizmy v sportivnoĭ terminologii russkogo yazyka' (Anglicisms in the Russian Sports Terminology), unpublished avtoreferat kandidatskoĭ dissertatsii (Tashkent), 19 pp.

By analysing three hundred words, five hundred translation loans, and ten thousand citations from periodicals of the nineteenth/twentieth centuries, the author defines the types and stages of their assimilation and the role of English terms in Russian sports terminology. In chapter II various kinds of translation loans are described in detail (morphological, semantic, and phraseological).

43. LOMAKINA, Z. I. (1985), *Zaimstvovanie i osvoenie russkim yazykom inoyazychnoĭ leksiki v 60–80 gg. XX v.* (Borrowing and Adaptation of Foreign Words of the 60–80s in the Russian Language) (Kiev), 24 pp.

44. LUKASHANETS, E. G. (1982), 'Leksicheskie zaimstvovaniya i ikh normativnaya otsenka (na materiale molodezhnogo zhargona 60–70 gg.)' (Lexical Borrowings and their Normative Estimation (with reference to the youth jargon of the 60–70s)), unpublished avtoreferat kandidatskoî dissertatsii (Moscow), 22 pp.

The work is based on two hundred lexical units of spoken sources collected by the author in Moscow and Tambov. She gives social reasons for the growing English influence on Russian. The interrelation between English and native jargonisms is also discussed.

45. LYCHYK, V. (1994), 'English Borrowings in Recent Soviet Russian', *Papers and Studies in Contrastive Linguistics*, 29: 141–56.

The author analyses the most recent decennial dictionary of Soviet Russian neologisms, *Novye slova i znacheniya: Slovar'-Spravochnik po materialam pressy i literatury 70-kh godov* (*NSZ-70*). He finds 198 loanwords, of which thirty-two are 'graphic' loans, and fourty-two phonetic loans, whereas others are compromises—or exhibit no conflict between spelling and pronunciation. Morphological adaptation is obligatory—but a few recently borrowed adjectives are invariable. By contrast, twenty semicalques and forty-eight calques are recorded—a noteworthy increase compared with earlier periods when loanwords were almost the only type of borrowing. Technology, social sciences, and art/entertainment were—in the 1970s—the domains most affected.

46. MARTINEK, V. M. (1971), 'Leksiko-semanticheskaya assimilyatsiya angliĭskikh zaimstvovaniĭ v russkom literaturnom yazyke' (Lexico-Semantic Assimilation of English Borrowings in the Russian Literary Language of the Soviet Period), unpublished D.Phil. thesis (Dnepropetrovsk), 160 pp.

According to Martinek, lexico-semantic assimilation is a slow and long process due to which anglicisms not only enlarge their semantic range but also acquire stylistic, phraseological, and other ties with the words of the receptor language. The author shares the point of view worked out by Akulenko according to which anglicisms are characterized by the following stages of adaptation: 1) When first used they denote English or American realia: *drug-store, horror-fan*, and are quotations, not part of the linguistic system. 2) If they remain, the words are no longer strikingly alien to the Russian ear. 3) Some of these become assimilated loanwords. Finally, 4) loanwords become structurally and semantically assimilated and are used to denote objects of the receptor language.

47. MAXIMOVA, T. V. (1996*a*), 'Anglitsizmy-terminy v sovremennom russkom yazyke' (Anglicisms-terms in Contemporary Russian), *Vestnik Volgogradskogo universiteta*, vypusk 1, seriya 2: 58–62.

The analysis shows that derivationally long words can penetrate into Russian, thus contributing to the appearance of new derivational morphemes in Russian.

48. —— (1996*b*), 'The Phonetic and Morphological Assimilation of Anglicisms in Russian', *Vestnik Volgogradskogo universiteta*, vypusk 1, seriya 2: 62–6.

The article is devoted to changes of newly adopted English words on the level of pronunciation, spelling, and morphology in the process of integration. Phonetic-orthographic variability is typical of words before they become completely assimilated. Variable morphological adaptation is also justified as demonstrating the flexibility and creativity of the Russian language.

49. —— and E. A. PELIKH (1994), 'Angliĭskie zaimstvovaniya v russkom i drugikh evropeĭskikh yazykakh' (English Loanwords in Russian and other European Languages), *Materialy XI nauchnoĭ konferentsii professorsko-prepodavatel'skogo sostava* (Volgograd), 356–60.

The authors investigate the sociolinguistic aspects of English borrowings; the distinction between motivated and occasional borrowings is considered important in observing language development. The comparative study of anglicisms in different languages presents very useful material for bringing out the universal and specific motives in the process of borrowing and the results of their assimilation.

50. MZHEL'SKAYA, O. S. and E. I. STEPANOVA (1983), 'Noveĭshie anglitsizmy v russkom yazyke' (The Latest Anglicisms in the Russian Language), in *Novye slova i slovari novykh slov* (New Words and Dictionaries of New Words) (Leningrad), 125–39.

The authors treat anglicisms in Russian denoting both Western concepts and phenomena, and those typical of Western and Russian society/culture. In addition they analyse the difference between the semantic structure of anglicisms in Russian and their English etymons.

51. NAUMOVA, I. O. (1982), 'Frazeologicheskie kal'ki angliĭskogo proiskhozhdeniya v sovremennom russkom yazyke (na materiale publitsistiki)' (Phraseological Loan-Translations of English Origin in Contemporary Russian (from Press Material)), unpublished avtoreferat kandidatskoĭ dissertatsii (Moscow), 18 pp.

The author describes the process of phraseological calquing of English items in the Russian language. A semantic classification of the calques, their structural organization and the principal types of their transformation are treated in the work. The chronological stages of their formation in the social and political terminology are defined and the main principles of their stylistic usage are shown. The research material has been extracted from the periodical and special reference literature of the nineteenth/twentieth centuries.

52. NOVIKOV, L. A. (1963), 'O semanticheskom pereoformlenii zaimstvovannykh slov v russkom yazyke' (On Semantic Changes of Loanwords in the Russian Language), *Russkiĭ yazyk v shkole*, 3: 5–10.

The author focuses on the transformation of the semantic structure of borrowings and underlines the reasons for splitting the relationship between historically cognate words (e.g. *block—blockade*).

53. NOVIKOVA, N. V. (1992), 'Zvonkoe inoyazychie' (The Fresh Foreignism), *Russkaya rech'*, 3/4: 49–54, 56–60.

Problems of language purism are discussed in the article. The author argues that the forced elimination of foreignisms in Russian will not bring the desired effect, but unscrupulous use of anglicisms in the mass media and in translations of foreign literature arouses natural protest and requires a careful distinction between what is good and what is bad in the culture. The author criticizes the import of some anglicisms (e.g. *impichment*, *butleger*, *sheĭping*, etc.) into Russian.

54. PANOV, M. V. (ed.) (1968), *Leksika sovremennogo russkogo literaturnogo yazyka: Russkiĭ yazyk i sovetskoe obshchestvo. Sotsiologolingvisticheskoe issledovanie* (The Vocabulary of the Contemporary Russian Literary Language: the Russian Language and the Soviet Society. Sociolinguistic Studies), I. (Moscow).

The authors deal with types of semantic changes, ways of enriching the vocabulary, and the importance of terminological lexis. Chapter II is devoted to borrowings from the 1920s to the 1960s; the analysis shows that some decades were more favourable to this process than others.

55. PODCHASOVA, S. V. (1995*a*), 'Novye slova advertaĭzinga' (New Words of Advertising), *Russkaya rech'*, 2: 71–6, 3: 61–6, 4: 48–51.

56. —— (1995*b*), 'Vsë dlya ofisa' (Everything in the Office), *Russkaya rech'*, 5: 54–7.

The author's aim is to analyse the origin of some foreign words, mostly anglicisms. She provides first occurrences and traces semantic changes in the process of assimilation.

57. POLLOCK, R. W. W. (1969), 'Lexico-morphological Characteristics of Twentieth-century Russian Terminology with Special Reference to the Usage of the Theoretical Sciences', unpub. Ph.D. thesis (Bradford).

58. PREOBRAZHENSKY, A. (1910–18), *Étimologicheskiĭ slovar' russkogo yazyka* (Etymological Dictionary of the Russian Language) (Moscow).

59. PROTCHENKO, I. F. (1962), 'Iz nablyudeniĭ nad internatsional'noĭ leksikoĭ' (On the Observation of International Vocabulary), *Russkiĭ yazyk v shkole*, 3: 5–12.

60. —— (1975), *Leksika i slovoobrazovanie russkogo yazyka sovetskoĭ épokhi* (Vocabulary and Word-formation in the Russian Language in the Soviet Age) (Moscow).

61. REINTON, J. E. (1978), 'The Relationship between English Loanwords and their Synonyms in Russian Sport Terminology', *Scando-Slavica*, 24: 213–37.

After discussing various definitions of 'synonymy' and 'complete synonymy' and giving reasons for the choice of his material, Reinton presents a list of 350 English loanwords including a statistical investigation of their frequency in relation to the Russian synonyms.

62. ROTHSTEIN, R. (1985), 'On Reading Dictionaries of Russian Neologisms', *Slavic and East European Journal*, 29: 461–70.

63. SCATTON, E. A. (1980), *Slovar' inostrannykh slov* (Dictionary of Foreign Words) (Moscow).

64. SEN'KO, E. V. (1980), *Novoe v leksike sovremennogo russkogo literaturnogo yazyka* (New Words in the Vocabulary of the Contemporary Russian Literary Language) (Leningrad), 21 pp.

65. SERGEEVA, E. V. (1996), 'Zaimstvovaniya 80–90-kh godov v sotsiolingvisticheskom aspekte' (Borrowings of the 80–90s in Sociolinguistic Aspect), *Russkaya rech'*, 5: 42–8.

The author describes the result of interviews with one hundred students on the understanding of anglicisms not yet included in dictionaries but often used in the mass media. A comparison of dictionaries of foreign words is also provided.

66. SÉSHAN, SHARMILA (1996), 'Sushestvitel'nye na -ing simvol amerikanskoĭ yazykovoĭ ékspansii?' (Are Nouns Ending in *-ing* a Symbol of the American Language Expansion?), *Russkaya rech'*, 3: 46–9.

The author defines five thematic groups of anglicisms ending in *-ing*. She concludes that the words have undergone regular shifts in meaning mainly caused by new contexts and loss of motivation.

67. SHANSKIĬ, N. M. (1963), *Étimologicheskiĭ slovar' russkogo yazyka* (Etymological Dictionary of the Russian Language) (Moscow: Izdatel'stvo Moskovskogo universiteta).

68. SHANSKIĬ, N. M. (1972), *Leksikologiya sovremennogo russkogo yazyka* (Lexicology of Contemporary Russian) (Moscow), 327 pp.

69. —— (1997), 'Inostrannye yazyki na urokakh russkogo yazyka' (Foreign Languages Lessons in Russian), *Russkiĭ yazyk v shkole*, 1: 3–11, 2: 26–9.

The article is devoted to the problems of teaching the spelling of foreign words and their adaptation in Russian. The author suggests referring to correlative facts known from the study of foreign languages at school. English words are treated in the context of other foreign words.

70. SHKOL'NIKOV, L. S. (1974), 'Pa-d Espan' ili Padespan'? Rok-énd-roll ili rok?' (Pa-d Espan' or Padespan'? Rock-énd-roll or rok?), in L. P. Kalakuckaya *et al.* (eds.), *Nereshënnye voprosy russkogo pravopisaniya* (Moscow), 153–61.

71. *Slovar'-Poputchik: Malyĭ tolkovo-étymologicheskiĭ slovar' inostrannykh slov.* (1994) (The Dictionary: a Travel Companion: a Small Explanatory Dictionary of Foreign Words) (Moscow: MGU), 191 pp.

The dictionary was compiled in the laboratory of etymological investigation at MGU. It includes 1500 entries, including borrowings from English, giving spelling, stress, the most important grammatical data, definition, and date of borrowing.

72. SOROKIN, Y. S. (1968), *Razvitie slovarnogo sostava russkogo literaturnogo yazyka (30-e gody XIX v.)* (The Development of the Word-Stock of the Russian Literary Language) (Moscow, Leningrad), 565 pp.

This monograph centres on the nineteenth-century Russian lexis including the impact of borrowings (such as anglicisms). The first part of the study has a theoretical description, the second deals with lexical borrowings, the third considers new coinages, and the last scrutinizes semantic changes in the language. The author tries to explain motives for the borrowing and use of anglicisms, changes they undergo in Russian and thoroughly investigates some English words in terms of their history and development.

73. *Sportivnye terminy na pyati yazykakh.* (1979–80) (Sport Terms in Five Languages) (Rowing-canoeing, judo, equestrian sports, athletics, yachting, swimming, diving, handball, modern pentathlon, shooting, archery, weight-lifting, fencing, football) (22 vols., Moscow).

For the 22nd Olympics Russian Language publishers prepared a series of dictionaries of sports terms. These include the most common sports terms in five languages (Russian, English, German, Spanish, French). In compiling the dictionaries the authors used analogous foreign publications, materials of the preceding Olympics, and the Statutes and Regulations of the International Amateur Federation.

74. TIMOFEEVA, G. G. (1985), 'Fonetiko-orfograficheskoe osvoenie novykh zaimstvovannykh slov' (Phonetic and Spelling Adaptation of New Loanwords), unpub. D.Phil. thesis (Leningrad), 185 pp.

The author investigates not only the most recent anglicisms but also treats Kirgiz and Uzbek loanwords in Russian. She finds tendencies in assimilation of loanwords which can be explained by peculiarities of the donor languages.

75. VASMER, M. (1950–58), *Russisches etymologisches Wörterbuch* (Heidelberg: Winter), translated from German and supplemented by O. N. Trubachëv (1964–73), *Étimologicheskiĭ slovar' russkogo yazyka* (Etymological Dictionary of the Russian Language) (4 vols., Moscow: Progress).

76. WADE, T. L. B. (1984), 'Russian Pop: Thematic Vocabulary in Context No. 7—Pop Music and Disco', Supplement to *ATR Journal of Russian Studies*.

77. WARD, D. (1965), *The Russian Language Today—System and Anomaly* (London).

78. —— (1973), 'Appositional Compounds in Russian', *Slavonic and East European Review*, LI 122: 1–10.

Ward gives both structural and stylistic reasons for the creation of appositional compounds which are treated as evidence of the 'degrammaticalization' of Russian. He suggests that the type is native and non-learned in origin, though the possibility of external influence through words such as *vagon-restoran* should not be dismissed.

79. —— (1981), 'Loanwords in Russian', *ATR Journal of Russian Studies*, 41: 3–14, 42: 5–14.

80. —— (1984), 'Charting the Lexical Flood—Some New Works on Russian Neologisms', *Scottish Slavonic Review*, 3: 140–51.

After discussing two productive types of compounding in Russian—appositional and 'abutted' compounding, Ward finds that the latter are most striking; they remind us of the simple juxtaposition in English compounds, which are, at least in part, the source.

81. WARD, D. (1986), 'The English Contribution to Russian', in *Viereck and Bald (eds.), 307–32.

Ward discusses English loanwords in Russian on the basis of the historical background covering the eighteenth century up to the 1980s.

82. WÓJTOWICZ, M. (1973*a*), 'Ob angliĭskikh imenakh sushchestvitel'nykh mnozhestvennogo chisla, zaimstvovannykh russkim yazykom' (On English Plural Nouns Borrowed by the Russian Language), *Studia Rossica Posnaniensia (SRP)*, 4: 151–6.

83. —— (1973*b*), 'O rzeczownikach zapożyczonych z języka angielskiego przez rosyjski język literacki w epoche radzieckiej' (On Nouns Borrowed from English by the Russian Literary Language in the Soviet Period), *SRP* 5: 61–76.

84. —— (1974), 'O foneticheskikh variantakh slov, zaimstvovannykh russkim yazykom iz angliĭskogo' (On Phonetic Variants of Words Having Been Borrowed by the Russian Language from English), *SRP* 9: 173–8.

85. —— (1984), *Kharakteristika zaimstvovannykh iz angliĭskogo yazyka imën sushchestvitel'nykh v russkom yazyke* (The Characteristics of Noun-borrowings from the English Language by the Russian Language) (Seria Filologia Rosyjska 18; Poznań: Wydawnictwo Naukowe Universytetu im. Adama Mickiewicza), 142 pp.

A synchronic analysis of nouns belonging to the type of loanwords proper (without morphological substitution). The study contains a concise characterization of the process of borrowing, types of loanwords, criteria of identification of loanwords, and periods of most intensive borrowing. The analysis distinguishes phonetic, graphic, and mixed borrowings, to establish the principles of substitution and identification of phonemes and graphemes, determine the reasons of deviation from a regular substitution, formation of phonetic variants, and the phonetic properties of loanwords. The author also discusses the place of accent in conjugation and analyses loanwords on the morphological, word-formation, and semantic plane. The work describes factors determining the inclusion of a word into the lexical and semantic system of the Russian language.

86. YURKOVSKIĬ, I. M. (1988), *Aktivnye protsessy v russkoĭ sportivno-igrovoĭ leksike* (Active Processes in the Russian Lexis of Sports and Games) (Kishinëv: Shtiintsa), 117 pp.

The author analyses the influence of English loanwords on the development of the Russian sports terminology, gives detailed etymological and historical data (of the time and circumstances of borrowing) and information about semantic specialization, determinologization, and word-formation.

Spanish (Félix Rodríguez González)

(see also *45)

The relatively abundant bibliography on anglicisms in European Spanish that has been mounting up over the years in the form of articles, glossaries, and dictionaries constitutes a good barometer of the growing influence of English on this language. The interest of these studies for the researcher varies according to the extent and nature of the subjects dealt with. On account of their general character, one should underline the issue of the influx of anglicisms in Spanish and their descriptive aspects, which have been brilliantly examined by Emilio Lorenzo and Chris Pratt in their classic studies. Sufficient attention has also been paid to the typology of borrowings as a whole (Gómez Capuz), the delimitation of the concept of anglicism in particular (Colin Smith), calques and translations (García Yebra, Vázquez Ayora), phonological and lexical variation (Lorenzo, Rodríguez), the presence of anglicisms in the press (Marcos) and in the colloquial language (Gómez Capuz, Rodríguez), and dialectal differences in South American Spanish (Haensch, Lorenzo).

Finally, one should mention lexicography, both in its theoretical aspects (Rodríguez) and in regard to the compilation or recording of anglicisms and the discussion of their etymology (Alfaro, Fernández García, Lorenzo, Rodríguez, and Lillo).

As to the specialized studies in which anglicisms flourish, and as a reflection of the vitality which the study of language for specific purposes (LSP) has reached in the last few years, one should note the research that has been done in the fields of economics, computing, and medical sciences.

Bolletino dell' instituto di lingue estere	Genova-Sampierdarena
Cauce	Sevilla
ES	Universidad de Valladolid
Estudios de Filología Inglesa	Granada
Hispanic Journal	Indiana, PA
Las Nuevas Letras	Almería
Miscelánea	Zaragoza
Notas y estudios filológicos	UNED-Navarra

1. Aguado de Cea, Guadalupe (1992), 'Problemas de traducción de la terminología informática en España', unpublished Ph.D. thesis (Madrid: Universidad Complutense de Madrid).

An account of the neologisms used in computing sciences—typically of English origin—with their equivalences and problems of translation.

2. —— (1994), *Diccionario comentado de terminología informática* (Madrid: Paraninfo). (Based on her Ph.D. thesis.)

3. Alcaraz, Mª Ángeles (1995), 'Anglicismos en las ciencias médicas', unpublished MA thesis (Universidad de Alicante), 153 pp.

A discussion of patent anglicisms and calques found in medical writings.

4. Alcoba Rueda, Santiago (1985), 'La lengua española, entre la provincia y la aldea global. I. El español, provincia del inglés', *Las Nuevas Letras*, 3–4: 17–25.

An account of the phonological, morphological, semantic, and syntactic changes caused by the influence of English.

5. Aldea, S. (1987), 'Función del préstamo en el discurso propagandístico', *Miscelánea*, 8: 5–19.

Discusses the connotative and associative aspects of the publicity lexicon of foreign—mainly English—origin, and their word-formational processes.

6. Alejo González, Rafael (1993), 'La influencia del vocabulario económico inglés sobre los textos de economía españoles posteriores a la II Guerra Mundial', unpublished Ph.D. thesis (Universidad Complutense de Madrid).

7. Alfaro, Ricardo J. (1948), 'Los anglicismos en el español contemporáneo', *Boletín del Instituto Caro y Cuervo*, 4: 102–28. (Reprinted as the 'Introduccíon' to his dictionary.)

8. —— ([3]1970), *Diccionario de anglicismos* (Madrid: Gredos). ([2]1964; 1st ed., Panamá, 1950).

The first dictionary of anglicisms in Spanish, with particular reference to South American Spanish, is flawed by the author's conspicuously prescriptive approach and the lack of distinction between European and South American usage. (Reviews: Boyd-Boyman, *Nueva Revista de Filología Hispánica*, 5 (1951), 431–2; Fente, *Filología Moderna*, 6 (21–2): 143–4.)

9. ALVAR EZQUERRA, MANUEL (dir.) (1994), *Diccionario de voces de uso actual* (Madrid: Acro Libros).

Contains a large number of recent neologisms, many of which are anglicisms and calques, accompanied with various contexts.

10. ALZUGARAY AGUIRRE, JUAN-JOSÉ (1979), *Voces extranjeras en el lenguaje tecnológico* (Madrid: Alhambra).

11. —— (1982), *Extranjerismos en el deporte* (Barcelona: Editorial Hispano Europea), 172 pp.

12. —— (1983), *Extranjerismos en los espectáculos* (Barcelona: Editorial Hispano Europea), 144 pp.

An account of some five hundred foreign terms used in the jargon of Spanish show business, half of which are anglicisms. The author classifies the collected items according to semantic fields (opera, modern music, etc.) and explains the reasons for their use.

13. —— (1985), *Diccionario de extranjerismos* (Madrid: Dossat), 192 pp.

Contains 2,400 entries of patent borrowings, some 1,300 of which are anglicisms.

14. ANON. (1992), *El idioma español en el deporte. Guía práctica.* Longroño: Gobierno de La Rioja; Agencia Efe. 74 pp.

Contains glossaries of the foreign terms used in various sports, most of which are anglicisms.

15. ARANGO, GUILLERMO (1975), 'Nuevos anglicismos en el español peninsular', *Hispania*, 58 (3): 498–502.

The reasons for the influx of anglicisms in Spanish in the 1970s and the different reactions towards this phenomenon are briefly described.

16. BEARDSLEY, T. S. (1979), 'Los galo-anglicismos', *Boletín de la Academia Norteamericana de la Lengua*, 4–5: 9–16.

Critical examination of the etymology of a good number of anglicisms coined or used in French by the 1960s, in some cases even with a French etymon (*block*, *boom*, *camping*, *clearing*, *parking* etc.), and later borrowed by Spanish and other languages. It also underlines the British origin of most of them.

17. BERNAL LABRADA, EMILIO (1992), 'La injerencia lingüística', *Boletín de la Academia Norteamericana de la Lengua Española*, 8: 111–27.

The author discusses purist attitudes as well as syntactic interferences, and advocates actions in defence of the Spanish language.

18. BOOKLESS, TOM C. (1982), 'Towards a Semantic Description of English Loan Words in Spanish', *Quinquereme*, 5 (2): 170–85.

Using principles of structural semantics, the author sets up categories concerned with the degree of abstractness of the referent and the overlap with other elements in the receiving language. Particular mention is made of 'unique loans', which may have many features in common with one or more Spanish words (e.g. *sandwich* ~ Sp. *bocadillo*).

19. —— (1984), 'The Semantic Development of English Loanwords in Spanish', *Quinquereme*, 7 (1): 39–53.

The author discusses three main factors which influence the semantic development of a loanword: 1) the relationship between word and referent, especially with regard to the degree of abstractness involved (e.g. extended meanings of *esnobismo* and *esnob*); 2) the role of the semantic field, with a tendency for loans to extend their semantic features (e.g. *test, slip*), especially in the case of abstract nouns (e.g. *handicap, bluff, establishment*); and 3) figurative usage, which may involve playful extensions of meaning (e.g. *estar offside* 'not to pay attention') or generalized figurative usage, which exhibits similar developments (e.g. *handicap* 'obstacle') or moves away from English usage (*sport*, in *ir de sport, vestirse de sport* 'dress casually').

20. BRASELMANN, PETRA M. E. (1994), 'Syntaktische Interferenzen?: Zum englischen Einfluss auf die spanische Syntax', *Iberoromania*, 39: 22–46.

The author considers the increasing use in Spanish of some typically English grammatical structures such as premodifying qualitative adjectives and gerunds with an adjectival value as parts of the Spanish system; therefore the English influence only relates to the frequency of their use.

21. Cabarello Férnandenz-Rufete, Salvador (1994), 'Anglicismos: Un trabajo de campo', *ES* 18: 143–59.

This sociolinguistic study based on empirical evidence explores the degree of penetration of anglicisms in relation to some social factors, especially the socioeconomic status and the place of residence, city or country. The data are from questionnaires containing ten anglicisms, handed out among Primary School students (fifth and sixth year of EGB) in Valladolid and its province.

22. Carnicer, Ramón (1969), *Sobre el lenguaje de hoy* (Madrid: Prenso Española).

This general study contains scattered references to anglicisms, especially in the following articles: 'Vamos a Kahlahtahyood' (21–4); 'Los falsos amigos' (25–8), 'Anglicismos' (205–9).

23. —— (1972), *Nuevas reflexiones sobre el lenguaje* (Madrid: Prensa Española).

The book contains two relevant short articles: 'Algunos anglicismos', 33–6; and 'Más sobre los anglicismos', 231–5, devoted to semantic borrowings such as *romance* and *balance*, and a few other articles treating individual anglicisms such as: *playboy* (183–7) and *sexy* (201–8).

24. —— (1983), *Desidia y otras lacras en el lenguaje de hoy* (Barcelona: Planeta).

25. Castañón Rodríguez, Jesús (1992), 'Anglicismos de fútbol en el periodismo español', *Notas y estudios filológicos*, 7: 128–47.

This study is based on part of the author's (1987) unpublished MA thesis (Universidad de Valladolid), here expanded and updated to include data from 1988–89. It examines the use of anglicisms in sports journalism as well as the historical, political, and social context, their development and change.

26. —— (1993), *El lenguaje periodístico del fútbol*. Valladolid: Universidad.

Contains a glossary of terms used in soccer terminology, many of which are anglicisms, with their Spanish equivalents, pp. 117–83.

27. —— (1995), 'El problema de los extranjerismos en el Nuevo Estado: 1936–75', in Jesús Castañón, *Reflexiones lingüísticas sobre el deporte* (Valladolid: the author), 95–104.

On the linguistic and extralinguistic causes that led to the proposal for the elimination of foreign terms, the linguistic criteria employed (translation, etc.) and the problems raised.

28. Castillo, F. J. (1990), 'El vocabulario de una modalidad del español. Algunas notas sobre los anglicismos de las hablas canarias', in *Actas del Congreso de la Sociedad Española de Lingüística*, I.XX aniversario (Tenerife, April 2–6, 1990) (Madrid: Gredas), 354–62.

On the reasons for the use of some borrowings restricted to the Canary Islands and the possible means of transmission.

29. Chiareno, Osvaldo (1973), 'Anglicanización del léxico mercantil español', *Bolletino dell' instituto di lingue estere*, 9: 3–17.

30. *Clave. Dictionario de uso del español actual* (1996) (Madrid: SM).

Contains around four hundred anglicisms, most of them recent adoptions, with their pronunciation and recommendations on their use.

31. Corbella Díaz, Dolores (1992), 'Los anglicismos en el español de Canarias: Interferencias lingüísticas', *Cauce*, 14/15: 61–9.

32. England, John and J. L. Caramés Lage (1978), 'El uso y abuso de anglicismos en la prensa española de hoy', *Arbor*, 390: 77–89.

33. Estrany Gendre, Manuel (1970), 'Calcos sintácticos de inglés', *Filología Moderna*, 38: 199–203.

34. Fernández, Joseph (1988), 'La fonología en la televisión española: violencias fonéticas', *Revista de Dialectología y Tradiciones Populares*, 43: 249–58.

35. Fernandéz Galiano, Manuel (1966), 'Sobre transcripciones, transliteraciones y traduciones', *Revista de Occidente*, 95–106.

The author discusses three main ways of incorporating foreign terms to a native language, through transliteration, transcription, and calquing or translation, apart from the risky preservation of the borrowed term in its original spelling. A distinction is made between nouns and proper names (anthroponyms and toponyms); the latter tend to preserve the spelling, especially in modern times.

36. Fernández Garcia, Antonio (1970), *Anglicismos en el español* (Oviedo: Gráficas Lux).

A well documented book on the introduction and etymology of the earliest anglicisms in Spanish, based on the *Blanco y Negro* news magazine from 1891 to 1936.

37. —— (1970–71), '*Sport y Deporte*. Compuestos y derivados', *Revista de filología Moderna*, 11: 93–110.

38. Fonfrías, Ernesto Juan (1986), *Anglicismos en el idioma español de Madrid. Afluencia e influencia de anglicismos en el español habloado y escrito de Madrid* (San Juan Bautista de Puerto Rico: Editorial Club de la Prensa), 96 pp.

This account of the anglicisms in the press of Madrid is written in a light and unphilological manner, including many anecdotes.

39. Fuster, Miguel (1995), 'La romanización del inglés y la anglización del español peninsular', in Mª Echenique *et al.* (eds.), *Historia de la lengua española en América y en España* (Valencia: Tirant lo Banch), 245–59.

The article underlines the role of French as a mediating language in the introduction of anglicisms in Spanish and also the influence of English in the adoption of many Latin-Hellenisms spread internationally.

40. García Yebra, Juán V. (1982), *Teoría y práctica de la traducción* (Credos; Madrid).

The book includes two chapters on foreign terms and constructions, particularly from English and French, in translated texts. Ch. IX, 'Calcos y anglicismos' (333–52) discusses the typology of foreign terms and the attitude that the translator should adopt, and ch. X, 'La interferencia linguística' (353–84), examines lexical, morphological, and syntactic errors (such as the misuse of prepositions and conjunctions, mood, and tense, abuse of passive voice, and excessive brevity).

41. —— (1988), 'Préstamo y calco en español y alemán. Su interés lingüístico y su tratamiento en la traducción', in *Problemas de la Traducción* (Madrid: Fundación 'Alfonso X El Sabio'), 75–89.

A discussion of advantages of using calques, with some reference to calques from English sources.

42. GIL SALOM, MARÍA LUZ (1986), 'El anglicismo en el campo de informática', unpublished MA thesis (Universidad de Valencia).

43. GIMENO, FRANCISCO and MARÍA VICTORIA (1991), 'Estado de la cuestíon sobre el anglicismo léxico', in C. Hernadez *et al. El español de América, Actas del III Congreso Internacional de El Espagñol de América*, 741–9.

44. —— —— (1996), 'Hacia un análisis cuantitativo del anglicismo léxico', Paper read at the *XI Congreso International de la Asociacíon de Lingüística y Filología de la América Latina* (ALFAL) (Universidad de las Palmas de Gran Canaria).

45. GIMENO, VICTORIA (1996), 'Análisis cuantitativo de los anglicismos léxicos en la prensa español de los Estados Unidos y de España', unpublished Ph.D. thesis (Universidad de Alicante).

46. GODDARD, K. A. (1980), 'Loanwords in Spanish: a Reappraisal', *Bulletin of Hispanic Studies*, 57: 1–16.

General remarks on the typology, attitudes, and causes of borrowings, with particular reference to anglicisms in Spanish.

47. GÓMEZ CAPUZ, JUAN (1991*a*), 'Notas para un estudio de los anglicismos en español', unpublished MA thesis (Universidad de Valencia), 183 pp.

48. —— (1991*b*), 'Para una clasificacíon tipológica de los anglicismos en español actual', in J. Calvo (ed.), *Lingüística Aplicada y Tecnología. Actas del I Simposio* (Valencia, February 1990). (Valencia: Departamento de Teoría de los Lenguajes), 63–70.

Examines the most relevant classifications of borrowings, in particular those proposed by Haugen, Weinreich, and Humbley, and pinpoints the levels at which the influence of English is considered most harmful.

49. —— (1992*a*), 'Anglicismos en las noticias sobre la guerra del Golfo Pérsico. Visión actual del problema e intento de clasificación', *Lingüística Española Actual*, 14 (2): 301–20.

An account of the various classes of anglicisms used in the political language during the Gulf War, of which semantic loans were the predominant type.

50. GÓMEZ CAPUZ, JUAN (1992*b*), 'La problemática de los extranjerismos en los libros de estilo. Purismo y defenso del idioma', *I Congres Internacional de Periodisme. València, 1990. Actes*, 899–909.

The author comments on the different recommendations on the use of foreign terms in stylebooks of Spanish newspapers, in particular de *Manual de español urgente* ([4]1987) and the *Libro de estilo de El País* ([3]1990). Most of the data refer to anglicisms.

51. —— (1993), 'Calcos y malas traducciones en los doblajes del inglés al español. Estudio y taxonomía de un corpus reciente y su contribución a la traductología y la enseñanza de lenguas', in J. Fernández-Barrientos (ed.), *Actas de las Jornadas Internacionales de Lingüística Aplicada* (Universidad de Granada, January 11–15, 1993). (Granada: ICE/Universidad), vol. 1, 627–38.

52. —— (1994), 'Calcos sintácticos, fraseológicos y pragmáticos en los doblajes del inglés al español', *Actas del XII Congreso Nacional de la Asociación Española de Lingüística Aplicada AESLA (AESLA) Barcelona*, 171–8.

The author discusses the most frequent errors of translation recorded in dubbed telefilms shown on Spanish TV during the period 1984–94.

53. —— (1996*a*), 'Tendencias en el estudio de las diferentes etapas de la influencia angloamericana en español moderno', in Alonso González *et al.*, *Actas del III Congreso Internacional de Historia de la Lengua* (Madrid: Arco Libros), II: 1289–307.

A discussion of the different stages of the introduction of anglicisms in Spanish and a review of previous studies.

54. —— (1996*b*), 'Observaciones sobre la función de los extranjerismos en el español coloquial: Valores estilísticos, semánticos y pragmáticos', in A. Briz *et al.* (eds.), *Pragmática y Gramática del Español Hablado (Actas des II Simposio sobre análisis del discurso oral)* (Universidad de Valencia, Depto. de Filología Española), 305–10.

Most data refer to anglicisms.

55. —— (1997), 'Anglicismos en español actual: Su estudio en el registro coloquial', unpublished Ph.D. thesis (Universidad de Valencia), 792 pp.

The treatment focuses on anglicisms in colloquial language; the study is based on candid recordings obtained at the University of Valencia by a group of researchers on colloquial Spanish known as VAL.ES.CO. under the direction of A. Briz. The study contains useful data on the pronunciation and extended meanings of the English etymons.

56. GÓMEZ DE ENTERRÍA, JOSEFA (1992), 'Los anglicismos léxicos en el vocabulario de la economía', *Actas de las I Jornadas Internacionales del Inglés Académico, Técnico y Profesional, Universidad de Alcalá de Henares, December 1991*, 216–20.

57. —— (1993), 'Los préstamos en los vocabularios técnicos y científicos: el vocabulario de la economía', in G. Hilty (coord.), *Actes du XXe Congrès International de Linguistique et Philologie Romanes*, IV: 639–50.

Particular reference is made to anglicisms and calques.

58. GÓMEZ TARREGO, LEONARDO (1992), *El buen uso de los palabras* (Madrid: Arco Libros). (Review: Gómez Capuz, *Anuario de Lingüística Hispánica*, 10 (1994), 462–70.)

59. GONZÁLES MONLLOR, ROSA Mª and MAGNOLIA DÉNIZ TROYA (1997), 'Tratamiento lexicográfico de los nuevos anglicismos en el diccionario académico', in *Contribuciones al estudio de la lingüística hispánica. Homenaje al prof. Ramón Trujillo* (Barcelona: Montesinos).

60. GONZÁLEZ CRUZ, Mª ISABEL (1993), 'El contacto lingüístico anglocanario: algunas consideraciones para su estudio', *Revista Canaria de Estudios Ingleses*, 26–27: 131–48.

61. GOOCH, ANTHONY (1971), 'Spanish and the Onslaught of the Anglicism', *Vida Hispánica*, 19 (2): 17–21.

Most of the examples are paronyms and semantic borrowings drawn from the press, dictionaries, and other written works.

62. —— (1986), 'El lenguaje político español y el factor anglosajón', *Revista de Estudios Politicos*, 52: 125–45.

Underlines the influx of English expressions (patent anglicisms and calques) which occurred in the last period of Franco's rule and in the advent of democracy, and explores some of the semantic pitfalls and the psychological significance of such phenomena.

63. *Gran enciclopedia Larousse* (GEL) (1988) (Barcelona: Planeta).

64. Gubern Garriga-Nogues, Santiago (1974), '¿Pánico ante los anglicismos?', *Yelmo*, 18: 24–8.

65. Guitarte, Guillermo L. and Rafael Quintero Torres (1968), 'Linguistic Correctness and the Role of Academies'. *Current Trends in Linguistics, 4: Iberoamerican and Caribbean Linguistics* (Paris and The Hague: Mouton).

Reference to anglicisms on pp. 596–601.

66. Guzmán González, Trinidad (1984), 'Anglicismos léxicos en el lenguaje de las revistas de cinematografía (1981–3)', unpublished MA thesis (Universidad de Oviedo).

67. —— (1986), 'Algunos aspectos de los anglicismos cinematográficos. Razones de su empleo', *Actas del IX Congreso Nacional de la AEDEAN* (Asociación Española de Estudio Anglo-Norteamericanos, Murcia, December 17–20, 1985), 175–82.

On the linguistic, psychological, and social reasons for the use of anglicisms in the cinema. The corpus for this study is based on magazines published during the period 1981–3.

68. Haensch, Günther (1963), 'Der Einfluß des Englischen auf das amerikanische Spanisch als weitere Ursache für dessen Differenzierung gegenüber dem europäischen Spanisch', *Lebende Sprachen*. (Festschrift for Hans Rheinfelder on the occasion of his sixty-fifth birthday) ed. H. Bihler and A. Noyer-Werdner (München: Hueber).

69. —— (1969), 'Einflüsse des Englischen auf den Wortschatz der spanischen Gegenwartssprache', *Neusprachliche Mitteilungen*, 22: 25–32.

70. —— (1995), 'Anglicismos y galicismos en el español de Colombia', in Klaus Zimmermann (ed.), *Lenguas en contacto en Hispanoamérica: Nuevos enfoques* (Vervuert: Hispanoamericana), 217–51.

71. Herrera Soler, Honesto (1993), 'Un análisis sobre la evolución de los préstamos que provienen del inglés económico', *Estudios Ingleses de la Universidad Complutense*, 1: 97–110.

Classification and analysis of anglicisms attested in *El País* during the period 1988–1991 in the *Negocios* section included in the Sunday Supplement. The lexical items collected are classified according to their process of incorporation into the Spanish language.

72. HOYO, ARTURO DEL ([1]1988, [2]1995), *Diccionario de palabras y frases extranjeras* (Madrid: Aguilar).

Includes an extensive number of anglicisms, with historical data on their introduction in Spanish.

73. JIMÉNEZ SERRAN, ÓSCAR (1993), 'El papel del inglés en la terminología de informática en español', *Analecta Malacitana*, 4 (36): 373–80.

74. LAPESA, RAFAEL (1966), 'Kahlahtayood: Madariaga ha puesto el dedo en la llaga', *Revista de Occidente*, 4 (36): 373–80.

Reply to the article by Madariaga (1966), in which he adopts a more balanced and moderate position on neologisms.

75. LATORRE CEBALLOS, GUILLERMO (1991), 'Anglicismos en retirada: Contacto, acomodación e intervención en un sistema léxico', in C. Hernández *et al.* (eds.), *Actas del III Congreso Internacional de El Español de América* (Valladolid, July 3–9, 1989) (Junta de Castilla y León—Consejería de Cultura y Turismo), II: 765–73.

General remarks on these topics with examples taken from Chilean and Peninsular Spanish. Criticism of Pratt in regard to some aspects related to the definition and etymology of anglicisms.

76. LODARES, JUAN R. (1993), 'Penúltimos anglicismos semánticos', *Hispanic Journal*, 14 (1): 101–11.

Comment on the new meanings of *conductor*, *cosmético*, *ganga*, *parafernalia*, *perfil* and *plausible*.

77. LORENZO, EMILIO (1955), 'El anglicismo en la España de hoy', *Arbor*, 119: 262–74; repr. (1980) in *El español de hoy, lengua en ebullición* (Madrid: Gredos), 96–121.

This first scholarly article published in Spain on the influx of anglicisms advocates from a moderate position, 'an attitude inspired in the unshakable belief that the foundations of language building are firm'.

78. —— (1987), 'Anglicismos en la prensa', *Actas de la I Reunión de Academias de la lengua Española: El languaje y los medios de comunicación* (Madrid: Comisión permanente de Academias), 71–9.

On the contrastive use of some anglicisms in Spain and South America.

79. Lorenzo, Emilio (1991), 'Anglicismos y traducciones', in *Studia Patriciae Shaw Oblata* (Oviedo), II: 67–79.

On the necessary, superfluous, and 'pernicious' anglicisms in the Spanish language, including semantic, syntactic, and orthographic anglicisms, and the so-called anglicisms 'of frequency'.

80. —— (1992), 'Anglicismos', *Boletín Informativo de la Fundación Juan March*, November, 3–14; reprinted in M. Seco and G. Salvador (eds.), *La lengua española, hoy* (Madrid: Fundación Juan March), 165–74.

81. —— (1994), 'Tratamiento del vocalismo inglés en español. Los diptongos', in *Sin fronteras. Homenaje a Mª Josefa Canellada* (Madrid: Editorial Complutense), 359–71.

On the different adaptations of English diphthongs in Spanish borrowings.

82. —— (1995), 'Anglicismos', in M. Seco and G. Salvador (eds.), *La lengua española, hoy* (Madrid: Fundación Juan March), 165–74.

83. —— (1996), *Anglicismos hispánicos* (Madrid: Gredos).

This extensive compilation of patent and semantic anglicisms in the form of an etymological dictionary includes the author's two best-known articles on the introduction of anglicisms in Spanish and the phenomenon of anglicisms today. (Review: Rodríguez, Félix, 1998, *IJL* 11, 66–72; Pratt, Chris 1997, *Estudios Ingleses de la Universidad Complutense*, 5: 81–9).

84. —— (1997), 'Tratamiento del vocalismo inglés en español', *Estudios Ingleses de al Universidad Complutense*, 5: 81–9.

Classification and description of the ways in which the vowels of both British and American English have been accommodated to Spanish.

85. Madariaga, Salvador de (1962), 'El español, colonia lingüística del inglés', *Cuadernos del Congreso por la libertad de la Cultura* (París), 59: 45–9.

On the anomalies introduced in the transliteration of proper names.

86. —— (1966), '¿Vamos a Kahlahtayood?', *Revista de Occidente*, 4 (36): 365–73.

In this influential article the author voices his purist position in response to the influx of anglicisms.

87. MARCOS PÉREZ, PEDRO-JESÚS (1971), *Los anglicismos en el ámbito peridístico: algunos de los problemas que plantean* (Valladolid: Departamento de Inglés), 71 pp.

The first study to analyse an extensive corpus of anglicisms drawn from a newspaper and the various phonological, morphological, and semantic problems raised by their use.

88. MARRONE, NILA (1974), 'Investigación sobre variaciones léxicas en el mundo hispano', *Bilingual Review*, 1: 152–8.

89. MARTÍNEZ DE SOUSA, JOSÉ (1996), *Diccionario de usos y dudas del español actual* (Barcelona: Bibliograf Vox).

Includes a great number of anglicisms, both general and specialized, and provides synonyms and recommendations on their use.

90. MARTÍNEZ GONZÁLEZ, ANTONIO (1976), 'Estudio de algunos anglicismos del léxico de la economía', *Estudios de Filología Inglesa*, 1: 27–39.

91. —— (1979), 'Anglicismos en el habla viva de los pescadores andaluces', *Estudios de Filologia Inglesa*, 6–7: 91–8.

92. MEDINA LOPEZ, JAVIER (1991), 'Los anglicismos: A propósito de los rótulos publicitarios', *Lexis: Revista de Linguistica y Literatura*, 15 (1): 119–28.

93. —— (1994), 'Nuevos datos del español canario', *Revista de la Sociedad Argentina de Lingüística*, 2, 7–18.

94. —— (1998), *Anglicismos en español* (Madrid: Arco Libros), 69 pp.

95. MEUNIER-CRESPO, MARIETTE (1987), 'Les Anglicismes dans la presse d'information economique espagnole', *Meta: Journal des Traducteurs / Translators Journal*, 32 (3): 273–7.

On the different types of anglicisms attested in a dozen issues of *El País*, under the section *Economía y trabajo*.

96. MIGHETTO, DAVID (1991), 'Las palabras-cita y los libros de estilo', *Moderna Språk*, 82/2: 180–5.

97. NAVARRO, FERNANDO A. and FRANCISCO HERNÁNDEZ (1992), 'Palabras de traducción engañosa en el inglés médico', *Medicina Clínica* (Barcelona), 99: 575–80.

List of false friends (including anglicisms) used in translation.

98. PÉREZ RIOJA, JOSÉ ANTONIO (1990), *La España de los años veinte en el lenguaje* (Madrid: Asociación de escritores y artistas españoles).

Contains anglicisms used in Spanish by the 1920s.

99. PÉREZ RUIZ, LEONOR and MAGDALENA VIVANCOS (1997), 'Usos y abusos de los anglicismos en el inglés técnico informático: préstamo y calco', *Actas del XVIII Congreso Nacional de la AEDEAN* (Universidad de Alcalá: Servicio de Publicaciones), 343–50.

100. PÉREZ SABATER, C., C. SOLER MONREAL, and B. MONTERO FLETA (1993), 'Análisis de anomalías lingüísticas: cambios producidos por la influencia del inglés en el español oral', in J. Fernández Barrientos (ed.), *Actas de las Jornadas Internacionales de Lingüística Aplicada* (Granada: ICE/Universidad), I: 405–11.

101. PRATT, CHRIS J. (1970–71), 'El arraigo del anglicismo en el español de hoy', *Filología Moderna*, 40–41: 67–92.

102. —— (1980), *El anglicismo en el español contemporáneo peninsular* (Madrid: Gredos), 276 pp.

The first rigorous and fairly comprehensive monograph on anglicisms in Peninsular Spanish discusses etymological problems, the typology, and etymology of anglicisms and provides a critical review of previous studies. Data are drawn from radio and television rather than from the press. (Reviews: Sánchez (1981), 'El anglicismo en *Anuari* (Universidad Autónoma de Bellaterra, Barcelona), 99–105; Coletes, *Revista de Bachillerato*, 21 (1982), 136; Höfler, *Zeitschrift für Romanische Philologie* (1983), 466–8.)

103. —— (1986), 'Anglicisms in European Spanish', in *Viereck and Bald (eds.), 345–67.

The article concentrates 'on questions of definition, identification, description, and analysis', restricted to the influence from the early 1950s. The author discusses ways how to classify anglicisms on various linguistic levels and the causes that have led to their adoption.

104. —— (1992), 'The Status of Loanwords in Modern Monolingual Dictionaries', *Actas del IV Congreso Internacional de EUROLEX* (Barcelona: Bibliograf), 506–16.

105. —— (1994), 'Colón, colonización y cocacolanización: 500 años de historia de la lengua española', in R. Penny (ed.), *Actas del Primer Congreso Anglo-Hispano. (I) Lingüística* (Madrid: Castalia), 205–14.

106. Quilis, Antonio (1984), 'Anglicismos en el español de Madrid', in *Athlon, Satura Grammatica in honorem Francisci R. Adrados* (Madrid: Gredos), 413–23.

The author discusses the lexical anglicisms in José C. de Torres Martínez (1981), *Encuestas léxicas del habla culta de Madrid* (Madrid: CSIC). Including references to frequency of use and synonyms.

107. Ramírez García, Mª Rosa and José L. Vázquez Marruecos (1984?), 'Aportación a la sociolingüística giennense', *Actas del 2° Congreso de AESLA*, 383–92.

On the recognition and use of one hundred anglisms among secondary school students in Jaén and other places in Andalucía.

108. Ramoncín [José Ramón Martínez Márquez] (1989), *El tocho cheli: Diccionario de jergas, germanías y jerigonzas* (Madrid: Ediciones Temas de Hoy).

109. Riquelme, Jesuchristo (1998), *Anglicismos y anglismos: huéspedes del idioma* (Alicante: Aguaclara), 117 pp.

Panoramic view of anglicisms with a didactic and divulgative purpose. Includes reference to Anglo-Saxon cultural influences and the label of *anglismos*.

110. Rodríguez Díaz, José Antonio (1996), 'Anglicismos y germanismos en el lenguaje de la publicidad del español peninsular contemporáneo'. (Unpublished MA thesis: Universidad de Santiago), 244 pp.

111. Rodríguez González, Félix (1989), 'Lenguaje y contracultura: Anatomía de una generación', in Félix Rodríguez González (ed.), *Comunicación y lenguaje juvenil* (Madrid: Fundamentos), 135–66.

The study refers to anglicisms as an expressive device of the language of youth.

112. RODRÍGUEZ GONZÁLEZ, FÉLIX (1994*a*), 'Rémarques sur les glissements de sens dans l'argot de la drogue. Les anglicismes en espagnol', *Cahiers de Lexicologie*, 64 (1): 147–54.

This article shows the very large number of figurative terms—especially metaphors—which are currently found in drug-users' slang, and how they relate to one another; it also brings out both the denotative and connotative differences of certain Spanish terms compared to other languages, and gives the social and contextual reasons for this. Certain terms, anglicisms in particular, have positive connotations when compared with their English equivalents. (Most of the terms treated are calques rather than loanwords.)

113. —— (1994*b*), 'Anglicismos en el argot de la droga', *Atlantis*, 179–216.

An overview of the penetration of anglicisms in the drug world, and their linguistic variants.

114. —— (1996*a*), 'Functions of Anglicisms in Contemporary Spanish', *Cahiers de lexicologie*, 1: 107–28.

A stylistic and pragmatic approach to the functions of anglicisms in Peninsular Spanish.

115. —— (1996*b*), 'Lexicografía de los anglicismos en español contemporáneo. A propósito del proyecto *Nuevo diccionario de anglicismos*', in Christian Schmitt and Wolfgang Schweickhard (eds.), *Die iberoromanischen Sprachen aus interkultureller Sicht. Akten der gleichnamigen Sektion der Bonner Hispanistentage, Bonn, 2–4 March 1995* (Bonn: Romanischer Verlag), 300–14.

116. —— and ANTONIO LILLO BUADES (dir.), (1997), *Nuevo diccionario de anglicismos* (Madrid: Gredos), 562 pp.

The first comprehensive dictionary dealing exclusively with anglicisms in contemporary Peninsular Spanish. Entries provide information on pronunciation, morphological variants, definition, synonyms and/or proposed translations, citations, etymon, and labels or markings for field of usage, relative frequency and stylistic uses of the anglicisms in question.

117. ROS PÉRZ, PABLO and RAFAEL ABELLÁN ROCAMORA (1998), 'La influencia de anglicismos en el sector turístico de la región de Murcia', *Cuadernos de Turismo*, 1: 117–28.

118. Rubio Sáez, José (1977), *Presencia del inglés en la lengua española* (Valencia: Ezcurra), 174 pp.

An extensive account of the reasons for the adoption of anglicisms and their presence in certain fields, notably the media, tourism, and sports.

119. Salvador, Francisco (1996), 'Incidencia del anglicismo en el español hablado de España y América', *Anuario de Letras*, 32: 321–32.

Contrastive study of the impact of anglicisms in Latin American and Spanish cities: Santiago de Chile, Ciudad de México, Granada, and Madrid.

120. Sampedro Losada, Pedro José (1998), 'Anglicismos en el lenguaje informático', *Hispanorama*, 79, 11–18.

The article discusses the problem of asssigning gender and the attitude towards the translating of computer technology.

121. Sánchez Macarro, Antonia (1993), 'La invasión del anglicismo en el español contemporáneo', *Actas del Simposio sobre el español de España y el español de América* (Valencia: Universidad de Valencia/University of Virginia), 19–34.

A panoramic study in which a review is made of the different types of anglicisms and the attitudes towards their adoption.

122. Sánchez, María F. (1995, in prep.), *Clasificación y análisis de préstamos del inglés en la prensa de España y México* (Lewiston, New York: Edwin Mellen Press).

Examines the anglicisms found in two issues of *El País* (Madrid) and *El Universal* (Ciudad de México) in the following sections: news; culture, art, show-business, and society; economy and work; sports; and advertising.

123. Santoyo, Julio-César (1987), 'Traduction, fertilisation et internationalisation: Les calques en espagnol', *Meta*, 3: 240–9.

124. —— (1988), 'Los calcos como forma de traducción', in *Problemas de la Traducción* (Madrid: Fundación Alfonso X El Sabio), 91–7.

125. Schweickhard, Wolfgang (1991), 'Anglizismen im Spanischen', *Terminologie et Traduction*, 1: 75–86.

126. Schweickhard, Wolfgang (1998), 'Englisch und Romanisch', in Günter Holtus, Michael Metzelin and Christian Schmitt (eds.), *Lexikon der Romanistischen Linguistik* (*LRL*), vol. 7 (Tübingen: Niemeyer), 291–309.

127. Seco, Manuel (1977), 'El léxico de hoy', in Rafael Lapesa (coord.), *Comunicación y lenguaje* (Madrid: Karpós), 183–201.

On the assimilation of foreign terms and the attitudes towards this phenomenon, 197–201.

128. —— ([9]1992), *Diccionario de dudas y dificultades de la lengua española* (Madrid: Espasa Calpe).

This classic usage dictionary includes many anglicisms in general use, with equivalences and recommendations.

129. Smith, Colin (1975), 'Anglicism or not?', *Vida Hispánica*, 23: 9–13.

130. —— (1991), 'The Anglicisms: No Longer a Problem for Spanish?', *Actas del XIII Congreso Nacional de AEDEAN* (1989: PPU), 119–36.

The author defines the term and investigates the attitude of English and Spanish speakers towards the phenomenon examining fully integrated terms (change of meaning, derivation)—as well as some syntactic constructions due to English influence.

131. Stone, Howard (1957), 'Los anglicismos en España y su papel en la lengua oral', *Revista de Filología Española*, 41: 141–60.

The author examines the adaptation, translations, and changes of meaning of anglicisms in use in the 1950s and provides a glossary of some five hundred items, drawn from various sources, especially from speech.

132. Teschner, R. V. (1972), 'Anglicisms in Spanish: a Cross-referenced Guide to Previous Findings, together with English Lexical Influence on Chicago Mexican Spanish', unpublished Ph.D. thesis (University of Wisconsin).

Reproduced partially in 'A critical annotated bibliography of anglicisms in Spanish', *Hispania*, 57 (1974): 631–78.

133. Torrents dels Prats, Alfonso ([1]1976, [2]1989), *Diccionario de dificultates del inglés* (Barcelona: Juventud).

Contains suggestions for the translation of English terms and proposals for their substitution.

134. VÁZQUEZ-AYORA, GERARDO (1977), 'Anglicismos de frecuencia', in *Introducción a la traductología: Curso básico de traducción* (Washington: Georgetown University Press), 102–40.

The article treats syntactic and lexical constructions found in translations into Spanish calqued on English and recurring with a certain frequency such as *-mente* to render adverbial *-ly*.

135. VEGA, PEDRO (1996), 'Evolución lingüística en relación con la armonización legal en Europa', in Christian Schmitt and Wolfgang Schweickhard (eds.), *Die iberoromanischen Sprachen aus interkultureller Sicht. Akten der gleichnamigen Sektion der Bonner Hispanistentage* (Bonn: Romanischer Verlag), 91–105.

On the borrowing of some legal terms through adaptation and calquing: *auditar*, *directiva*, *imagen fiel*, etc.

136. VIVES COLL, ANTONIO (1989–90), 'Los anglicismos económicos en los DRAE de 1970 y 1984', *Revista de Filología de la Universidad de la Laguna*, 8–9: 405–11.

137. VV.AA (1992), *El idioma español en el deporte. Guía práctica* (Logroño: Gobierno de La Rioja; Agencia Efe), 74 pp.

Contains glossaries of the foreign terms used in various sports, most of which are anglicisms.

138. ZAMORA MUNNÉ, JUAN C. (1994), 'Teoría y descripción del proceso de transferencia en el nivel léxico: indigenismos y anglicismos en el español', *Anuario de Lingüística Hispánica*, 10: 421–33.

139. —— and EDUARDO C. BÉJAR (1987), 'El género de los préstamos', *Revista Española de Lingüística*, 17 (1): 131–7.

General observations on the gender of anglicisms and review of some studies on this subject. On the uses of *meeting*.

Catalan (Félix Rodríguez González)

Since the number of studies does not justify an independent section and the problems discussed are closely related to those of Spanish, the nine entries are here appended.

1. Badía i Margarit, Antoni (1953), 'Anglicisms in the Catalan Language of Menorca', *English Studies* (Groningen), 34: 279–82.

2. Bruguera, Jordi (1985), *Història del lèxic català* (Barcelona: Enciclopèdia catalana).

Includes a chapter on anglicisms, pp. 90–6.

3. Clarassó, M. (1981), 'Anglicisms in Contemporary Catalan', *Polyglot*, 3: 1–7.

After compiling more than 280 terms, the author comments on the various categories and means of transmission of anglicisms.

4. Faura i Pujol, Neus (1985), 'Els anglicismes futbolístics a la premsa catalana fins al 1936', in Rolf Eberenz *et al. Estudis de llengua i literatura catalanes, X (Miscellania Antoni M. Badia i Margarit)* (Barcelona: Publicacions de l'Abadia de Montserrat), II: 145–90.

The author discusses the borrowing and adaptation of English words in football terminology since the beginning of the century based on evidence from Barcelona sports magazines.

5. —— (1986), 'Els anglicismos futbolístics a la premsa catalana fins al 1936', *Llengua i Lit.*, 1 (1): 251–74.

This is a continuation of the previous study, examining semantic anglicisms or calques.

6. Ortells, Vicente and Xavier Campos (1983), *Els anglicismes de Menorca. Estudi históric i etimològic* (Palma de Mallorca: Moll), 124 pp.

A compilation of more than 140 anglicisms used on the island, with their meaning and etymology.

7. Pujol Gorné, Ramón (1993), 'La influència de l'angles en el català actual', unpublished Ph.D. thesis (Barcelona: Universidad Autónoma), 2 vols., 748 pp.

The first volume deals with theoretical aspects of description, following Pratt (1980); the second describes the specific vocabulary in the form of an etymological and usage dictionary.

8. Recasens, M. (1982), 'Anglicismos en el léxico catalàn', unpublished MA thesis (Barcelona: Universidad Autónoma).

Cites 437 anglicisms, without contexts.

9. Ruiz y Pablo, Àngel (1908), 'Rastre que varem deixar en el llenguatge menorquí les dominacions angleses', *Primer Congrès Internacional de la Llengua Catalana* (Barcelona, 1906), 345–9.

Index of Topics

Note: Items are quoted by page(entry number).

Index of Words